George H. Taylor

An exposition of the Swedish movement-cure

Together with a summary of the principles of general hygiene

George H. Taylor

An exposition of the Swedish movement-cure

Together with a summary of the principles of general hygiene

ISBN/EAN: 9783337723835

Printed in Europe, USA, Canada, Australia, Japan

Cover: Foto ©ninafisch / pixelio.de

More available books at **www.hansebooks.com**

EXPOSITION

OF THE

MOVEMENT-CURE.

AN

EXPOSITION

OF THE

SWEDISH MOVEMENT-CURE,

EMBRACING

THE HISTORY AND PHILOSOPHY OF THIS SYSTEM OF MEDICAL TREATMENT,
WITH EXAMPLES OF SINGLE MOVEMENTS, AND DIRECTIONS FOR
THEIR USE IN VARIOUS FORMS OF CHRONIC DISEASE,
FORMING A COMPLETE MANUAL OF EXERCISES;

TOGETHER WITH

A SUMMARY OF THE PRINCIPLES OF GENERAL HYGIENE.

BY

GEO. H. TAYLOR, A.M., M.D.,

PRINCIPAL PHYSICIAN TO THE REMEDIAL HYGIENIC INSTITUTE OF NEW YORK CITY

New York:

FOWLER AND WELLS, PUBLISHERS,
No. 308 BROADWAY.
1860.

Entered, according to Act of Congress, in the year 1860, by

GEO. H. TAYLOR,

In the Clerk's Office of the District Court of the United States for the Southern District of New York.

DAVIES & KENT,
STEREOTYPERS AND ELECTROTYPERS,
113 *Nassau Street*, *N. Y.*

To his Friends,

PROF. GABRIEL BRANTING,

FOR FORTY-FIVE YEARS DIRECTOR OF THE SWEDISH CENTRAL GYMNASTIC INSTITUTE,

AND

HERMAN SATHERBURG, M.D.,

PROFESSOR OF ORTHOPOEDIC SURGERY IN THE CAROLINIAN MEDICO-CHIRURGICAL INSTITUTE, STOCKHOLM,

AS A TESTIMONIAL OF GRATITUDE

FOR

THEIR KIND PERSONAL INSTRUCTIONS AND GENEROUS HOSPITALITY,

This Work,

BEING AN ATTEMPT TO CARRY OUT, IN A NEW DIRECTION,

THOSE PRINCIPLES

TO THE ELUCIDATION AND PRACTICE OF WHICH THEY HAVE SO ASSIDUOUSLY AND SUCCESSFULLY DEVOTED THEMSELVES,

IS

AFFECTIONATELY AND RESPECTFULLY DEDICATED

BY

The Author.

PREFACE.

To do what he can to encourage and assist people in a rational endeavor to acquire and maintain an intelligent control of their entire physiological being—to bring into and keep in healthful and effective play all the complex machinery of their organism, has been the sole aim of the writer in this work. The importance of the agency proposed to effect this is conceded in general terms by all; it never was disputed, indeed. But this admission, so freely and so gracefully rendered, amounts to very little; it is not much better, really, than a virtual confession of inability to rebut the arguments directly or indirectly advanced in every sound physiological treatise.

The plan of the present work, so far as I am

aware, is quite new, no attempt having been hitherto made to analyze *single movements*, with a view to the production of such a combination of effects as are wanted to meet the various pathological needs of the system. This object, I am quite certain, has been, at best, very imperfectly accomplished; but I would feign indulge the hope that I have at least done the work of a humble pioneer, in breaking the ground and throwing out some hints and suggestions that may prove useful to the future laborer in this wide and fertile field.

The Author can not but hope, too, that he has furnished to his medical readers some food for thought that may lead to results in their practice that shall more than compensate for the time and strength expended in the work.

To a thorough understanding of all the principles of the MOVEMENT-CURE, an intimate acquaintance with *Anatomy* and *Physiology*, and, indeed, with medical science generally, is absolutely essential. Of course, skill in *diagnosis*, and in the practical application of these principles in the treatment of the countless ills of human flesh, can be acquired only by long and patient training and study. I do not expect, for I know it would be quite impossible in the nature of things, to turn every good-natured person who may do me the kindness to peruse these chapters into a good doctor. I should be entirely satisfied—the height of my ambition would be reached—could I but prevent a few hundreds of my Christian fellow-men and women from *making bad doctors of themselves.*

I have not endeavored to shake my reader's faith in the wise, prudent, conscientious, and learned physician. No one honors him more than does the writer. Blessed, say I, is the man or woman who has a *good doctor*, but more blessed he *who can do without him!* To enable my reader *so to do* has been my main aim in the preparation of this *manual.*

In Part I. is given what I conceive to be the more important principles upon which is based the practice of the *Movement-Cure.* These principles are mostly simple deductions from physiological science, and the *cure* is only the practical application of demonstrated physiological truths

In Part II. are given a number of examples of the method of carrying these principles into practice.

In Part III. the pathology of various common chronic affections is briefly discussed, and certain means of preserving the health and improving the strength are noticed.

Part IV. contains a concise statement of some of the relations of the system to *temperature, air, food, light, heat,* etc., with observations upon the superior advantages of obeying the laws of life, with a view to the maintenance or the restoration of health and vigor, over irrational and indiscriminate drug dosing.

GEO. H. TAYLOR.

No. 67 West 38th Street, New York.

TABLE OF CONTENTS.

Part One.

PRINCIPLES CONNECTED WITH THE USE OF MOVEMENTS.

CHAPTER I.

INTRODUCTORY.
                                                                                                   PAGE

Physical Self-Training, and the Classes of Persons for whom it is specially needful.. 17
1. After Duplicated Movements.. 19
2. Those who are but Slightly Affected by Disease........................... 20
3. Sedentary Persons... 21
4. Persons Engaged in Mental Toil... 21
5. Young Students of both Sexes.. 22
6. Tendency to Diminish the Drug Practice..................................... 24

CHAPTER II.
HISTORICAL SKETCH OF MOVEMENTS.

Movements among the Chinese... 32
Movements in India... 39
Movements among the Greeks and Romans..................................... 41
Biography of Ling... 47
Ling's Statements of Principles... 53
The Movement System in Stockholm... 59
Testimony of Philosophers—Dally, Hoffman, Rousseau, Pliny, Galen, Plato, Bacon, Georgii... 62

CHAPTER III.
THE RELATIONS OF CHEMICAL AND MOLECULAR CHANGES TO THE ORIGIN OF FORCE IN THE BODY.

Importance of First Principles.. 68
These Forces a Product of Vital Action.. 71
Different kinds of Motion... 77
Reciprocity of Actions.. 80
The System as a Reservoir of Force.. 82
Description of Muscle... 83
Physiological Effects of Exercise.. 85
Effects of Muscular Contraction on the Local Circulation................... 86
Effect on Respiration.. 87
Effect on the Secretions... 88
Effect on the Excretions... 89
Effect on Absorption.. 89
Effect on the Quality of the Blood... 90
Effect on the Digestion... 90
Effect on the Organizing Process... 91
Movements Stimulate the Vitalizing Processes............................... 92
Co-ordination of Motions by the Nerves... 93
The foregoing Effects... 96

CHAPTER IV.

MOVEMENTS, AND THE PRINCIPLES GOVERNING THEIR APPLICATION.

	PAGE
Definition	97
Different kinds of Movements, Active and Passive	98
Single and Duplicated Movements	99
Concentric and Eccentric Movements	102
General and Localized Movements	105
Influence of Movements in Regulating the Forces of the Body	109
Relations of the Action of the Will and of the Muscles in Movements	112
Movements as a Specific Medical Agency	116
Movements as related to Pathology	120
Province of Movements	121
Morale of Movements	122

CHAPTER V.

MOVEMENTS COMPARED WITH GYMNASTICS.

The Muscles a Medium of Language, and of the Manifestation of Character.. 129

CHAPTER VI.

DIRECTIONS FOR PRESCRIBING AND APPLYING MOVEMENTS.

Time Considered	135
Manner	136
Rhythm	136
Exertion	137
Number	137
Order	138
Relation to Diseased Parts	139
Regions of the Body	140

CHAPTER VII.

TERMINOLOGY OF POSITIONS.

Importance of System	142
Positions and Movements	144
Commencing Positions	145
Principal Positions of the Trunk	145
Standing Positions—Erect, Fall, and Bent Standing	145
Kneeling Positions—Erect and Fall Kneeling	146
Sitting Positions—Sitting, Short, and Long	146
Lie-Sitting, Half-Lying, Fall and Stride Sitting	147
Lying - Forward, Backward, Sidewise, Trunk, and Leg	147
Head-and-Heels, Elbows-and-Toes, Sidewise and Balance Lying	148
Hanging	148
Positions of the Arms and Legs	148
Arm Positions seen in a Front View of the Body	150
Arm Positions seen in a Side View of the Body	152
Leg Positions	154
Lower Leg Positions	155
Stride, Walk, Step-Standing, and Foot-Support-Standing	155
Squat and Leg-Angle Positions	156

CONTENTS. xiii

Part Two.

EXAMPLES OF SINGLE MOVEMENTS.

CHAPTER VIII.

REGION OF THE FEET.

	PAGE
Remarks on Movements of the Feet	157
Examples of Movements of the Region of the Feet	160
1. Standing, Feet-Extending	160
2. Toe-Support, Half-Standing, Heel-Pressing	161
3. Wing-Walk, Toe Wall-Standing, Foot-Bending	162
4. Long Sitting, Feet Sidewise-Bending	162
Long-Sitting, Feet-Rotation	163
Foot-Percussion	164
Foot-Rotation (Passive)	165
Support Half-Standing, Leg-Swinging	165

CHAPTER IX.

REGION OF THE LEGS.

Remarks on Movements of the Legs	167
Walking	167
Examples of Movements of the Legs	170
Wing-Stride-Standing, Curtseying	170
Half-Standing, Curtseying	171
Balance-Standing, Curtseying	172
Wing-Kneeling, Knee-Stretching	172
Half-Standing, Alternate Twisting	173
Wing-Walk, Forward-Fall-Standing, Knee-Bending	174
Leg-Angle, Half-Standing, Leg-Clapping	174
Region of the Hips	175
Remarks on the Region of the Hips	175
Wing-Stride, Short-Sitting, Leg Outward-Stretching	176
Leg-Angle, Half-Standing Knee-Stretching	177
Wing-Recline, Support-Sitting, Knees-Raising	177
Half-Standing, Leg Forward-Raising	178
Half-Standing, Leg Backward-Raising	179
Half-Standing, Leg Sidewise-Raising	179
Forward-Fall, Head-Support-Standing, Leg-Raising	180
Half-Standing, Leg-Rotation	181
Wing-Sitting, Double Leg-Twisting	181
Legs-Angle, Lie-Sitting, Knees-Stretching	182
Shelter Trunk-Backward-Lying, Legs-Raising	183
Kick Backward-Lying, Legs-Separation	184
Sidewise-Lying, Leg-Raising	184
Backward-Lying, Legs-Rotation	185
Wing Leg-Angle Half-Lying, Knee-Stretching	185
Thigh-Rotation	186
Chine-Knocking	187

CHAPTER X.

REGION OF THE TRUNK.

Remarks on the Region of the Trunk	188
Movements of the Digestive Organs	189
Movements of the Respiratory Organs	193
Stretch-Stride Short-Sitting, Trunk Forward-Sidewise Falling	198
Stretch-Stride Short-Sitting, Trunk Backward-Sidewise Falling	199
Stretch-Sitting, Trunk Backward-Falling	199
Half-Stretch, Half-Wing, Stride Short-Sitting, Trunk Sidewise Bending	200

	PAGE
Half-Stretch, Half-Wing, Stride-Sitting, Trunk-Twisting	201
Shelter Stride-Sitting, Change-Twisting	202
Yard-Sitting, Arms Swaying	203
Stretch-Stride-Kneeling, Trunk Backward-Bending	204
Half-Stretch, Half-Wing, Reclined Stride-Kneeling, Trunk-Twisting	206
Half-Stretch, Half-Wing, Walk-Kneeling, Trunk-Twisting	206
Arms-Angle, Reclined Kneeling, Arms Stretching	207
Rack-Reclined Stride-Kneeling, Arms Backward-Striking	208
Wing Stride-Kneeling, Ringing	208
Yard Stride-Kneeling, Swaying	209
Stride-Sitting, Arms Sidewise-Raising	210
Stretch Half-Walk, Half-Kneeling, Trunk Backward-Bending	211
Half-Wing, Half-Curve (weight held) Step-Reclined-Standing, Trunk Sidewise-Bending	211
Half-Wing, Half-Stretch, Step-Standing, Trunk Sidewise-Bending	212
Half-Stretch, Half-Wing, Half-Kick, Reclined Standing, Trunk Sidewise-Bending	213
Half-Stretch, Reclined Kick-Standing, Trunk-Twisting	213
Shelter Long-Sitting, Trunk Forward-Bending	214
Arms-Angle, Half-Kick (foot supported) Reclined-Standing, Arms-Stretching	214
Yard-Reclined, Half-Kick Standing, Swaying	216
Half-Stretch, Half-Wing, Walk, Trunk Sidewise-Bent, Standing, Trunk-Twisting	216
Yard Walk-Standing, Trunk Backward-Bending	217
Upward-Sidewise Stretch Doorway-Standing, Walking	217
Shelter, Sidewise-Bent Stride-Standing, Trunk Rotation	218
Head-and-Heels Lying, Holding	219
Elbow-and-Toes Lying, Holding	220
Elbow-and-Leg Sidewise-Lying. Hips Raising	221
Shelter Back-Lying, Head-and-Legs Raising	222
Back Lying, Holding	222
Wing-Stride Leg-Angle Standing, Trunk Vibration	223
Operations upon the Digestive Organs	223
Kneading, Shaking, Stroking, Circular Stroking, Point Pressure, Clapping	224
Agitation of the Abdomen and Diaphragm	226

CHAPTER XI.

REGION OF THE ARMS.

Remarks on this Region	227
Stretch Backward-Lying, Weight-Holding	229
Rack Grasp, Forward Fall-Standing, Arms Angling	230
Stretch-Grasp Standing, Hip Rotation	231
Half Stretch Grasp Standing, Arm Twisting	232
Yard Stride-Sitting, Arms Twisting	232
Standing, Arms Rotating	233
Hanging, Swinging	234
Swing-Hang-Standing, Trunk Rotating	236
Trunk Forward-Fall Hanging, Holding	237
Backward-Fall Elbows-Support Lying, Holding	238
Half-Stretch Support Half-Standing, Stretching	239
Stretch-Stride Standing or Star-Standing, Stretching	240

CHAPTER XII.

REGION OF THE HEAD AND NECK.

Remarks on the Region of the Head and Neck	241
Head Turning	242
Head Forward Bending	242
Head Backward Bending	243
Head Backward Bending and Twisting (Screw-Raising)	243

Part Three.
THE PATHOLOGY OF SEVERAL FORMS OF CHRONIC DISEASE.

CHAPTER XIII.
THE RELATIONS OF MOVEMENTS.
                                                                    PAGE
Remark 245
Indigestion, Dyspepsia 247

CHAPTER XIV.
NERVOUSNESS.
Nervousness 262
Seminal Disease 271
Neuralgia 273

CHAPTER XV.
Scrofulous Affections 277

CHAPTER XVI.
Pulmonary Affections—Consumption 286

CHAPTER XVII.
Paralysis of the Nerves of Motion 300

CHAPTER XVIII.
CONSTIPATION, DIARRHEA, AND PILES.
Constipation 308
Diarrhea 315
Piles 317

CHAPTER XIX.
Deformities of the Spine 320

CHAPTER XX.
Female Diseases 323

CHAPTER XXI.
MISCELLANEOUS APPLICATIONS OF MOVEMENTS.
Movements to Remove Fatigue 340
To Stop Nose-Bleed 341
To Induce Vomiting 342
To Remove Chilblains 343
To Relieve Headache 344
Worms in Children 345
Hernia 346
Prolapsus of the Womb and Bowels 347
To Relieve Backache 347
Amenorrhea 347
To Excite Action of the Lower Bowels 347

CHAPTER XXII.
DIFFERENT EFFECTS OF VARIOUS COMMON EXERCISES UPON PERSONS IN HEALTH.

	PAGE
Walking	348
Running	348
Dancing	349
Sewing	349
Agricultural Labors	350
Painting, etc.	351
Study	351

CHAPTER XXIII.
MOVEMENTS ADAPTED TO THE USE OF SCHOOLS.

Order of Command for Free-Sitting Movements 355

Part Four.
HYGIENE.
CHAPTER XXIV.
THE PHILOSOPHY OF HYGIENE.

Food	358
Quantity	359
Quality	360
Salt	362
Preparation of Food—Cooking	363
Proper Times for Eating	364
Drinks	366
Milk	366

CHAPTER XXV.
TEMPERATURE.

Physiological Effect of Heat and Cold	368
Origin of Colds	371
Effect of Continued and Great Extremes	373
Importance of Cold	374
The Water-Cure	374
The Cold Bath	375
The Warm Bath	376
The Hot Bath	377
Local Baths	377
Effect on the Nerves	378
Compresses	379
The Air Bath	379
The Cold General Bath	380
Reaction	381
Shower and Douche Baths	381

CHAPTER XXVI.

Light 383

CHAPTER XXVII.

Mental Hygiene 386

A MANUAL OF EXERCISES.

PART I.
PRINCIPLES CONNECTED WITH THE USE OF MOVEMENTS.

Chapter One.

INTRODUCTORY.

PHYSICAL SELF-TRAINING, AND THE CLASSES OF PERSONS FOR WHOM IT IS SPECIALLY NEEDFUL.—There are not in nature nicer or wiser adaptations of means to ends, than are exhibited in the arrangements of the human system for the maintenance in perfect order and health of its functions. Such provision implies the reverse of chance or accident as its controlling cause, and in fact *intelligence* in the arrangement of its activities and relations, if indeed safety and perpetuity be the object contemplated in it. That all may have to a certain and sufficient extent the control of their own physical systems, will scarcely be denied; for it is on this fact that human actions and human responsibility are based. The acknowledgment of this evidently throws the responsibility for his health, efficiency, and happiness upon his own shoulders, where every man should feel that it belongs.

84551

The moral and intellectual natures of man have ever been regarded as proper subjects for training and development, in order to secure their due healthful exercise. The physical system is manifestly a subject for corresponding attention; and its right to this advantage should be recognized, and receive in civilized communities no less regard. That physical culture should claim the precedence, would seem to be indicated by the fact that the physical is prior in the order of development, not only as respects the individual, who is, *through the physical,* fitted for his destiny as an *intellectual* being, but also in the progressive unfolding of the powers of the race.

Physical culture, then, should be promoted both as a science and as an art, in all the numerous applications of which it is susceptible, till it assumes a position in the public esteem commensurate with its importance. The particular form it shall take, and the modes of carrying it out, will long remain a matter of abstract and experimental investigation; each person interested contributing something of his experience and thought toward the realization of the grand object —the highest efficiency and well-being of mankind, physical and moral.

This subject is one that receives much superficial attention. It is one concerning which an abundance of "vague and glittering generalities" have been expressed, but only a very few practical precepts or definite directions given. While all seem familiar with the subject of exercise, in its relations to the health, but very few admit that they are prepared to meet, with suitable applications, any given case requiring treatment. The feeble person and the invalid are constantly advised to take exercise. The popular lecturer, books, friends, physicians unite in confirming the dictates of his common sense in this respect; but the inquirer looks almost in vain to all these sources for any definite and satisfactory information based on physiology and the laws of life, such as will tell him *how* the remedy operates, and also *how it should be applied.*

The present treatise, it is hoped, will assist in supplying the needs here referred to, in the several directions now to be named.

1. The class of persons who will best understand the meaning as well as the method of the present treatise, consists of those who have been, or are, under my medical direction. Indeed, this is the class that loudly call for the work, and who have constantly spurred me on to its completion. After receiving for a while a full prescription of *duplicated* movements, until their health has become much improved, such persons require, at every stage of their progress toward the goal of perfect health, directions for self-treatment —for a continuation, in a modified form, of the measures previously employed. I have felt, as others have and will, the need of such particular directions as each patient may require, and which this treatise is an attempt to furnish. In this way, the purposes of both physician and patient are equally served, and the desired object of extending the practice of movements in a domestic way is to a limited extent realized. But the reader must understand at the outset, that the movement-cure can be practiced in this way *only* to a limited extent, both on account of the obscure nature of the diseases for which it is applied, and also from the kind of processes which it employs.

The present treatise is therefore confined to the discussion of a few *single movements*. With those who have had a previous training with the *duplicated movements*, the directions herein contained will be of the greatest service, not only for the purpose of carrying on the curative processes to results of greater perfection, but also for *preventing* a recurrence of the complaint, since it is the prime object of the treatment to secure to the invalid the intelligent and permanent *command of himself*.

2. There is in the community a very large class of persons who might be called *half-invalids*—persons who do not possess a satisfactory amount of health, but who at the same time feel that they are not the proper subjects for medical care. Such persons feel that they are forewarned of disease, and would gladly attempt to avert it, could they obtain such directions for doing so as would meet the approbation of their reason or instinctive sense of physiological propriety. Current medical practice takes no cognizance of these cases; or if it does, it is in such a way as often to confirm the subject in serious and prolonged disease. Aware of this fact, many keep aloof from medical advice of any kind, and insist that suffering in any of the more moderate forms is less a misfortune than the habit of gulping drugs for the palliation they afford. For persons of this class, it is evident that it is not drugs, but such *easily performed self-training* as that of which examples and directions are here given, that is required. By this means, the abundant latent powers which they possess are developed into activity and harmony, and they soon rejoice in health, while the neglect or continued misdirection of these would eventually have degenerated into grave, and perhaps fatal, disease.

INTRODUCTORY. 21

3. Besides these, there are many whose avocations are sedentary, yet such as require the continued and often severe employment of a part of their muscles. This tends to an undue and disproportionate activity of some parts of the body to the detriment of others. Such avocations constitute in many constitutions a potent cause of ill health; but the ill effects of them can, in general, be easily counteracted by a recourse to such means as are prescribed in this treatise. Persons suffering from the causes here alluded to, will be enabled to remove fatigue and congestion from the parts of the body that have been abused by too continuous exercise, and thus to prevent the occurrence of the grievous symptoms so commonly resulting from such causes.

4. Persons of *literary* and of *business habits* require a similar aid to preserve them from falling into habitual ill health. The habit of this class of persons is, to employ all the available forces of their organism through a particular channel—the brain and nerves, and of course to excite nutrition chiefly in a single department of their organism. This is contrary to the laws of the system, and ill consequences are necessarily ere long felt. This disproportionate use and unbalanced nutrition, whereby *one* set of functions is heightened, is, of course, to the detriment of *another* set of functions, which, becoming reduced in power, are, at last, literally *starved out*. Examples of this class of persons are met with everywhere, and generally recognized at sight. It is to be hoped the time will come when such physiological abuse will meet the general reprehension it so much deserves.

The principles advocated, and the practical examples

afforded in this work, are adapted to obviate all such unfortunate results. Persons whose tastes or necessities lead them to employ the *nervous* department of their being chiefly, *may*, if they choose to learn *how*, counteract any disproportionate nervous wear, and by attending to its cultivation, maintain their physical vigor.

5. As a necessary element in the education of the young, *physical* culture should hold a place co-ordinate with that of the intellect—it should be a part of all academic training. For the want of this culture, educational means and appliances too often defeat their own purposes; for the due co-ordination of the powers of the body, under the order of civilizational development, can not with safety be left to chance. If we are to judge of the utility of institutions of learning by many of the specimens of manhood which they turn out, our decisions respecting them can not be unqualifiedly favorable. Sadly true will this appear when we come to set against the fulfillment of the highest hopes of parent, teacher, and friend, in regard to intellectual advantages, the destruction of the power to use them. With physical health broken down, and stamina destroyed, we are led to inquire if the advantages are not quite counterbalanced. We are at least justified in making the inference, that *the processes tending to such results are radically defective.* The hardy teamster or plowman, with few intellectual resources, has, with nothing to boast of, in fact, besides an excellent physique, in the comparison, plainly the best of it; for though the college youth has satisfied the ambition of his friends in the matter of intellectual culture, his success proves of little avail as a source of rational enjoyment, or as contributing to the world's advance-

ment; since he has at the same time acquired a fearful drawback in the form of the life-lease of a narrow chest, shrunken and flabby muscles, and a general dyspeptic or consumptive habit. While learning was being put into him, his natural *pluck* was driven out of him—an exchange of very questionable advantage.

With females, the case is even worse. The girl is sacrificed to society's conventionalisms, senseless and even vicious though they may be; while the boy may rudely thrust these aside. Many of the world's leaders have acquired the power to be such, by shocking their friends in their boyhood. But, her parents or teachers knowing nothing nor caring for vital laws, the girl is restrained in the opportunities for bodily activity that nature would seek; and by the time that her education is "finished," she is rendered, physically, thoroughly useless, both from want of power and of disposition to be otherwise. Regardless of the necessary physical conditions, her intellectual powers can not be sustained; and, in too many instances, she is rendered incapable of reaching or appreciating the higher ends of life, and becomes satisfied with a merely sensorial existence.

We may conclude, then, that the prevalent amount of disease among females is not a sacred birthright derived from the providential constitution of things, but that it is *acquired*, and follows as the necessary consequence of the inharmonious action of the organism, imposed by the customs of society and the neglect of bodily culture. It is thus that the chlorosis, the nervousness, the dyspepsia, the deformity of spine and chest, the loss of the attractions that should belong to the sex, and divers other afflictions, so common with females, are fully accounted for.

It may be said that physical training, when subjected to rules, is *unnatural*, and that this matter is better left to the spontaneous suggestions of nature.

I would reply to this, that if so, *all* education, *any* training, is equally "unnatural." The object of all true culture is to aid the designs of nature; and our plans must be carried out conformably to her laws, in order that we may attain satisfactory results. We are purposely so constituted as to be susceptible of improvement in every department of our being; and such improvement becomes a duty we owe ourselves. Civilization proceeds by steps; and when any custom or mode of life exists that is attended by unwholesome effects, it is an indication that further knowledge is required for their counteraction; for that civilization is faulty which does not prevent the evil results of any habits that cultivated society may impose.

The *principle* of cultivating the body along with the mind, so as by preserving the health to render mental culture available, is far from being new. It has been often recognized and put in practice; and laudable and successful examples have existed both in ancient[*] and in modern times. But it has been culpably overlooked or slighted by us, the American people; and for such neglect we, as a nation, are now receiving the castigation necessary to correct our short-comings in this respect.

6. It need not be concealed that the influence of the principles of physical culture, such as it is my present

---

[*] The Greeks made the education of their children of both sexes an affair of state —it was done at the public expense. In this way they became the type of the human race in its best characteristics. In form they were all but perfect; in courage unequaled; they excelled in the arts and sciences; in polite literature, in poetry and history, they are still our masters. Their theory of education, and the practical results of it, were better than ours at this day.—DR. CHAPMAN.

purpose to inculcate, is to a considerable extent inimical to the interests of the current medical practice. So far as this influence is based upon the *truth*, it must inevitably prevail, and to a certain extent will enable us, eventually, to dispense with the old style of medication.

It must be conceded, upon a little reflection, that current medical science does not answer the requirements of the age. Its scope is too narrow—it does not *attempt* to supply the most pressing wants of a civilized community. For the chief want is, not some mighty *cure-all*, much less the faltering, unsatisfactory *attempts* at curing, so exhausting to the limited vital resources —but to be *kept well*. In spite of the antiquity and respectability of the medical art, the community is not restrained through its influence from wasting in the most prodigal manner its precious boon of health.

The popularity of the received medical practice depends on the common belief, that there really exists a connection, yet not well understood, between the drug and certain curative results. It is plain that the implied promise to cure thus furnished, so far as credence is given it, in effect lessens the fear of the pain, *which is the penalty of physiological misdeeds;* and thus the barrier to the perpetration of such acts is taken away. Such credence is palpably demoralizing in its influence, for it not only countenances the infringement of physiological law, but discourages the desire to understand, and to practice according to the dictates of a correct physiology.

It behooves us to look more closely than is the general habit, to the *principles* involved in drug-practice. Suppose all the expectations and hope held out by the administrator of this means of cure to be completely fulfilled, would it not discourage inquiry in regard to physiological relations, and really offer a premium to indulgence and the consequent physiological crime? Does not the assurance of delivery from danger annihilate the fear of it, and are not men ready to rush into danger in proportion to their belief in speedy and complete delivery? To what else are we to refer the general ignorance and misunderstanding of the laws of health, but the indifference to such knowledge, which medicine, indirectly, to be sure, but powerfully, inculcates?

Let us contrast this principle with its opposite, viz., that there is no scape-offering for physiological sin, but that suffering and diminished power are its due, direct, and inevitable consequences. Must not this stimulate to such inquiry as would lead to exact knowledge, rigid care, and correct practice? Self-preservation and self-interest, which it is impossible to despise, would tend directly to this result.

It is apparent that the true physician has a higher duty resting upon him than those who bear that name are accustomed to acknowledge, namely, that of carrying instruction to the popular mind in regard to the natural capabilities and requirements of the body, so as to enable men to preserve their powers, and to repel the first insidious approaches of disease. There is scarcely any discreet physician or well-informed person who will not admit that the department of hygiene that is here advocated and rendered practical, is the most powerful of agencies in securing this desirable result. Upon the physician rests plainly a duty in this matter, because the duty confessedly exists, and it can fall to no one else. Here is opened a broader field for his labor than he now enjoys, and one compatible with the dictates of a noble and generous mind.

7. The importance of the special hygienic system of *movements*, for the recovering invalid, for the weakly, for those whose position requires too little or improper kinds of exercise, for youth of both sexes, and for preventing disease, must be manifest to all. But that the subject is invested with an interest which is strictly medical, in the highest sense of that term, will not be so readily admitted. It is conceived by the author, that the importance of movements as a curative resource is hardly second to that of any other heretofore brought before the public.

It is the purpose of the present treatise only to supply some hints toward a practice based on the phenomena of motion in the body. And in order to render it useful for the purposes above indicated, it is restricted to what I have denominated *single movements*. This limitation, while it fits the treatise for the use of a larger number of individuals in the community, renders it, at the same time, imperfect as a *medical guide*, and confines its applications to a limited number of diseased conditions. In short, the work aims to do nothing more than to introduce the idea of the remedial application of movements, which, to be complete, must employ also, and perhaps chiefly, the *duplicated movements*, of which there is an account here included.

Movements have incontrovertible *remedial* effects, and may therefore be considered a legitimate remedial agent. The application of this system has been known and practiced to a limited extent in all ages; and in modern times it has been much extended, and has received the appellation of the *Movement-Cure*.

This practice is not pretended in any quarter to be a universal panacea, nor to include all that is valuable in the present domain of medical art. It is an invaluable contribution to a system of practice based on physiology, which, to be complete, will embrace, by separate and distinct methods, every avenue through which the health of the body is influenced, either from external or internal causes. The tendency of current medical practice is to narrow down medical means to the use of drugs; whereas these are but *one* of the many kinds of agents that affect the health of the body. All the variations and perturbations of the health are a true record of the effects of the slighter variations in the use of the materials and of the forces that are adapted by nature to functional employment, and that, acting together in appropriate adjustment, produce that condition which is termed health.

An enumeration of these elements available to the restoration as well as to the maintenance of the health would include many forces and agents that have to do mainly with man as an *animal*, such as heat, cold, food, drink, labor, recreation, rest, and all the inter-relations and adjustments of these, considered both in reference to their effect upon the vegetative life, and the animal functions of the body.

This system regards man as a *spiritual* being—recognizes all the various influences that operate upon his intellectual and moral life flowing from physical causes, and the power of the mind over the exercise of functional acts of the body, of every kind. The fact that man is subject to these relations, and that they directly modify and control his health, is undoubted. How this control is to be exercised as a remedial means has not yet been shown; except, perhaps, in such a fragmentary way as does not admit of any organic construction. The practice of *duplicated movements*, wherein the mental powers of both the invalid and friend co-operate to the production of certain effects, affords many new facts and interesting illustrations of the control of the mental and nervous states over those functional acts of the body that constitute the health; and such as may lead to higher results than have yet been conceived—in building up, indeed, what may be called a system of *moral* medicine.

But the Movement-Cure, as a specialty of medical practice, depends entirely on *purely physiological means* for the accomplishment of its purposes. It may be considered as a means of enabling the natural tendencies of the system toward health to act more powerfully and effectually. It points out the means of directing the corporeal energies into just those channels in which they are most needed, in order to perfect the balance of the physiological processes. It enables the system to develop and maintain its forces in greater amount, because it employs them naturally and without undue waste. And because the Movement-Cure thus limits itself to a realm of facts concerning which there is no question, it has a right to expect the approval of physicians of all the different schools, even of those advocating opposing theories. It requires assent only to the plainest and most obvious facts and inferences of physiology. In the Movement-Cure, all physicians meet on common ground and blend their differences. This proves, we hold, that the practice is founded in *common sense*, as well as upon the rigorous deductions of science and experience; and that the rapid dissemination of its principles and practice may be prophesied with a degree of certainty.

Chapter Two.

HISTORICAL SKETCH OF THE PRACTICE OF MOVEMENTS.

The desire of men to become more complete, comely, vigorous, and healthy—to approach as nearly as possible to the ideal man—has existed in all ages, and has impelled them to make special efforts to secure these ends. The suggestion of the necessary means would seem to arise from an instinct of our nature; and these evidently consist in simply *calling into action the power whose improvement we desire*—or in giving direction to the capabilities of which we are in conscious possession. Such a process is based on anatomy and physiology, and is limited by these sciences; and it deals with the very instruments and laws of vitality.

In recent times, the term "movements" has been employed to designate the processes by which this control of the bodily powers is secured. Theoretically, then, *movements* are capable of being reduced to an art, hygienic and remedial, as perfect as the principles upon which the natural operations of the body are based; and though, as a training or healing art, it may *always* have been successfully practiced, yet that success becomes necessarily more perfect, as less empirical, when it employs the facts and principles developed by modern research in physiology.

In glancing at the history of *movements*, the reader will wonder *why* an art so easily practiced, the elements of, and the demand for, which exist in the constitution of every one, while its principles are so fundamental and leave so little room for improvement, should not in modern times have come more generally into popular favor. The answer to this inquiry will be found in the fact of the maze of obscurity that has prevailed in the general mind in regard to the true curative value of drugs. But while all possible things have been both asserted and denied in regard to drugs, the value of *movements has never been denied or questioned*, but only at times *neglected*, in the general interest with which the popular mind has invested the other questions. In the last few centuries, *chemistry* has at each of the successive epochs of its development, furnished medicine with the means of toying with the credulity, the hopes and fears of the suffering public; and it requires all of the present amount of knowledge, and more time than has elapsed, to enable the scientific, supported by the popular mind, to turn the influence of the full-fledged science into its proper channels, to consummate a revolution that may be delayed, but must eventually be realized.

The employment of movements for hygienic and medical purposes is by no means a new thing, but is, on the contrary, older than any other means proposed for the same purpose. Movements have been employed in every age, and if not suggested by the natural instincts of the rude mind, their imperfect use is very soon suggested by experience. Among Indian and African tribes, various manipulations, flagellations, etc., have been practiced, generally connected with superstitious rites, incantations, prayers, etc., to which more enlightened people attribute the least portion of the benefit that is obtained. It is well known that certain movements produce vertigo, nausea, palpitations of the heart, and various other effects corresponding to actions that are brought about by chemical means. And so a primitive people, even, would make a beginning that would soon become extended with their extending experience, till checked by their ignorance of the general scientific principles underlying what they rudely practice.

Such primitive people, who know nothing of the brain wear, the confinement, and the defective exercise connected with the in-door and sedentary occupations of civilized society, have no need of other physical training than results from the *chase* and the *dance*, to which they are always devoted. But as civilization is developed, which always implies training, the physical powers must also be trained to maintain the general harmony, and if not by accident, then by design; or the constitution suffers in the way we see it so apt to do in old and enfeebled nations.

Thus it happens that there is developed from causes naturally and inevitably operating, a system of regulating the health, and overcoming diseases by the employment of movements. But this system has, with but few exceptions, been practiced in an incomplete manner, owing to the imperfect development of chemical and physiological science, upon which such a practice is necessarily founded.

MOVEMENTS AMONG THE CHINESE. — The traditional history of this people affords us many instructive examples of the employment of various exercises to preserve and restore the health. This history informs us that the humidity of the atmosphere and the stagnant waters were considered a prolific source of epidemic and endemic diseases, and that the efficient means of preventing these consisted in regular exercises of the body, by a kind of *gymnastic dance*. These movements tend to produce action from the center to the circumference of the body, or *centrifugal* — an action very appropriate for the renewal of the functions of the liver, and to give tone and vigor to the whole economy. *This matter was considered so important as to be under governmental regulation.*

The Chinese writers support this practice with the tradition that the life of man depends on a union of earth and heaven, together with the use that the creature makes of these. A subtile material, they think, circulates in the body; if then the body is not in action, the material accumulates; and, according to their theory, all diseases come of such obstruction.

The devotion of the Chinese to bodily exercises suggested the fundamental principle, which in China has always been considered the basis of progress and moral development, viz., that of *self-development.*

It appears that the Chinese have long practiced an art of medical movements, which they denominate the *Cong Fou*. The meaning of this term is, simply, the *art of exercising the body, and its application to the treatment of disease.* Says P. Amiot, a missionary, "Volumes might be written of the traditions, stories, and extravagant virtues of the *Cong Fou*, which are implicitly believed; even the majesty of the throne not exempting many emperors from a stupid credulity. Notwithstanding the priestly superstitions connected with it (for the priests persuade the people that it is a true exercise of religion), it is really a very ancient practice of medicine, founded on principles, and potent in many diseases."

From the statements of the learned missionary and others are deduced these conclusions:

1st. That this art is founded on a genuine experience and original scientific principles, and may be freed from the superstitions and charlatanry that at the present day surround it—that it dates back to Hoang-Fi, 2698 years before the Christian Era.

2d. It consists of three essential particulars, to wit:

a. Various positions of the body.

b. Rules for varying these attitudes.

c. During these exercises and attitudes, a management of the respiration according to certain rules of inspiration and expiration.

3d. This method has its own proper technical language.

4th. *It does really effect the cure and relief of many diseases.*

5th. *The Chinese of every rank eagerly resort to this remedy when every other means of cure has been tried in vain.*

Thus it is affirmed that the *Cong Fou* has really all the characters and pretensions of an ancient scientific mode of medical practice.

"The priests (who are the physicians) enter into an extensive detail of the positions of the body in all their shades of variation. These are so numerous, that we do not fear to say that all the postures and attitudes of comedians, dancers, tumblers, and artistic figures are but a small portion of those which have been introduced into this practice. The different modes of *stretching, folding, raising, falling, bending and ex-*

tending, separating and approaching, the arms and legs, in the standing, sitting, and lying positions, form a prodigious variety."

M. Amiot proceeds, at considerable length, to explain the methods and principles of this Chinese system of medical movements, and the diseases and symptoms for which it is applicable; and from this account the following is extracted:

"The *Cong Fou* consists in certain positions in which the body is placed a certain length of time, in which the patient breathes in peculiar methods. These methods must be chosen and combined according to the disease that is treated.

"The morning is the proper time for the treatment; after the night's repose the circulation is more equable, the secretions more balanced and uniform. Persons plethoric or charged with humors are always profited by fasting in the evening; and this is absolutely necessary in certain diseases.

"In practicing the movements, the body is either completely or partially clothed, and has weights upon the head and shoulders, according to the complaint; and in the respiration, the mouth should be half full of saliva or water.

"The physical and physiological principles concerned seem to be these:

"1. The mechansim of the body being entirely hydraulic, with a free circulation of the fluids, health consists only with the proper equipoise of these fluids in their reciprocal relations; and to restore health, this equilibrum must be established.

"2. As the air constantly enters into the blood and vital fluids through the lungs, tempers and purifies it and preserves its fluidity, these last qualities can only be maintained through respiration, and of course are restored by the same instrumentality.

"From these two principles they draw conclusions after their own fashion, which we will give for what they are worth.

"1. As the circulation of the fluids of the body has to overcome the two great obstacles of weight and friction, all that tends to diminish these, aids to establish the circulation which is disturbed.

"2. As the motion and impetus of the air increases the fluidity of liquids, and thus facilitates their movements, therefore all that tends to increase or diminish the force of the air in the body must increase or retard the circulation.

"These principles and deductions being understood, the disciples of the *Cong Fou* enter into very lengthy details in order to show the sympathetic correspondence of the different parts of the human body, the action and reaction of the great organs of the circulation, of the secretion, and of the digestion of food.

"*Theory.*—The Chinese physicians make use of reasoning like the following, after the principles and consequences above expressed. There are two essential parts of the *Cong Fou*—the first embraces the positions and attitudes that are given to the body, the second the manner in which the respiration is accelerated, retarded, or modified.

"1. If we regard the circulation of the blood and fluids as being opposed by their gravity or their friction, which tends to retard the flow, it is evident that the degree in which the body is straight or bent, lying or raised, the feet and hands stretched or folded, raised, lowered, or bent, ought, in the hydraulic mechanism, to effect a physical change, either to retard or to facilitate the circulation.

"The horizontal position being that which diminishes the weight most, is therefore most favorable to the circulation; while the erect position, on the contrary, augments the weight to its utmost, and must, necessarily, render the circulation most difficult; for the same reason, the position, according as the arms, the feet, or the head are raised, inclined, bent, etc., ought to affect the circulation more or less.

"This is not all; that which hinders the circulation in one part, gives more force in the direction in which the obstacle does not exist; and hence the fluids are made to overcome the engorgements that obstruct its passage.

"Another fact is this, that when the circulation has been hindered in a part, the greater is the force and impetuosity of the current when the obstacle is removed.

"It follows that the different postures of the *Cong Fou*, well directed, ought to produce a salutary relief in affections that arise from an embarrassed, retarded, or interrupted circulation. Now what are the affections that have other causes? Except fractures, bruises, etc., *it is difficult to find other than these causes to derange the organization of the human body.*

"2. It is certain that the heart is the grand power concerned in the circulation, and the force it exhibits in producing and maintaining it is one of the wonders of the universe.

"It is also certain that there is an obvious connection, continually existing, between the movements of the heart, in filling and emptying itself of blood, and the movements of dilatation and contraction of the lungs, which fill and empty themselves of air by inspiration and expiration. Their connection is so intimate, that the beats of the heart increase and diminish directly in proportion to the increasing and retarding of respiration.

"Now, if more air is inspired than is expired, or the contrary, its volume should increase or diminish the total mass of the fluids of the body, and recruit or curtail more or less the blood of the lungs; if the respiration is hastened or retarded, the result should be a quickening or retarding of the heart's action, so that both the mode of the circulation in the different parts of the body and the volume of the fluids of the body are controlled by the respiration," etc.*

It would appear from the above extract, that the Chinese *were acquainted at an early day with the circulation of the blood*, and tolerably versed in the mechanism of the body. And although, in the light of modern science, their reasoning in medical matters appears to a degree fallacious, one can not but be persuaded that their practice of the movements must have been salutary and efficient; and that this primitive practice, suggested by the most obvious facts pertaining to the constitution, when improved upon and modified by modern science, would be infinitely more salutary and efficient. The effect of increased respiration would now be explained by the well-known oxydizing power of the air upon the blood, and its consequent eliminatory effect upon the system oppressed with incompletely oxydized matters.

The patrons and priests of the *Cong Fou*, let it be said to their credit, seem to have had in mind the higher ends of existence—the good of the soul.

---

* CINÉSIOLOGIE: *ou, Science du Mouvement. Par* N. DALLY.

They believed the true mode of ministering to it to be primarily through the body. P. Amiot says that the Chinese "regarded the *Cong Fou* as a true exercise of religion, which, by curing the body of its infirmities, liberates the soul from the servitude of the senses, and gives it power of accomplishing its wishes on earth, and of freely elevating itself to the perfection and perpetuity of its spiritual nature in the *Tao*, the realm of the great creative Power."

MOVEMENTS IN INDIA.—Intermingled with the superstitious religious practices of the ancient Indians there were also many bodily exercises, bearing a great resemblance to those of the Chinese. The most prominent among them was the *retention of the air* in respiration. They insisted that air produced the same effect in the body that fire produces upon metals exposed to its influence, namely, to *purify* it. The Greek physicians entertained similar ideas, and had rules for the application of a similar practice. The retention of the air, said they, will increase the heat of the internal parts, dilate the capacity of the chest, strengthen the organs of respiration, clear the chest of its impurities, enlarge the pores, attenuate the skin, and drive out moisture through that membrane.

It was from these well-known powers of this movement, that it was employed to purify the mouth, throat, stomach, chest, intestines, and to remedy yawning, hiccough, laryngitis, cough, asthma, gastritis, and enteritis; while in the intervals of movements, and after each series of exercises, friction was employed as an auxiliary means.

A Greek historian who was on a mission to India, in the third century before our era, relates that "among the Brahmins there is an order of physicians who rely chiefly upon diet and regimen, together with external processes, having great distrust of any more powerful means. For this reason it was said that they called charms to their aid. Probably these external processes were a system of therapeutic movements. An order of Brahminites exists at present whose chief medical recourse is hygienic shampooing.

The English who reside in India frequently give accounts of the shampooing and friction, which they find a great source of delight as well as of health. The person receiving the operation is extended on a seat, while the operator manipulates his members, as he would knead dough for bread. He then strikes him lightly with the side of the hand, applies perfume and friction, and terminates by cracking the joints of the fingers, toes, and neck. After this operation, *the subject experiences a sensation of ineffable happiness and energy.* It is said that the Indian ladies seldom pass a day without being thus shampooed by their slaves.

In India, the best qualified practitioners belong to Brahminic families, with whom the art of treating disease was hereditary; and there is every indication that the sacerdotal orders, who were faithful observers of primitive traditions, secretly possessed some Vedic treatise upon the art, of which the preceding is the substance of fragments that have come down to us.

Thus it is seen, that the oldest nations of the world fully believed in and practiced various external mechanical operations upon the body, both as a luxury, and to relieve them of their chronic ailments. And whatever superstition of a religious nature was connected with these operations, by these or other and ruder people, *no one is prepared to assert that they were inefficacious.* All that was required was a larger amount of the science of physiology with which to direct and extend the application, to render this resource legitimate and complete.

MOVEMENTS AMONG THE GREEKS AND ROMANS.—In the remains of statuary that have descended to us, we have ample demonstration of the appreciation the ancient Greeks had of perfectly developed and beautiful physical forms. These representations in marble are enduring monuments of the perfection of the physical education of that people. Even without these evidences, we feel from the character of their literature that such must have been the case; for it is impossible to connect the idea of physical weakness and deformity with such sound philosophical and poetical genius as they possessed. At the very mention of *Greek*, there arises in the imagination of the student a robust and beautiful human form, as near to perfection as it is possible for any child of Adam to approach.

The *Gymnasium* was, with the Greeks, the place for both physical and intellectual culture. The training of body and mind went hand in hand. It was in the gymnasium that persons of all ages daily congregated; and while some were reciting poetry or delivering lectures on philosophy, others were performing, or criticising the performance of, various exercises adapted to develop all their physical parts and powers, or to qualify them especially for arms. Probably no Greek town of any importance was destitute of these schools of exercise.

The education commenced at the seventh year, and consisted of music, grammar, and physical training. Some authors assert that as much time was employed in the culture of the body, as in that of the mind. In Sparta, the idea of physical culture overtopped every other, and the excess to which it was carried excluded that attention to letters which obtained at Athens and the other Grecian states.

Even the women were subjected to treatment similar to that which men received. For, said the lawgivers, "female slaves are good enough to stay at home and spin; but who can expect a splendid offspring, the appropriate gift of a free Spartan woman to her country, from mothers brought up in such occupations?"

The Olympic games were a perversion of the objects of exercise, and produced effects in opposition to those contemplated by rational movements; for they stimulated to excess single faculties for the purpose of winning a prize, instead of producing general excellence and power. Neither true health nor power are possessed by athletes, no matter what astonishing feats they may be able to perform.

The Romans were less appreciative in regard to movements as an educational or as a curative means. The genius of that people was eminently warlike, and they slighted everything that did not look directly to the promotion of physical force for *warlike purposes*. No soldiers were better developed by educational drill than the Roman, both for feats of arms and for endurance.

The Romans had gymnasiums also; but these were perverted, especially in the later days of the empire, to exhibitions of the most brutal and degrading sort, such as pugilistic shows, and encounters with wild and ferocious animals.

To the preceding accounts we may add the following extract, relating to ancient "movements," mainly derived from Oribasius, a Greek physician of the fourth century.

"By the term *exercise* the ancients understood physiological movements pursued according to determined rules. They prepared for exercise by special frictions. They divided movements according to their effects, into three kinds:

"1st. Movements which proceed from within, having their origin in the depths of the body, and depending on the will of those that produce them; these are *active* movements.

"Of these there are several kinds. One requires the exertion of force, as using the spade, driving four horses at once, raising a weight and holding it at arm's length, walking up a steep ascent, climbing a rope, clinching the fists close, stretching the arms, and maintaining them in this position for a long time, resisting the efforts of one trying to lower the extended arms.

"There was also used in the *palestra* (part of the gymnasium) many other movements that required the exertion of power, but all were directed by the *pedotribe*, or director of movements, a person as different from the gymnast as a cook is from a physician.

"Other movements were rapid, but neither intense nor violent; as the mock combat, gesticulation, the play with the *corycos* and the little ball; running in a circle that constantly diminished till a point was reached; walking upon the points of the toes, raising the arms and causing them to move very rapidly, alternately forward and backward. Other rapid movements not requiring exertion, performed in the *palestra*, consisted in *rolling*, either together or alone.

"A third kind are *violent* movements, consisting of such exercises as unite force with rapidity of execution.

"The following may be classed as violent: using the spade, the lance, leaping constantly without resting, throwing heavy projectiles, or working rapidly in heavy armor.

"2d. Movements that proceed from exterior causes, or *passive*. Among these, in general, are sailing, the motion of horse and carriage riding, movement in beds suspended, or with foot supports; in the cradle or their nurse's arms, for infants.

"*Friction* may also be classed among exercises that come from exterior sources. Pressures and pinchings also belong to the same class. Many other movements are included in the kneadings that the ancients employed so frequently.

"3d. *Mixed movements*, or those which proceed partly from exterior and partly from interior sources. Riding is given as an example, for while one is shaken by the vehicle, he must also maintain his posture and his form erect by his own exertions.

"They mention also other kinds of movements, such as speaking, hallooing, breathing, retention of breath, dancing, slow walking with stretching the legs, upon the feet, toes, or heels, up or down an artificial hill, in the sand or soft earth, the play of grace-hoops, swimming, jumping, etc. All these are of the active kind.

"Wrestling, in which there is established an action and reaction between two persons, appertains to mixed movements. There should be reckoned in this class friction, with retention of the breath to stretch the muscles of the chest, and to relax those of the abdomen, or conversely, and the effect of the application of a ligature, which causes the part to become distended, or when the same effect is produced by certain movements.

"It is evident that these movements are of a mixed kind, both *concentric* and *eccentric;* and that the ancients, to have made applications so ingenious to each particular organ of the body, as well as to the entire organism, must have had a knowledge of the different physiological effects of movements.

"We are reminded every day, in our more intelligent applications of these principles, of our indebtedness to the sagacity and patient efforts of the ancients.

"Each of these kinds and species of movements, we see, had its distinct rules and its supposed physiological effects. These effects were modified according to position of the body, upright sitting, lying, or as bent in different ways, forward, backward, or to either side. They were sometimes slow, sometimes quick, sometimes moderate, but *always regular.* The movements being general or partial, precise in their quantity, quality, duration, rhythm, etc., and the director of the ancient exercises being a skillful physician, knew how to adapt them to the age, constitution, or disease of the individual."

In modern times, the literature pertaining to the science of movements in its various branches has been very abundant. But most of it has either related to special topics, or its applicability in special cases and forms of disease or exigencies of the system; or else it has been of too general and philosophical a character to be of popular use, and has not included such practical directions as are demanded for successful general application. There has heretofore been so great an intermixture of error in the prevailing physiological systems, as to prevent the simple, obvious, and eminently practical truth from shining clearly out and exerting its due influence.

The philosophical reader will readily appreciate the causes that have prevented so manifestly true and successful a practice as the *movement* from becoming paramount. Men are ever inquiring. As the reward of these struggles of the growing mind of man, new truths and new ways leading to truth are constantly disclosed. Each of these naturally fills the mind with high hopes in regard to the ultimate results of present knowledge and effort. Inorganic chemistry yielded its riches to the modern physician; and as its facts preceded those of vital chemistry, he naturally made a misapplication of them; for his practice is an outgrowth of, and is limited by, his knowledge. Neither the chemist nor the metaphysician could form a correct statement of physiological truth, and so practice must necessarily remain empirical to a great extent, waiting for the new light that shall bring out those elemental truths that are instinctively seized upon by all primitive people.

The current medical practice has for its foundation these scattered, incongruous, and shifting facts; but so greatly modified is it, however, by the additions of more modern science, that now it seriously threatens to lead us back at last to the first principles of physiology as the only reliable basis after all.

The system of *Ling*, though probably invented by him, is really but the collecting together, on a philosophical plan, of the fragments that had long existed. It comprehended, as it were, by an instinctive grasp, all the truth that had been previously realized at various times and places. What in China, Hindoostan, and Greece had been but empiricism, he put upon the ground on which his successors and followers may hope to build a system of philosophical accuracy.

BIOGRAPHY OF LING.*—The present state of the science of remedial treatment by movements, and the development of this doctrine, is intimately connected with the life of Ling, so that his biography is necessarily a part of its history.

Peter Henry Ling was born on the 15th of November, 1766, at Smaland. His father, who was a curate, died soon after his son's birth, and his mother, who married again, died a short time afterward. Possessing no remembrancer of his father, except a small portrait, which he received from his mother, as a souvenir of love and reverence, the growing boy passed the days of his childhood under the too severe training of a capricious tutor. The young Ling was afterward sent to the schools of Wexio for further instruction. Here he soon distinguished himself for his great talents, and his energy and devotion to study.

When Ling left the schools, he saw life open before him in its roughest aspects; he found himself exposed to incessant vicissitudes, reduced at times to absolute poverty and want. During this period he resided for the most part in Upsala, Stockholm, Berlin, and Copenhagen; but it is not known in what manner he was employed. All we know is, that he studied at Upsala, and passed his theological examinations at Smaland, in December, 1797; afterward he was tutor in several families; at one time at Stockholm, at an-

---

* Extracted from Rothstein.

other in the country. Suddenly he left Germany, and went to Denmark. In 1800 he studied in Copenhagen, and the following year took part in the naval battle against Nelson, as a volunteer in a Danish ship. He afterward returned to Germany, and passed on to France and England, whence he returned to Copenhagen, with a perfect knowledge of the languages of these different countries.

During this period he received on different occasions military appointments, the character of which are unknown to us. It is said that during his travels he was frequently reduced to the most trying circumstances, even suffering the pangs of hunger. At one time he was glad to shelter himself in a miserable lodging in a garret at Hamburgh; he was even forced to wash, with his own hands, his only shirt.

These privations, however, did not depress him; although without means, the desire of continuing his travels, to develop and improve his knowledge, buoyed him up, and enabled him to surmount all difficulties. He was proud of his ability to endure privations, and to do without what are thought by most to be indispensable necessaries.

The same impulsive energy which previously induced him to take part in a sea-fight, determined him to study the art of fencing during his second sojourn at Stockholm. Two fencing-masters, French refugees, had founded there at this time a fencing-school. Ling was there every day, and his great skill in this art soon became notorious, and his passion for it grew with his skill. He was now only at the commencement of that career which was already providentially marked out for him, and which from deliberate choice, and with characteristic energy, he steadily pursued. His reflections upon fencing, and his own experience (for he suffered then from gout in his arm), taught him to infer the wholesome effects which may be produced on the body, as well as the mind, by movements based on rational principles; and he began to realize that fencing, however valuable as an exercise, could not accomplish all that was desirable.

About this time the idea struck him that an harmonious development of the body, of its powers and capabilities, by suitable systematized exercises, ought to constitute an essential part in the education of a people.

The realization of this idea now became his grand aim, the more so as he pictured to himself the brilliant image of mankind restored to health, strength, and beauty. Ling thought not, like his predecessors, of merely imitating the gymnastic treatment of the ancients, but he aimed at its reformation and improvement.

At this period of Ling's life begins that part of his history which for us possesses the deepest interest. Quite unknown, but attracting the attention of every one by his appearance, he made his *début* at Lund in the spring of 1805. Versed in several modern languages, and a thorough master of fencing, he began to teach them both, and being proud of all that concerned his fatherland, he lectured with enthusiasm on the old Norse poetry, history, and mythology.

In the same year he was appointed professor of fencing at the University, and began at once to re-fit the fencing-saloon connected with it, and prepare it for several gymnastic exercises, which were commenced without delay. He soon excited the attention not only of the inhabitants of Lund, but of the other towns in the kingdom.

Ling wished to put gymnastics in harmony with nature, and began in 1805 to study anatomy, physiology, and the other natural sciences. The high value he set on these studies, and the enthusiasm with which he pursued them, are forcibly expressed in his own words.

"Anatomy, that sacred genesis, which shows us the masterpiece of the Creator, and which teaches us how little and how great man is, ought to form the constant study of the gymnast. But we ought not to consider the organs of the body as the lifeless forms of a mechanical mass, but as the living, active instruments of the soul."

Ling looked on anatomy and physiology as the essential and necessary basis of gymnastics. But according to his idea, these and other natural sciences were not at all sufficient for the gymnast, whose aim is the elevation of man, in his corporeal and mental nature, to the ancient *beau-ideal*. He must, therefore, know what effects movements produce upon the bodily and psychological condition of man, a knowledge which can be obtained only by investigating human nature as a whole, and by the most careful and untiring analysis of details.

Not only to himself, but to others also, must the gymnast be able to give an account of the application of his art. Ling opened a new field for physical investigation, hitherto untried, and almost unknown, even to the most learned physicians and naturalists. He conducted his researches with the most scrupulous exactness, and in the most earnest manner frequently recommended his companions to do the same. He did not acknowledge a new movement to be a good one until he was able to render an exact account of its effects. His intention was not merely to make gymnastics a branch of education for healthy persons, but to demonstrate it to be a remedy for disease.

Herein we find the explanation of the strong public interest taken in Ling's ideas. Laymen who had always looked upon bodily movements as a deception, in their sickness, anxious for the re-establishment of their health, were easily induced to seek relief for their ailments by the new method, and were not disappointed.

The curative movements were first practiced in 1813, while Ling remained at Stockholm; but before this time they were neither disregarded nor treated with neglect at Lund.

During his stay at Stockholm, a change fortunate for Ling's usefulness took place, which, in the improvement of his circumstances, extended itself rapidly. At first he was appointed master of fencing at the military academy in Carlberg, near the Swedish capital. Soon afterward he became the director of the Central Institution, founded at his own suggestion. He projected such an establishment at Lund, and addressed, in 1812, the Minister of Public Instruction, soliciting the support of the Government. He received the following answer:—"There are enough of jugglers and rope-dancers, without exacting any further charge from the public treasury." This did not at all diminish his zeal, for after his arrival at Stockholm he had the happiness (in consequence of the propositions he personally made, which were examined by a royal commission) to be appointed by a royal ordinance, with a regular salary of 500 rix-dollars, as the founder and director of this Institution, for the setting out and preparation of which not more than 200 rix-dollars were voted.

The royal ordinance, issued in the year 1814, states that the statutes proposed by Ling, and presented to the commission, were confirmed and legally established. Active and indefatigable, Ling continued his attempts at realizing his great ideas with these scanty facilities, and pursued his philanthropic efforts with a disinterestedness and self-denial which can be attributed only to his enthusiasm for the cause, and to his noble patriotism and humanity. Not only by the zeal and circumspection with which he performed his duty as director, but by the manner in which he taught and practiced his art, the public were at last forced to acknowledge his merits, and its importance. Although in the last days of his life he may have seen his task still incomplete, he was yet able to enjoy a feeling of satisfaction, in comparing the degree of perfection his art had already attained with the state in which he found it at the beginning of his gymnastic career.

The important increase of public support which was accorded to the Institution in the year 1834, was a mark of the increasing general favor conferred on him and it by his country. His sovereign raised him to the dignity of a Professor, and Knight of the Order of the North Star. He thankfully accepted both, but used neither the title of the first nor the insignia of the latter. He was much gratified by the proof of the love of his friends and pupils, when on a festive occasion they presented him with a silver medal. He had the deeper gratification of seeing at length his ideas realized, his art established in Sweden, made use of in every grade of society, and incorporated, as an important element, in the education of the people.

Ling's gymnastics were introduced many years ago, not only into all the military academies of Sweden, but into all town schools, colleges, and universities, even into the orphan institutions, and into all country schools. In the rooms of the Central Establishment at Stockholm, persons of every condition and age, the healthy as well as the sick, executed, or were subjected to, the prescribed movements. The number of those who adopted their use increased every year, and among them were physicians who, in the beginning, had been the most opposed to Ling.

In the Central Institution clever teachers are educated, and no one obtains a diploma, or an official license to act as a practical teacher, without having finished the course, and passed an examination in anatomy, physiology, and the bodily movements.

Ling being convinced of the unity of the organism, and of the importance of the mechanical and physical laws to be observed in its education and remedial treatment, based his system on these truths. He says:

"It is perhaps not readily understood that a movement, or a mechanical action, is competent to affect interior portions of the organism. It is necessary first to understand that the human system is a *unit, complete* and *indivisible*. It can not exist in distinct parts, for then it would not be one organism, but several. All that we find in the body, whether inherent, or foreign matter, in any movement, to whatever extent, engages in each displacement of any one part, and this implies a corresponding change in neighboring parts, according to the extent of the primary action.

"Every little act of changing the attitude, or the relation of the members of the body, an exterior pressure upon a nerve, a vein, or muscle, must necessarily produce a displacement of neighboring parts, and produce an action more or less sensible upon organs, in the proportion of their distance and intensity, resembling those wave-circles we notice on the surface of water.

"Experience shows that the different professions affect differently the physical and moral stamina of those engaged in them. It shows us that a very slight pressure upon a nerve irritates it, that a greater pressure produces pain, and if we add still to the pressure, engorgement, and at last paralysis is produced. It is well known that a certain position is more convenient than all others for the ease of the body and the tranquillity of sleep. Do not persons affected with internal maladies find that they are more comfortable in some positions than in others, and therefore seek those positions?"

Ling arrived at these results by repeated experiments and by direct observation, being nearly always himself the subject of his trials. Still young, and affected with a grave disease of the lungs, and already given up by physicians, he noticed the favorable influence that the movements produced upon his health. In the course of these experiments he succeeded in curing himself of a disease that had been deemed incurable. He was thus enabled to corroborate the observations he had made upon the effect of movements of the body in general, and so to progress in the establishment of his system.

Observation and experiment soon led him to the following law:

"*Nutrition, or muscular development of any part of the body, occurs in direct relation with the active movements to which the part has been subjected.*"

His researches and persevering studies upon the skeleton, muscular attachments, etc., led him at last to a great law, and enabled him to draw the correct inference therefrom. Hence the discovery of a series of movements capable of provoking muscular contractions wherever the hygenic or therapeutic needs indicate them.

He gives the following definition of *movement:*

Every exercise of which the direction and duration are determined, is a movement.

Each movement, according to Ling, *is an idea expressed by the body.*

Ling contended that mechanical agencies could be employed therapeutically as well as chemical and galvanic agencies, as it is an established fact that the "living fiber equally reacts from mechanic as from chemical or galvanic excitation."

He summed up his experiments on the motory phenomena of the human organization in this formula: "To render any movement definite and exact, a point of departure, a point of termination, and a line through which the body or any portion of it must pass, are to be clearly and severally determined as well as the velocity and rhythm of the motory act itself."

The following are the general laws which Ling has laid down in his treatise on physical development:

1. Every just attempt to develop the powers of the human being—mental or corporeal—is properly education.

2. Every movement should have proper relation to the organization of the body; whatever transgresses the laws of that organism is irrational.

3. The sphere of the activity of the muscles and the laws of gravitation determine the limits of a movement of the body.

4. Every movement, however simple and slight it may appear to be, acquires its character from the nature of the whole organism, and each part of the body,

within the limits of its own function and office, ought to participate in that movement.

5. To arrive at a healthful development of the body, it is necessary to begin at the primitive type of each movement; this study should be exact, and can never be considered trifling or unimportant by any one who knows that every movement is either simple or composite.

6. In physical order, as in moral order, simple things are the most difficult to apprehend, thence one can not too zealously study simple movements.

7. A movement is nothing worth if it is not *correct*, that is, if it is not in conformity with the laws of the organism.

8. The body, whose different parts are not in harmony, is not in harmonious accord with the mind.

9. The aim of movements as a science is the proper development of the human organism.

10. Correct movements are such as are founded on the character and temperament of the individual to be developed thereby.

11. The organism can only be said to be perfectly developed when its several parts are in mutual harmony, corresponding to the different individual predispositions.

12. The possible development of the human body must be limited by the faculties, mental and bodily, belonging to the individual.

13. A faculty may be blunted by want of exercise, but can never be utterly annihilated.

14. An incorrect and misapplied movement may pervert the development of such a faculty. Consequently an incorrect movement tends rather to the dis-

advantage than to the gain of the harmonious development of the body.

15. All one-sided development impedes the practice of corporeal exercise; general and harmonious development, on the contrary, facilitates it.

✔ 16. Stiffness or immobility, in any part of the organism, is, in most instances, only an over-development, which is always attended by corresponding weakness in other parts.

✔ 17. The over-development of one part may be diminished, and the weakness of other parts remedied, by equally distributed movements. *f*

18. It is not the greater or lesser power of any part that determines the strength or weakness of an individual, so much as the proportion and harmony of the several parts. Congenital and accidental disorders are not considered here, of course.

19. A real and healthful power consists in a simultaneous action of the several parts (or in action and reaction). In order that motion and power may be developed to their highest point, they must co-operate simultaneously in all parts.

20. Perfect health and physical power are consequently correlative terms; both are dependent on the harmony of the several parts.

21. In corporeal development, commencing with the simplest, you may gradually advance to the most complicated and powerful movements; and this without danger, inasmuch as the pupil has acquired the instinctive knowledge of what he is or is not capable.

Some of Ling's physiological and therapeutic views are contained in the following statements:

"The vital phenomena may be arranged in three principal or fundamental orders: 1st, *Dynamical phenomena*, manifestations of the mind, moral and intellectual powers. 2d, *Chemical phenomena*, assimilation, sanguification, secretion, nutrition, etc. 3d, *Mechanical phenomena*, voluntary and organic; respiration, mastication, deglutition, circulation, etc.

"The union and harmony of these three orders of phenomena characterize a perfect organization, and every vital act is accomplished under their combined influence.

"The shares these phenomena take in a certain vital act give it its peculiar character. If any serious derangement occurs in any of the phenomena, the result is always a disturbance of the vital functions, which we call disease.

"The state of the health depends, accordingly, on the degree of equilibrium and harmony existing between the functions of those tissues or organs in which these three orders of phenomena occur.

" When this harmony is deranged, in order to re-establish it, we should endeavor to increase the vital activity of those organs whose functions have a relation to that order of phenomena whose manifestation is decreased or weakened."

In accordance with these views, he includes among therapeutic means three different kinds of influence on the human organism. 1st, *Chemical agencies;* 2d, *Physical and mechanical agencies;* 3d, *Dynamical agencies*. And he observes that the physician has accordingly to regulate, not only the food and medicine requisite for the sick, but also position during resting, and the manner in which the irritable mind is to be calmed. Due attention to these matters is necessary to constitute a rational treatment of disease.

Ling was a man of unwearied energy and unceasing

activity. He had but few hours to spare for the enjoyment of domestic life, for which no man had a keener relish. It was with reluctance that he wrote on the subject of his art; he preferred to practice and teach it. He was a poet of eminence, of whose genius his nation may well be proud. His poetical writings have been collected in five volumes, consisting of *epic*, *dramatic*, and *lyrical* pieces; the latter are very popular at this day. He took pleasure in dictating verses to his young friends; and it is recorded of him that his flow of verse was so rapid that they often could not keep up with him, a thing which not seldom provoked an outbreak of impatience from the poet. During his last years he suffered much bodily pain, but habitually walked from his country seat, Annelund, to Stockholm, through the last summer of his life, besides performing his fatiguing professional labors. He conversed on his death-bed till the last hour, and gave instructions regarding the science to which he had so nobly devoted himself through a long life. He died on the 3d of May, 1839.

A fine cast of Ling's head may be seen in the cabinet of Prof. Rezius, of Stockholm, the celebrated Swedish ethnologist. It is remarkable for its great length and height, as well as for its general intellectual expression.

The Movement System in Stockholm.—The Swedish capital contains about 95,000 inhabitants, and it has several public institutions for the practice of movements. Having resided there for some time for the purpose of studying the system at its fountain-head, I will give a brief account of the most prominent of these institutions as I found them.

The Central Gymnastic Institute.—This is the original establishment founded by Ling in 1813 under the royal patronage. Professor Branting, the present director, is the immediate successor of Ling. He has lived at the institution as patient, pupil, and director for forty-four years. He is a man of extensive medical reading, a profound anatomist and physiologist, conversing easily in nearly all the European languages, and of a bountiful and sympathetic nature. Ling's widow also resides there, and two or three of his children assist at different responsible posts in the institution.

This establishment consist of several buildings, adapted to the different purposes in view, on a large plot of ground, in a central portion of the city. The *locale*, originally an armory, belongs to the government, and the director and teachers are salaried from the same source.

The especial objects contemplated at this institution are the following:

1. The training of boys to health and the perfecting of their physical powers.

2. The instruction of teachers of the schools, throughout the kingdom, in the modes of physical development by movements.

3. The instruction of youths in sword and bayonet exercise.

4. The instruction of officers and teachers in practical anatomy and in physiology, as connected with the application of movements for the purposes of their professions.

5. The treatment of the sick by the exclusive means of movements.

This latter department, in both the male and female

divisions, is under Professor Branting's personal supervision. A yearly report is made to the government, setting forth the progress of the institution in each of its departments. The total number of persons that avail themselves of the advantages of the institution is about fifteen hundred each year, of whom about 350 are invalids. The number of patrons is constantly varying, but is much greater in winter, when about twenty teachers are required for all the different departments.

Dr. H. SATHERBURG's institution enjoys a medical reputation equal, if not superior, to that of the Central Institute; and it receives more patients, its purposes being entirely medical. It maintains a free clinique for a limited number of patients, in consideration of which it receives a large governmental stipend. Orthopedic surgery is the branch to which Dr. Satherburg makes application of the *movements*, and with extraordinary success. This institution requires about the same number of assistants as the Central.

There are generally one or two other institutions of the same kind, but on a smaller scale, in Stockholm. There is scarcely any chronic disease known that is not successfully treated at these institutions. I might mention a case that I witnessed of blindness, from *amaurosis*, to all appearance completely restored. Numbers of cases of deformity are constantly under treatment, which are in general quite restored before leaving. Pulmonary catarrh, chlorosis, and all diseases of weakness are treated with eminent success.

Institutions of a similar kind, but generally without governmental support, are scattered throughout northern Europe. The one at St. Petersburg is on a magnificent scale, far excelling anything else of the kind, and is patronized by the royal family. The director receives a salary of 10,000 roubles. The whole number of institutions in Europe based on Ling's system is about thirty.

To these historical statements we may append the corroborative testimony of several distinguished philosophers, physicians, and others, of both ancient and modern times, in regard to the utility and efficacy of this system.

DALLY.—"Physical and mechanical agents excite, augment, or diminish in organic bodies, as in inorganic bodies, light, heat, electricity, and magnetism.

"The intimate relation of these fluids, still too slightly appreciated, has given occasion to partial and incomplete applications of mesmerism, electro-vitalism, electro-therapeutics, and, quite recently, to odic-force and tellurism.

"Artificial movements, deduced from a knowledge of physics and mechanics on the one hand, and physiology and pathology on the other, are certainly, of all agents, the most rational and the most powerful for controlling by their action in the interior of the organs, in the gases, the fluids, and the tissues, the development of the so-called imponderable fluids essential to life.

"Movement is one of the primordial products of life and the regulator of all vital conditions. Artificial movements are the agents most specially adapted to excite natural, physiological, vital, organo-biological action, by which the human machine performs its functions, is developed, preserved, and repaired.

"These are the ordinary bases of physical education, of hygiene and therapeutics—bases at once traditional and established by modern experience in a manner the most thorough and positive, and which, in their essentially medical point of view, M. Bonnet distinguishes by that beautiful and legitimate title, 'treatment of diseases by the exercise of functions.'"

HOFFMAN.—" We can not perfect the art of healing till we learn to apply mechanics and hydraulics to medicine.

" Experience furnishes materials, but they ought to be worked up according to the rules of mechanical science, and the only way to introduce exactitude in medicine is not to admit as proved that which does not rest upon irrefutable principles. It is thus medicine may be raised, as well as geometry, to the rank of the exact sciences, and it is not less susceptible of a logical or geometrical precision than any branch whatever of the mathematics."

J. J. ROUSSEAU.—" It is a pitiable error to suppose that exercise of the body is injurious to the operations of the mind, as though the two actions were not intended to go together, and that the one ought not to direct the other.

" Do you wish to cultivate the intelligence of your pupils, cultivate the power that controls it. Exercise the body continually, make it robust and healthy, to make a wise and rational individual."

PLINY.—" The mind is stimulated by movements of the body."

GALEN.—" All the powers of the soul are increased and renewed by exercise.

" It is necessary to place health under the auspices of labor.

" The greatest danger to health results from complete inactivity. In the same manner the greatest benefit results from moderate exercise."

Speaking of his own manner of life, and which he

had caused to be adopted also by one of his friends, he thus discourses of movements: "We make it a duty to take exercise and to avoid improper food, and in this manner we have been very many years, even to this time, exempt from diseases."

ARISTOTLE.—A long time before Galen, Aristotle, replying to this question, "Why is it good hygiene to diminish the quantity of food and increase exercise?" says, "The cause of disease is the excess of excretions which result from the excess of nourishment, or from the want of exercise."

The great and venerable HIPPOCRATES remarks: "He who eats without taking exercise can not be well." And adds, "Perfect health results from a just and constant equilibrium between alimentation and exercise."

This illustrious author also says, "Those who do not eat to satiety, and are diligent in labor, preserve excellent health."

VEGECE informs us, that military men consider that the daily exercises contribute more than medicines to the maintenance of health in the soldiers.

Of the good ABBE SAINT PIERRE, author of the *Projét de paix perpetuelle*, member of the *Académie Français*, and the inventor of a kind of elastic *fauteuil* which he names *Trémousoir* (movement apparatus), upon which one may perform hygienic movements similar to those of equitation, Maupertuis, his successor in the *Académie*, relates the following anecdote: "A geometer proposed, on one occasion, to relieve certain organs where the blood accumulated, for the purpose of causing it to flow into other organs, to make use of centrifugal force, which he proposed to secure by means of a whirling machine."

It was a very rational idea, that of thus exciting in the human organization the centrifugal and centripetal forces for the purpose of modifying at will that organization which Ruysch, in his enthusiasm as an anatomist, declared to be only a tissue of vessels.

PLATO.—"A good education is that which assures to the body all the beauty, all the perfection, of which it is capable.

"To secure this beauty, it is only necessary that the body should be developed, with perfect symmetry, from the earliest infancy.

"The first stages of development are always most controlling and most enduring.

"If the exercise does not keep pace with the growth of the body, it becomes subject to I know not how many infirmities."

This is all very well; but, to obtain this result, it is necessary to know precisely the means; it is necessary, in the first place, to study hygienic movements, as related to the anatomy and physiology of the body; otherwise all is uncertainty and ignorance, and the experimenter is blind to the true nature of the means which he puts in practice, as of the result which he wishes to obtain.

BACON.—"The human organization, so delicate and so varied, is like a musical instrument of complicated and exquisite workmanship, and easily loses its harmony. Thus it is with much reason that the poets unite in Apollo the arts of music and of medicine, perceiving that the genius of the two arts is almost identical, and that the proper office of the physician consists in tuning and touching in such a manner the lyre of the human body as that it shall give forth only sweet and harmonious sounds."

While discussing the means of prolonging the ordinary term of human life, he thus writes:

"The living man wastes continually, and continually also repairs his loss. But this reparative power becomes exhausted, and the man dies. To diminish the activity of the forces which weaken and destroy, to maintain the power which repairs, to soften the indurated parts, which are opposed to the reparative powers, this is to prolong human life, as far as the organization of the body will permit."

As to the different kinds of exercises which contribute most to preserve or restore health, no physician has yet been sufficiently specific. Although there is scarcely any predisposition to any disease which may not be corrected by certain well-adapted exercises, it may be mentioned, by way of example, that bowling is valuable for diseases of the kidneys; archery, for those of the lungs; exercise in the open air, whether on foot or in a carriage, for a weak stomach, et cetera. "Everything in its own turn," to the end of the long list of ills to which our flesh is heir. A random, indiscriminate application of these means is rather hurtful than beneficial. Quackery is as injurious here as in any other department of practice.

Georgii.—"The education of the mind and that of the body are alike in this, that they both demand a special method, founded upon the physiological action of their respective organs.

"Hence, as education, moral or intellectual, should have for its object the exercise of those faculties whose action is deficient, so *physical* education should constantly tend to produce and maintain an equilibrium between the functions of the body, and to have for its end the harmony of all its operations.

"Having, then, need of a perfect body, let us try to secure that blessing by keeping up the equilibrium of the functions; let us multiply in ourselves the points of intelligent contact with the whole of nature, and we shall see the princely powers of the soul displayed in all their magnitude and dignity.

"The actual state of man may be considered as the product of the educational discipline to which the species has been submitted, from the most remote period, and also as a lamentable proof of his departure from the line of rectitude, and of the degree of it thus far."

Chapter Three.

THE RELATIONS OF CHEMICAL AND MOLECULAR CHANGES TO THE ORIGIN OF FORCE IN THE BODY.

IMPORTANCE OF FIRST PRINCIPLES.—It is needful to study the nature, origin, and relations of the powers of the body in order to become properly qualified to direct them healthward. For it is evident that the kind of health we possess must be determined by the kinds of actions that are going on in the elementary constituents of our physical being; since it is on these actions that the development of the powers of the body depends. In other words, bodily health is referable to conditions back of those symptoms, or good or ill feelings which we superficially regard as constituting the health; namely, to those primary motions of elementary matter that are concerned in organic growth and physiological manifestation; the sensorial indications being the last result of a series of actions, of which health and happiness constitute the result. Hence, all medical control of the health, of whatever name or origin, essentially consists in a control of these elementary actions, inasmuch as the causes of good or ill health, as we have seen, reside in these. Such medical practice as does not recognize the changes induced by its agency on these primary actions, as the basis and explanation of its power, is empirical. It appeals chiefly to the sensations, which are ever to be distrusted in the invalid, and in the end always prove unworthy of reliance. While the invalid is made comfortable by means of a drug, he is to be satisfied that its effects are good, and is disinclined to investigate further. Medical science must remain untrustworthy, and continue incompetent to command the regard of the philosophic mind, so long as it overlooks scientific principles in its search for remedies, and is not ashamed to ignore the first truths of physiology, or pour contempt upon the simplest dictates of enlightened reason.

To establish and maintain two great forces is the main object of all the operations of the human system. These are the *mechanical* and *nervous* forces. All the corporeal functions and actions, of whatever kind, are subservient to these chief purposes; and in the *muscular* and *nervous* systems it provides organs or instruments through which these powers are manifested. The one set of organs includes the great mass of the flesh of the body covering the skeleton, while the other set is, by its filaments, extensively and minutely distributed to the muscles, as well as to all other parts, besides existing in distinct local masses, in the head and central portions of the body. The nervous forces are of several distinct kinds or classes, each sustaining peculiar relationships to the organism, but all associated in one grand unit. These classes are, the sensorial and intellectual, relating to the mind; the reflex, connecting the mind and senses with the muscles, the medium of mechanical power; and the organic, relating to the various agencies concerned in the processes of growth.

These powerful instruments are evidently the means intended for the manifestation of the individuality and distinctive character of the man, the grade and quality of his being. It is through these that he impresses surrounding things, acts upon them in a thousand ways, modifies their relations to assist his purposes, and secures through their use the objects of his own desires. It is through the use of these agents, also, that he fathoms the designs of nature and of God, discovering the laws that appertain to surrounding things and to his own spiritual nature. The possession of these powers fulfills in him his utmost desires, and he can covet nothing more as respects the quality of these powers. They are capable of a progressive and almost limitless expansion, at least this may be said of those belonging to the nervous system. But they *may* act inharmoniously, feebly, painfully, or antagonistically.

The latter condition constitutes disease. As a man's possibilities of power in this mortal state can not be realized without instruments, so will they find imperfect expression through imperfect instruments. Hence we must go to the *source* of these manifestations, if we would correct or improve them whenever they are imperfect or defective.

To improve these capabilities, and to train them to their proper uses, is, in short, to put an individual in possession of himself. Ill health is evidence of loss of such control; medical efforts are merely endeavors to restore this control.

In order to acquire balance and perfection in the powers of the mind, the necessity of training them by due exercise, we have seen, has been acknowledged in society in all its grades, from the most rudimental up to the most civilized. This is everywhere the burden of the precept, and is taught in the examples of the most advanced minds. This principle is the basis of all wise education; it is that which raises men from the condition of the savage, who knows only to supply his immediate animal wants by the most simple and direct means, to that of civilized society, with its manifold resources for, and high appreciation of, intellectual enjoyments—to that, indeed, of philosophers, and expounders of the most important truths of life and nature.

The importance of this training by exercises is also conceded by most men—it is, indeed, so generally admitted as to make any argument in its favor apparently unnecessary for the purpose of arousing a proper sense of its value as a means of cure. The obligation to labor, in some sphere of genial activity, was kindly imposed on all men by nature at the beginning, and a sufficient penalty is sure to be visited upon all who transgress this primal law. Men in all states of society fully understand this principle; but they recognize it only in a general way, and scarcely ever inquire as to the *laws* of exercise, its bounds, and its special applications.

The physical exercise imposed by the necessity of supplying food and shelter, and of compassing the various ends of ambition, has served very tolerably the coincident but incidental purpose of developing both the physical and moral manhood of the race. Yet the laws respecting the effects upon the instruments of these powers themselves, and upon the connected and dependent functions produced by the different modes of manifesting the bodily powers, are generally too imperfectly understood to be made available.

These Forces a Product of Vital Action.—Though

we may not define correctly what life *is*, yet we may understand what it *does*, and what are the conditions of its highest development. The powers above described are the last products of a series of operations referable to this principle. These operations are conducted through material agencies, are chemical in a certain phase of their effects, and are influenced by the chemical nature of the agents that take part in them. The development of life and of the forces here considered is inseparably connected with elemental changes that are continuously going on in the system. These changes are kept in continuance by constant supplies of new material, which enjoys only a temporary residence in the body, being excluded from it in connection with the evolution of the above-named forces, giving place to fresh material of a similar kind that is as constantly provided. Vitality is an endowment of matter of the most transient kind; it is little more than the expression of the changes matter undergoes while in the body, both in regard to *form* and *chemical* composition. Hence it is apparent that whatever influence modifies the health, whether for good or for ill, effects this result by modifying in some way those elementary changes whereby vital power is evolved.

The vital acts through which animal power is manifested may be included under the general term, *nutrition*. The term *nutrition* covers the total process whereby the integrity of the organism is preserved, during its interstitial changes. It consists of many distinct actions, whether chemically or physiologically considered; but these are resolvable into two general classes, which, in health, are nicely balanced. These acts are variously named *construction* and *destruction* of organic forms; assimilation and disintegration; composition and decomposition, etc., etc.

In effecting these functional acts two distinct classes of materials are employed in the body, both of which are conveyed to the scene of vital activity by the blood. These are *food* and *oxygen;* one entering the blood through the stomach, by means of digestion, the other through the lungs, by respiration.

The general office of these materials is to maintain the actions that produce the two classes of effects under consideration, the food to build up, and the oxygen to change, by its chemical power, the composition of organic bodies, and to reduce them, at last, to the state in which they find their exit from the body. We may be able better to appreciate the extent of these operations by estimating the quantity of the materials that are employed in conducting them. According to Draper, the water taken into the system of a man weighing 140 pounds, in the course of the twenty-four hours amounts to 4.1 lbs.; the dry food, 2.25 lbs.; the oxygen, 2.19 lbs.; the whole amounting to about eight and a half pounds of material every day, furnished the system to sustain its powers. A proportionate amount, we discover, is discharged from the body in the same time, there being no increase of its weight. But in the mean time these materials have become greatly changed in consequence of chemical combinations with each other. About a pound and a half of water has been produced in the course of these combinations, half a pound of carbon has been dismissed through the lungs, and a great variety of organic and earthy salts have been concocted in the system and drained off by the kidneys. To convey oxygen and nutriment to the changing structures, about twenty-five pounds of blood have been kept in unceasing circulation through all, even to the minutest channels of the body; and about twenty-one pounds of solvent juices have been poured into the digestive canal to effect the solution of the food, to be again absorbed into the blood.

But a view of the results and the means of transformation in the body conveys but a very inadequate conception of the amount and extent of the change produced. For the final eliminatory product is generally the last result of a series of changes that must occur in regular order. So the food and oxygen received into the system enter into many distinct states of union, during their residence in the system, each of which is necessary to the advancement of the vital interests, while it forms a step toward their final dismissal from the body. At each of these stages of progress, malign influences will cause a deviation of the action, as well as of the product of action, from the physiological standard; the healthful process will be arrested, and other actions are substituted, which defeat the great end of evolving the forces mentioned; the perfect evolution of which it is the aim of all physiological actions to accomplish. Disease is a deviation from the usual and prescribed processes of atomic change.

Since the chief intention of the processes within the body is either to build up or to demolish, it follows that all the influences brought into relation with the organism must tend to *promote* one or the other of these results. Such is the normal intention of food and oxygen, both of which are received into the system in about equal quantities by weight. The product of the digestion of food is employed in the *organizing* processes; while the oxygen aids in dissolving the organized molecule into a soluble or volatile form, whereby its egress from the system is determined. According to the physiological plan of the system, such matters are applied to these specific purposes, and thus fulfill the intentions of Nature in respect to the development of the forces of which we are treating.

When the influences exerted upon the physiological processes are such as to promote equally and properly these actions of *waste* and *renewal*, through the use of the legitimate materials prescribed by the laws of organization, health is the necessary consequence. The theory and practice of the principles concerned in the maintenance of health are included in the term *Hygiene*.

By *Remedial Hygiene* is understood the intelligent application of certain principles and agents for the restoration of lost or impaired health. The employment of *Movements* is a powerful means of directing or enforcing nutrition. Movements are a device for aiding the organism in its efforts to derive sustenance from suitable materials, and for assisting the exit of waste matters; and they thus constitute a special application of hygiene; while hygiene, in general, embraces the means that in health are influential to control the waste and renewal of the body.

All substances incapable of supporting the growth of the vital parts, if not absolutely neutral in their relations to them, will modify and generally accelerate the *wasting* processes of the body. Such, indisputably, are the effects of drugs. When the living molecule is forced into unwilling contact with a drug which has been introduced into the system, one of two effects must ensue: the natural affinity of the molecule for oxygen is increased, or else it is impressed by the chemical or mechanical power of the foreign and unfriendly substance. The peculiar symptoms that appear are either the result of the unusual waste and of the consequent rapid evolution of the reserve powers of the organ, or the quality of the intermediate forms of wasting matter is made to differ more or less widely from that of the normal and usual series of products; thus rendering the ejection of these matters less easy, distending, as a consequence, the capillaries of the part, and impressing both its organic and sensitive nerves in a peculiar and painful manner. The cases of spontaneous or accidental disease, and the artificial effects produced by drugs, are admitted to be very similar. Hence, drugs are classed accordingly as their effects correspond with certain pathological conditions; but they may be considered as in general *favoring* the chemical changes in the body, sometimes accelerating, sometimes impeding the manifestation of power, but never promoting any conditions calculated to induce the production of that power, by contributing to the primary *organizing* processes. But this organic growth is the first condition for the manifestation of vital power, and, indeed, one without which such power can not be manifested in any degree.

To the securing of health, then, it appears to be indispensable that the interstitial changes taking place in the body shall be those which can proceed only in a normal condition of the organism. To effect this purpose, the incentives to the changes must be physiological in their nature.

The existence of the profession of medicine rests upon the general belief in or on the tacit consent of the world to the notion that the operations of the human system can be favorably excited or controlled by the employment of various agents; and accordingly the ingenuity of man has always been severely tasked for the discovery of such agents; but to this day the toil and search have been unrewarded by any result universally satisfactory. These remedial means have generally been of a character calculated either to promote, as their primary effect, the *disorganizing* operations of the body, or else to produce certain chemical effects without necessarily effecting the desired elimination of the refuse products, *carbonic acid, water*, and *urea;* affording also no assistance to the *organized* agencies.

Better results must be attained when the means employed shall directly evolve the proper product, which shall be at once liberated from the system, and in the same act shall promote in the highest practicable degree the activity of the organizing or reproducing forces. We must confine our researches, in pursuance of this purpose, to an investigation of the conditions of perfect health, instead of vainly searching for some wonderful specific, or panacea, or divine balsam among substances whose demonstrable effect on vitalized matter is only and forever to deteriorate and destroy.

DIFFERENT KINDS OF MOTION.—The chemical changes, or changes of quality in the organic tissues of the body, always imply change of place or *motion*. By motion, all vital phenomena are accomplished. But this motion consists of many kinds, or is presented to us in different phases, each bearing its individual relation, and being equally indispensable to the welfare of the vital whole.*

---

* Beclard gives the following summary of the natural internal movements of the body, a careful perusal of which will be advantageous to the studious reader:
Cerebro-spinal axis in the region of the neck: movement of alternate *raising* and *falling;* a kind of oscillation of the encephalic mass.

1. The first variety of these motions is that already described as being conducted among the elementary constituents of the body, and involving changes in the composition of organized parts; this is *chemical action*. Here *motion* occurs through the displacement of the ultimate atoms, and, as we have said, it is the inevitable consequence of such displacement.

Chemical action proceeds within the system on a scale of magnitude of which the sensible products afford us but an imperfect indication, since we can know only the last of a series of actions of which chemical power is the first cause. Some of these actions are but the concomitants of vital changes, of which vitality only supplies the conditions, the action itself being, meanwhile, independent of vitality. We might instance the metamorphosis of tissues, on the one hand, and the oxydation of hydro-carbons on the other, as

---

Spinal and sympathetic movement of the nervous fibers from the circumference to the center, and from the center to the circumference; movements *reflex* and *sympathetic;* movements of undulation and vibration, of quivering, of shuddering.

Respiration, inspiration, and *expiration.*

Related with inspiration: inhaling, expanding

Related with expiration: voice, speech, singing, crying, whistling, explosion of breath in excretory efforts, yawning, coughing, laughing, sneezing, sighing, sobbing, hiccough.

Peristaltic movements of the stomach, commencing at the large curve, and *Antiperistaltic* at the small. The revolution is completed in two or three minutes. *Concentric* movement is that which takes place in the circular fibers of the lesser end of this organ.

Small Intestine.—*Progressive* movement of the alimentary mass, conducted by the longitudinal and circular fibers of the intestine. The contraction is local, and moderate in force. The movements of the large intestines resemble those of the small, but are slower.

Organ of the Circulation. Heart: movement of *systole* and of *diastole.* These movemen's are correlative, and resemble those of a forcing-pump, the contraction of the walls of the heart answering to the operations of the piston, and plugged by its valves.

Movements of tension and distention; of torsion, pulsation; of shock, palpitation.

Arteries and capillaries: eccentric circulation.

Veins: concentric circulation.

Movements of electricity, contraction, compression, tension, distention, resistance, remittence, intermittence, rubbing, etc.

interesting examples of these varieties of chemical action.

2. *Growth,* or the reproduction of the wasting parts of the body, under the inspiration of vitality, may also be regarded as a peculiar kind of action, involving unceasing motion. In this action, the materials of growth, existing in a soluble state in the blood, are discharged through the membranes of the vessels, and the elementary constituents rearranged in a new form, generally without a very material change in their proportions. The matter in this instance assumes, under certain mysterious laws, the primary organic forms which, by repetition, build up or reproduce the various organs.

3. Muscular action, it has been discovered, results from a motion of contractility peculiar to the cells constituting muscular fibrillæ. These motions are found to be merely results of a change in their shape, by flattening of the little cells in such a way that while their length is diminished, their diameter is augmented.

4. The above motion, so inconsiderable in itself, results at last in that most conspicuous of corporeal motions, namely, that of a change of place effected by the whole body or of one or more of its members. When a muscle contracts, we know it carries the whole mass of bones, nerves, vessels, areolar tissue, fluids, etc., of which the moving part is composed, along with it through space, besides changing, in some degree, the relations of these parts to each other.

5. To the fluids of the body is imparted a motion by this muscular action. This motion of the blood is in fact required as a means of inducing this very muscular action. And the circulation of the blood throughout the system is supported by the joint action of the

countless and constant motions taking place in the substance of the various tissues.

6. By means of the force communicated by the muscular action of their walls, the contents of the canals of the body are caused to flow in regular tides through these organs in the direction of the outlets. In this way those matters for which the system has no use are ejected.

7. The walls of the chest and of the arterial blood-vessels have an established and rythmical motion in health. The one is designed to refresh the blood, and the other mainly to assist the circulation of this fluid throughout the body.

RECIPROCITY OF ACTIONS.—The different motions of which the body is the sphere, constitute that connected series of activities which it is the function of Physiology to explain. Their action is wonderfully complicated, and they all have a part to play in the development of that grand *mechanical force*, the countless muscles and nerves with which our bodies are supplied. An impediment to the fulfillment of any one of these actions necessarily vitiates them all, just as one defective link weakens the whole chain. In one respect these simultaneous motions resemble the successive elemental actions of the chemical state, before alluded to. All interference with the regular vital processes renders imperfect those several conditions of organic growth upon which all power absolutely depends.

An important principle is now to be noticed, to wit, that *the expenditure of power is necessary to its very evolution*. This expenditure is the phenomenon contemplated in the entire train of actions above alluded to, and without this there can be no mechanical motion, no molecular motion, no organic and no chemical action; and no demand, therefore, made upon the digestive organs, or upon the respiratory function.

The reader must not infer from this statement that all function ceases with the cessation of *voluntary* motion, or with the suspension of the will. Provision is made against any such fatal accident. In the economy of the system it so happens that a large amount of its muscular action is carried on *involuntarily* for the special furtherance of its organic operations. This is particularly true of all the rythmical motions, such as the movements of the chest, diaphragm, and abdominal muscles in respiration; of the heart and arteries; of the alimentary tube, etc.

While, then, the living body may be regarded as an admirably arranged theater in which these various motor forces have their full and harmonious play, *muscular motion* must be considered as the great mainspring of all the others. It certainly sets in operation many kinds of action; many seem to depend on it as their chief stimulant, and others appear to radiate from it as from a central force. By this far-reaching power of its own it controls to a good extent all the motions of the alimentary atoms, and disposes of them to the highest advantage of the whole system.

Nature, in her arrangements for the welfare of her children, saw fit to select *motion* as a chief means for the maintenance of the physiological harmonies of the body, and for the restoration of these harmonies and the health they confer, in cases in which the latter have been lost through accident or imprudence.*

---

* Leehmann corroborates this view of the influence of motion in the following passage: "Albinus took no superficial view of the organic activity in nature, when he established the axiom, that the essence of vital force consisted in motion.

THE SYSTEM AS A RESERVOIR OF FORCE.—The system, in health, is capable of supplying force at a certain *rate*, determined by the degree of perfection in which its organic processes are conducted. These processes are always, with more or less effect, engaged in producing force. Now, if this force be expended in a single channel, the production will probably about equal the expenditure; but if in several channels at the same time, the expenditure must not only exceed the production, but will even exhaust the reserved supply which the healthy system always possesses. This state of things is denoted by the feeling we call *fatigue*.

In the invalid, the force production is more or less limited. This is a necessary result of disease. Hence, such exercises as involve a large portion of the system at one time are harmful, because they are sure to exhaust the reserve fund of force, which is not readily restored by the defective organic processes, and so the disease will be increased in our very efforts perhaps to quell it. But if the exertion be confined to a single instrument or organ, or to a single set of muscles, the expenditure of force is made to correspond more nearly with its production; the system is not fatigued, but is refreshed, because the movements have helped to sup-

---

Even if this expression be far too general for organic action, it can not be denied that we assume life to exist wherever we perceive a constant alternation of phenomena and incessant changes induced by the constant motion of the molecules of the organized body, as well as of the organs themselves. * * * * *

"Metamorphoses are continually developed in the material substrata of the body. Physical forces continue to act upon matter after it has attained its position of equilibrium, for it is only by opposite actions that equilibrium exists. * * * * * The case is very different when motion occurs in organized bodies, for here we find a tendency to persistence; everything that is brought into the line of the direction of these concurrent forces is impelled to a similar motion, and equilibrium will not be produced, for equilibrium is rest, and in rest there is no life, and in equilibrium there is death."—Vol. ii., pp. 210, 211.

ply the true and proper conditions for the production or augmentation of the life-power.

Description of Muscle.—The mere fact of muscle entering so largely into the composition of the system, would indicate to any mind its importance in the physical economy. This tissue constitutes more than half of the weight and bulk of the body. It has but a single function, and that is, as it is technically termed, *contraction*, or the approximation of the extremities; for experiments show that the bulk is unvarying. By contracting, and in proportion to the vigor of the contraction, muscle is capable of *moving* the bones and other appendages with which it is connected. It also forms the walls of the hollow organs, and, by contracting, lessens the caliber of such organs, and impels their contents onward. The muscles are crowded with bloodvessels, the larger trunks of which pass through, and the smaller are distributed within them for the supply of nutrient matter. They are connected together by an areolar structure, consisting of elastic filaments, forming a network around them, which serves the double purpose of at once binding them together and keeping them separate.

Fig. 1.

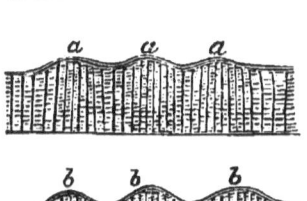
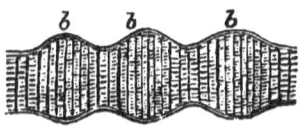

Muscular fiber, showing the cells; *a a a*, the waves of contraction, showing the flattening of the cells; *b b b*, similar waves, engaged in still stronger contraction, traveling along the fiber, and causing it to be thicker at the contracting portions.

Muscle is visibly distinguished from other structures by its red color. Masses of muscle are divided longitudinally into parallel fibers, visible to the naked eye, which are again divided into exceedingly minute fibrillæ; and these fibrillæ are crossed by transverse stripes which seem to divide each of them into microscopic dimensions. These cubes are the *ultimate muscle-cells.* In the act of contraction these cubes are flattened, and at the same time become proportionably broader.

The contraction of a muscle is effected by the contraction separately of the fibers of which it is composed. These fibers act through only a portion of their length at the same moment; the contractions seeming to travel from one portion to another of the fibrils, each portion becoming relaxed as the action travels beyond it. This becomes an important fact in the curative application of movements, as we shall see.

Muscular contraction never takes place independently of an exciting cause or *stimulus.* The power effecting this act is derived from the nerves distributed to the muscular structure. These nerves for the voluntary muscles have their origin in the spinal axis, and are also generally connected with the seat of the will. So that impressions received from without the body by the sensitive nerves, and those originating in the mind, are capable of directly inducing muscular action, and consequently motion, in all the organs that are connected with them.

M. BECLARD gives thus, with much clearness, the chemical phenomena which attend muscular contraction:

"The muscles develop a certain quantity of heat at the moment of contracting. The researches of MM. BEQUEREL and BRESCHET, and those more recent of M. HELMHOLTZ, have placed the fact beyond doubt, that the muscles during their contraction, as also during their state of repose, absorb oxygen and form carbonic acid. During contraction, the absorption of oxygen and exhalation of carbonic acid is doubled."

MM. Du Bois-Raymond, Liebig, Valentine, and Matteuci have demonstrated satisfactorily the fact by placing the members of an animal in a space exposed to a known gaseous composition. The chemical phenomena of oxydation are then manifested in the muscles, and these phenomena increase during contraction. M. Helmholtz caused a muscular group to contract by aid of a powerful induction-current for a long time, till exhaustion occurred; he then examined the chemical constitution of the muscular fiber, and found that the soluble materials contained in the muscle (creatin, creatnine, and inosic acid) had increased in proportion when compared with other muscles that had been in repose of the same animal. Du Bois-Raymond proved, on the other hand, that when a muscle remains for a long time at rest, it has a neutral reaction, and that its reaction becomes acid after repeated contractions. The absorption of oxygen increases in a contracting muscle, and the action has the effect of transforming a part of the muscle into an oxydized product, and this oxydation is the cause of the elevation of temperature observed.

In muscular action, generally, the products of combustion formed in the muscles pass toward the blood, and are carried off by the excretory passages; we have also seen that, in exercise, the products of expiration and the products of urinary secretion are increased.

PHYSIOLOGICAL EFFECTS OF EXERCISE.—It will be necessary to particularize at some length the more direct and distinct effects of muscular contraction, in order to bring out more clearly to the mind its claims to attention as an important hygenic and remedial agent.

EFFECTS OF MUSCULAR CONTRACTION ON THE LOCAL CIRCULATION.—*Muscular Contraction* affords powerful aid to the local circulation of the parts in which it takes place, in several distinct ways. 1st. Materials pass from the arterial to the venous side of the circulation according to a law common to all vital tissues. This occurs at a rate directly proportionate to the vital activity. 2d. The effect of the pressure of the contracting muscle upon the blood-vessels that penetrate it, or that are contiguous, is to hasten the flow of the contents of these vessels. The tendency to displacement of these contents can only operate in the direction allowed by the valves of the veins; that is, in the heart-ward direction. At the moment the contraction ceases, the vessels of the part contain less blood; but the pressure from the arterial side instantly supplies the part more abundantly, so as to distend the vessels. This is the condition favorable for the effusion of the vital *plasma* of the blood for the nutrition of the acting part; thus providing for a repetition of the act. 3d. Not only the blood, but the intermuscular juices are renewed by the act of muscular contraction, for the compression to which these organs have been subjected compels all the fluids to change place like the contents of a wetted sponge; and the previously mentioned circumstances give *direction* to the fluids thus set in motion.

The benefit derived from these effects on the circulation is by no means confined to the muscles. All other organs connected with the blood-vessels that supply the muscles participate freely in the same advantages; and it would seem that this is the appointed way in which to secure the nutritive supply in its perfection to the tissues generally.

The mucous membrane, skin, intervening areolar structure, nerves, and other anatomical constituents of the body, share equally in the advantages thus attained. It would seem to be the province of the muscles, numerous and powerful as they are, not only to secure their own health by the exercise of their function, but to minister to the good of all other structures; for all depend alike for their nourishment upon a common reservoir, whose distribution could not be efficiently maintained without the assistance so largely rendered by the muscles.

EFFECT ON RESPIRATION.—Increased respiration occurs simultaneously with every muscular effort. This follows from the fact that *arterial blood*, of which *oxygen* is an important ingredient, is essential in every muscular contraction; for in each contraction oxygen is required probably, as a second result, to effect the destruction of the acting muscular molecule; hence the necessity of a continual supply of this principle through respiration. It will be noticed that an increased inspiratory effort does not succeed, but immediately *precedes* the muscular exertion, and is simultaneous with the suggestion of the *will*, which it seems to render more vehement and energetic. As the arm is raised to strike, the breath is drawn in; and if a strong blow is contemplated, the glottis is for a moment closed, and a strong pressure is exerted upon the contained air of the chest, to force, as it were, the blood to take in an increased quantity of the power-liberating element. This involuntary "holding the breath" is without doubt a very important aid to the respiratory act. It at the same time expands the chest, and aids, by pressure of the respired air, the solution of the oxygen.

In respiration there are two things to be considered: the mobility of the walls of the chest, and the nervous arrangement by which this mobility is controlled. The nerves of respiration act independently of the consciousness in their ordinary operation; but *every effort of the will* increases their action by the stimulus it affords the muscles of the chest. Whether the effort of the will be directed to the muscles of any part of the body, or is confined to mental operations—in each case *waste* is produced, and the employment of an amount of oxygen is implied proportionate to the magnitude of the exertion. It may be remarked that there are other circumstances that influence respiration, as diet; but this is true of *temperature* especially, and respiration is deep just in proportion to the rapidity with which the body loses its heat.

But respiration is entirely a *mechanical* action. It is performed by the muscles of the chest and abdomen, and the degree of perfection with which it is performed is determined by the condition and habits of the organs performing it. If these muscles are badly nourished and imperfectly used, oxygen can be supplied to the blood to support the bodily need only in limited quantities. So it turns out that the amount of work a man can do is not so much dependent on his muscle as on his *breathing capacity*. If he can breathe well he can generally work well; if short-winded, though he may have the muscles of an Ajax, he will be left behind to a certainty in the race of life.

EFFECT ON THE SECRETIONS.—Anything that promotes renewal of the blood of the capillaries, promotes secretions; for whatever be the nature of the secreted product, or its origin, it is derived primarily from the blood of the capillaries, distributed to the membrane whose involutions form the secreting gland. The quality of the secretion will greatly depend, of course, on that of the blood whence it is derived, which, again, is subject to variation from many causes under the control of motion or exercise.

EFFECT ON THE EXCRETIONS.—Muscular action powerfully urges the blood into the skin and lungs, the two principal excretory organs, whence its excretory products are readily eliminated. The same action results in the production of an important element of the urinary excretion, without which this fluid can not be of normal quality. The channels for the egress of this principle are also kept free and open by exercise.

It is now well understood that the most common cause of constipation of the bowels is want of general muscular tone, and especially want of action in the tube through which the alvine discharges are conveyed. The expulsion of the contents of the bowels is only effected by muscular action, to induce which, the tube and the abdominal wells work conjointly, and too frequently tug in vain.

EFFECT ON ABSORPTION.—Nutritive matters, after being reduced to a fluid state by digestion, are prepared to pass the digestive boundaries into the blood. But there must first be a *demand* in the tissues for the materials. The unceasing wastes caused by muscular action, and the expenditure of the blood constantly taking place, must be made good with materials from the digestive surface. The connection between muscular action and absorption is direct.

But *local* action is also required of the digestive membrane. Hence nature causes the whole alimentary tube to take on a sort of rythmical, vermicular motion. The ordinary avocations of life accelerate this motion of the canal. But in sedentery occupations the causes of motion from without are lessened, and the health is sure to suffer as a consequence. Absorption from the digestive canal is incomplete, and the digestive organs become clogged, and soon diseased.

Physiologists have compared absorption to the passage of fluids of different kinds through membranes, known as *osmosis*. The conditions for maintaining this physical phenomenon are, that *the fluids on the opposite sides of the membrane shall be of different kinds.* Now the renewal of the fluids of either side of the membrane of the alimentary canal by motion preserves this difference.

EFFECT ON THE QUALITY OF THE BLOOD.—All the above enumerated processes, namely, *nutrition, respiration, secretion, excretion, absorption,* are the means whereby the blood itself, the great fountain from which life is supplied to the whole body, is maintained in its purity and fitness for its several purposes. Nutrition itself, so far as the blood is concerned, is an excretory act. The very matters destined to supply muscular power and bulk can not be retained in the blood without injury to its quality and damage to the health. The force-imparting properties of the blood can not long be maintained therein unless it gives them up as readily as it receives them.

EFFECT ON THE DIGESTIVE PROCESS.—Digestion is the

means whereby food is furnished to the system, as respiration is the means for supplying oxygen. It is not enough that good food be swallowed. Food is not only inert, but positively injurious, unless rendered fluid and made to proceed in the series of changes it is appointed to undergo. At the natural temperature of the body, food must, from its nature, undergo some change; and if this change is not *digestive*, it will be *chemical*, with the formation of poisonous products. Many persons are habitually poisoned with food taken even in small quantities, when the conditions for its digestion are wanting or imperfect.

Digestion is dependent on the *blood*, its quality and distribution, and on the demand arising in the system for the digested product. If the demand is small, and the amount of food taken be not also proportionably small, the function is injured, and repeated injuries inflict permanent disease. Exercise, in proper modes, is capable of preventing and of remedying such conditions, as is proved by the almost universally good digestive power of the habitual laborer, even when placed under the most unfavorable circumstances.

EFFECT ON THE ORGANIZING PROCESS.—All manifestations of force, muscular or nervous, are directly proportionate to the vigor of their instruments, the muscles and nerves; and it is no exaggeration of the truth to say that we may consider all other functions of the system as contributing to their increase and support. The *organization* or growth of these instruments is evidently a most essential link in the chain of actions between the digestion of food and the manifestation of force. Organization, or growth of organic forms, is to a great degree a vegetative act, and takes its character very much from the character of the nutriment afforded and the manner of its appropriations. Atomic absorption is necessarily preliminary to the process of renovation; the destruction of the organized form and the elimination of the effete material must precede growth, and muscular exertion is requisite in order to insure the vitalization of the material elements from which nature collects what she needs for the continuance of her renovating processes.

Movements Stimulate the Vitalizing Processes.— The modes in which movements, by their mechanical and chemical effects, contribute to the corporeal welfare, has been described, but the last result is of a higher order than any included in these effects. This consists, if we may use the expression, in an augmentation of the control exercised by vitality in the system. The body we have considered as the theater of two opposing actions, the *organizing*, and the *disorganizing*, and *chemical* actions. In the healthy body, those influences which promote the former preponderate, secured as they are by voluntary and involuntary movements habitually conducted, while the inactive body becomes diseased, for the simple reason that therein actions must transpire among its elementary particles which are purely chemical in their nature, and which must have the effect to deteriorate the organizing vital forces, and consequently vitiate the general health and sap the strength of the constitution. By means of rational movements, vital action is made to predominate over all opposing or simply chemical actions, and health follows as naturally and inevitably as night the day.

The part played by drug chemicals in the vital

domain may be easily understood. The presence of such substances is never uninfluential. They increase to a certainty the amount of chemical change going on in the system; and notwithstanding the impulse toward health that is oftentimes thought to be given, and which is the result of a temporary vital reaction, yet it remains true that the real tendency of the system, under their sway, is necessarily downward, because chemical, and consequently injurious, changes are thereby promoted.

Co-ordination of Motions by the Nerves.—Every organ and member of the body performs a distinct office, and its individuality is never merged in that of others. But it is also true that all the diverse parts are connected in an individual whole by means of the nervous system. The nerves, we know, pervade all vital parts, and not only preside over the peculiar function of every local element and member, but also cause each to act with reference to, and harmoniously with, all other organs, and with the whole economy. We are well aware, through our sensations, of many things that are going forward in the body; for the consciousness and intellectual functions are influenced through the nerves. The great majority of the operations of the system proceed *without* the consciousness, and are soon interrupted by it when it is brought to bear on them; but there is, so to speak, a kind of *organic understanding* maintained between the functions of the different parts harmonizing their motions. Some of the manifestations of this principle are termed *reflex action*. A person instinctively draws back from a danger that he *sees*, *hears*, and *feels*. The stomach and bowels also reject food which it would be harmful to tolerate; a limb retracts unconsciously if even a fly alights upon it, and the eyelid winks if a mote sails by it ; the pulse is quickened not more readily from the effects of a drug than by a passing thought of the mind or emotion of the heart. These results are *automatic*, that is, not connected necessarily with the consciousness and the will. Hence, on the same occult principle, during the natural performance of every organic act, there occurs a response of organ to organ, of part to part, throughout the system, in every direction along the nervous network. One sees a luscious peach, and the whole gustatory apparatus takes on a gentle excitement; the circulation of the part is instantly affected and the saliva commences to flow.

If now the fruit be taken into the mouth, not only is an abundance of saliva poured forth, but the stomach also enters upon a state of preparation ; the gastric and other fluids are secreted, and the whole system experiences a sense of satisfaction and enjoyment. The explanation of all this is, that the ultimate organic actions of the body have been impressed and brought into vigorous and harmonious play in accordance with natural and beautiful, though mysterious law.

The effect of muscular contraction upon the organs of the body, through the nerves, is perfectly analogous to that just noted. Whenever a great muscle acts energetically, the nerve-filaments distributed therein are powerfully affected, the terminal loops or extremities are suddenly approximated, and its sensibility is increased. The immediate effect of the flow of blood which takes place from other parts to the acting part, even the heaving of the chest sometimes, and the change of expression of the whole man, are very apparent. This consentaneousness in the action of the whole person is effected by the nerves; but these visible effects, great and striking as they are, are a mere representation of invisible, internal action still more important and wonderful. These actions may be made to supply special needs of the organism, and then they become *remedial*. We are *unconscious* of the intervening or connecting changes till we see their outward phenomena produced.

Another important influence that we may mention here, is that exerted upon organic motions through the medium of the *consciousness*.

When one notices the effects of the exertion of his muscles, and appreciates the consequences, the system becomes infused with a wholesome energy, *the consciousness of the possession of power*. This principle is understood by comparing the influence upon the mind, and through it upon the organic system of the *successful* with the unsuccessful effort. If one makes an exertion that is inadequate to overcome the resistance, discouragement results, and a general depression of all the organic forces is the consequence. Such is the influence of mental impressions upon the nutrient processes. A few unsuccessful attempts to do what ought perhaps never to have been attempted, will sometimes make an invalid for life; for the system is thus deprived of the stimulus of that nervous *vim* requisite for vigorous and healthful organic action. Now if in such a case exercise be *prescribed* so as to adapt nicely the quality and quantity to the condition of the invalid, the encouragement thus afforded to the failing forces imparts new energy to the whole man, and we often see him in a few days brought up out of his slough of despond and enjoying the sunshine of hope and renovated feeling.

THE FOREGOING EFFECTS.—What are ever contemplated as the ultimate results of medical prescription other than those here enumerated? Not that perfect health will always be secured by attending to these particulars, even if attended to in the best manner that a patient's opportunities, amount of knowledge and experience and constitutional capacity will allow; but we do say, and insist strenuously, that the mode here indicated of securing healthful effects is *direct and rational*, and more efficacious than those usually employed by medical practitioners; and that it is in many cases attended with *the most satisfactory results.* And when from causes already intimated imperfect results follow, we insist that it is less the fault of the means than of the mode of their application.

Chapter Four.

MOVEMENTS, AND THE PRINCIPLES GOVERNING THEIR APPLICATION.

DEFINITION.—It is necessary for the reader to bear in mind the distinction between *movements*, *gymnastics*, and *exercises*, as these words are here employed. By *exercises*, is understood all voluntary motions of the body whatsoever, without any reference to the object or objects had in view. Thus labor and recreation, practiced by either body or mind, whether general or partial, are exercise. The word *gymnastics* is used exclusively to indicate the means of developing the corporeal frame, whereby it is fitted for the business of life, or for any special purpose, by means of certain exercises. Gymnastics are employed by the well, and are recognized universally as a useful means of developing the healthy body into its due proportions, which, without exercise, it fails to acquire. Gymnastics, in its technical meaning, may indicate very many kinds and degrees of exercise, and it is only necessary that they should have this end in view in order to deserve this title.

The term *exercises*, however, does not include, by any means, all that is implied by *movements*. Movements are not limited to muscular action, instigated by the *will*, but include other motions also, employed according to certain rules, for certain specific, rational purposes. Movements, in short, are simply motions of specific kinds, having specific effects, practiced for specific purposes, and intended to secure definite results. *Movements are mechanical agencies, directed either upon the whole system or a part of it, for the purpose of inducing determinate effects upon its vital actions, and generally having reference to its pathological state.**

Hence, the kind of movements proper in a given case are determined by the *condition of the system*, and will vary with its variations, so as to correspond with its special as well as general needs, at the particular time when they are employed. Movements admit of extensive variation in regard to *kind*, *degree*, and *place*.

DIFFERENT KINDS OF MOVEMENTS, ACTIVE AND PASSIVE.—The division of movements into *active* and *passive* relates to the sources whence the moving power is derived. The motion of riding, for instance, is *passive*, if the body be supported. So also are the *clappings*, *knockings*, *strokings*, *kneadings*, *pullings*, *shakings*, *vibratings*, etc., of the duplicated movements, because both the motion and the will that gives it energy are derived from another person.

---

* Dally gives the following definition of movements:

A movement is a product of life, and is impressed with its essence; the natural interior invisible action which unceasingly creates the vital forces; which at the same time engenders other exterior visible vital manifestations—in a word, it is that by which the united organic individual manifests its intellectual and moral, physical and chemical life, whereby life is developed, maintained, deteriorated, repaired, or resolved into its elements.

If we carry this definition into the domain of animal mechanism, we shall be obliged to modify it thus: *A movement is the most direct and proper means for provoking naturally, or in harmony with physiological laws, vital or biological motions, by virtue of which last the human machine, in all its multiform organs and functions, is developed, maintained, and repaired.*

This philosophical idea of movements furnishes the grand basis of true physical **education, rational hygiene, and scientific therapeutics; the at first despised traditional basis that the progress of modern science more and more confirms as the true one.**

Among the *single movements* there are none that are *wholly* passive. While the muscles of some portion of the body are acting, they *act upon* other structures, which, in relation to the acting muscles, are of course passive. But the antagonizing muscles are also acted upon—compressed and distended, and are relatively passive. The condition of the *will* is an important element in determining whether the movement be active or passive.

Whenever the contractile power of a muscle is engaged in overcoming resistance, the resulting movement is active, whether the effort be successful or not.

SINGLE AND DUPLICATED MOVEMENTS.—A movement is called *single* when but a single person is engaged in its execution; *duplicated*, when more than one is engaged. In single movements the weight of the whole or of some portion of the body is overcome by muscular action; as when in a standing posture the feet are extended, or a leg or arm is raised. The movement is also single if the resistance of antagonizing muscles is overcome, as in twisting a limb or the trunk; or when a burden is added to the weight of the body, or of the extremity or part moved. The movements described in this treatise are of the variety termed Single Movements. But as frequent reference is made to the duplicated variety of movements, it is necessary to describe here their general qualities and purposes.

Duplicated Movements are of two kinds. In one, the movement is received by the patient, who is quite passive, while *motion* of some particular variety is given to some portion of the body, or to the whole of it, generally by a physician, or by an operator under his immediate direction. In the other kind the patient is required to bring into action some particular part designated in the prescription; while the *quality*, *amount*, and *duration* of the action is entirely controlled by the physician. This action is, of course, varied according to the therapeutical indications of the case, partly judged of by the physical symptoms brought to light by the ordinary modes of diagnosis, partly determined by the cultivated and delicate perception and experience of the operator. The operator, in manipulating, usually affords a certain kind and degree of *resistance*, which aids in effecting the desired physiological action of the part concerned in the movement. Even in the same movement, the resistance should be carefully varied in the different stages, and with all the nicety of manipulation that is required of the musician for giving expression and effect in an instrumental performance.

The range and variety of effects capable of being produced by the duplicated movements, when directed by tact and intelligence, are very great, meeting most of the indications of chronic disease, probably quite all that present themselves in ordinary cases. These effects may be realized either in interior organs or the extremities, and may be made general or local. They may be confined mainly to any particular anatomical division or physiological function, to the nerves, the muscles, or may influence all together. They are adapted to the most enfeebled invalid or to the stoutest persons, and never need produce effects beyond the requirements of the invalid or the intention of the physician.

A most important element in the treatment by duplicated movements is that of the co-operation, both by will and action, of the patient with the physician or operator; by which the superior power of the one becomes a source of strength to the other.*

Nothing, for a plain reason, so encourages a person to act, as the consciousness of abundant ability; and this is fully supplied to the mind by the auxiliary power afforded. So that, in addition to the control obtained over the chemical and vito-chemical actions, we secure in this way the favorable influence of the healthful play of the nerves, whose function it is to control organic operations. All medical systems acknowledge the immense value of this assistance in the treatment of invalids; but what can secure it in so high a degree as an intelligent and patient application of the duplicated movements?

But the employment of duplicated movements, it must be confessed, is attended with difficulties that will prevent their general use as a medical resource. An ordinary course of medical instruction does not confer the necessary qualifications for their successful application; the *tact* necessary to prescribe and apply them properly is only acquired by long and patient practice, and the labor is excessively severe.

---

* Some of the German practitioners of the Movement-Cure, adopting Reichenbach's theory of the *odic force*, contend that an influence of this kind is concerned in the production of the effects of this treatment; the nervous energy of the patient being thereby exalted, and the system consequently enabled to overcome disease. Dally gives a fine drawing of the human hand, in its minute anatomy, arguing therefrom that it is an instrument eminently adapted to perform the office, or a part of its physiological functions, of conveying something like vital electricity to another person; and that an important advantage is derived by the invalid from such a transference. The reader will perceive the similarity, if not the identity, of the ideas underlying these statements with those concerning *animal magnetism*, with which every one is familiar. But it is not necessary, in order to prove or explain the hygienic and the medical effects of the Movement-Cure, to resort to any statements outside of its own well-demonstrated facts, and the easily understood laws of physiology. Especially must it be injurious to the reputation of this practice to resort to any theory in explanation of its effects that involves anything, to the common mind, mysterious or equivocal; and such is confessedly the character of the theories alluded to.

Single Movements, on the other hand, being comparatively few in number and simple in character, are much more readily learned and practiced; and they are found very efficacious in combating the lighter forms of disease and in opposing the first approaches of graver maladies.

CONCENTRIC AND ECCENTRIC MOVEMENTS.—When the extremities of the muscle are approximated, the muscular contraction steadily increasing, the movement is said to be *concentric*. When the muscle is stretched, its contraction steadily *decreasing*, the movement is said to be *eccentric*. Thus, the raising of a weight, as a book, by the hand, requires a *concentric* movement; while in permitting the same object to fall gradually by the side, an *eccentric* movement is effected. In both cases the same muscles have been employed; but often the effect upon the circulation, and especially upon the innervation of the part, is entirely different. The advantages of this distention are however only imperfectly available in the single movements, because both the concentric and eccentric are necessarily used indiscriminately in many of them. In practicing duplicated movements, it is easy to render a given movement either wholly concentric or wholly eccentric, and thus to obtain whatever advantages may be derivable from this distinction.*

---

* Dr. Neuman, and some other writers on the Movement-Cure, insist on the great importance in practice of the distinction of *eccentric* and *concentric* movements. They suppose that not only the muscles, but also all vital cells, have the two qualities of contraction and relaxation, as inseparable from their nature. These two qualities, it is supposed, just balance each other in health, but in disease one or the other of them preponderates. In other words, they think that all diseases may be classed either as those in which the *contractility* of the primary cell of the organic structures prevails, or else as those in which *relaxation* prevails. The one case, according to this theory, is to be treated by *concentric* movements, and the other

PRINCIPLES CONSIDERED. 103

The accompanying cuts* will serve to illustrate concentric and eccentric movements. Fig. 2 represents the arm bent at the elbow. To accomplish this, it is necessary for the muscles of the upper arm, toward which the forearm is drawn in the action, and which are attached to the forearm near the elbow, to contract, or shorten the distance between the extremities. This mass of muscles is shown at $a\,b$ in the cut. This is *concentric* action. But the muscles of the opposite side of the arm are, meantime, by no means passive. If they were, the bending would be accomplished with a sudden jerk; this is prevented by the contraction of the opposing muscles. But this contraction is not sufficient to prevent the shortening of $a\,b$, and the consequent motion of the forearm. At the same time the

Fig. 2.

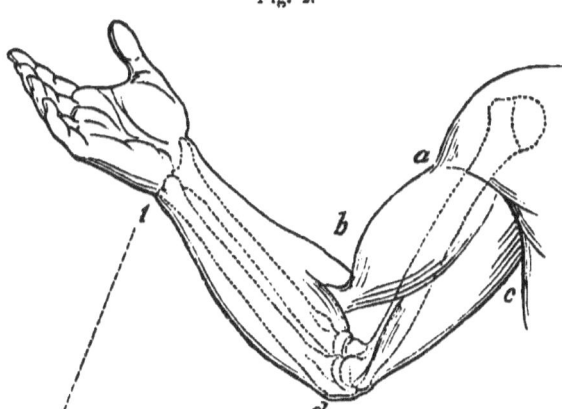

Bending of the arm at the elbow showing that while the contracting muscle, $a\,b$, shortens itself, its antagonist, $c\,d$, is drawn out.

by *eccentric*. Oftentimes the symptoms are supposed to indicate that *concentric* movements are appropriate to one organ or region of the body, while the *eccentric* are required for the other, and they are to be combined accordingly in the prescription.

* From "Theory and Practice of the Movement-Cure." By C. F. Taylor M.D.

muscular mass, c d, is steadily extended, in opposition to its efforts, and its contraction is called *eccentric*.

Fig. 3.

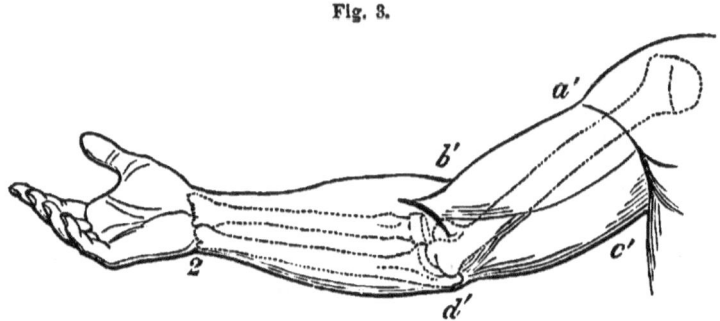

Stretching of the arm at the elbow, showing the action of the same muscles reversed.

If, while the muscle $d'\ c'$ is contracting, there be *resistance* applied at the hand, then $a'\ b'$ will not contract during the movement, for its opposing force is already supplied by the resistance from without, and though drawn out, it remains relaxed during the movement, having neither the physiological nor mechanical conditions requiring an influx of arterial blood. The whole effect of the movement is experienced in the contracting part.

Again, if *force* be applied to the hand, and $a'\ b'$ is drawn out by means of that force, instead of $c'\ d'$ acting, then the muscle $c'\ d'$ will not contract, and it will possess neither the physiological nor mechanical conditions for propelling forward the venous blood, but will remain entirely inactive. The only result of the movement is the contraction of $a'\ b'$ with the resulting influx of arterial blood. Furthermore, if the movement be made with *resistance* both ways, from 1 to 2 and from 2 to 1, the contraction would be first concentric in $c'\ d'$, then also in $a'\ b'$, without any eccentric action. But if *force* be used to move the limb in the directions specified, while the muscles oppose the force which overcomes them, then both actions are *eccentric*, and there are no *concentric* actions. The understanding of these principles is of the first importance in the application of movements for the removal of disease.

In fig. 3 it is plain that the action of the muscles d' c' overcomes that of a' b'; hence the action of the former is *concentric*, while that of the latter is *eccentric*. In either case both sets of muscle act, but with different effects.

The difference in the physiological effects of these two modes of muscular contraction is thus explained:

The pressure resulting from the contraction of a' b' forces the contained blood into the venous capillaries, while at the same instant the drawing out of the muscles c' d' extends the arteries, relieves them of pressure, and admits more arterial blood into the capillaries than before. In both cases the conditions are supplied for a new contraction; in the one case, by excluding waste matter, and in the other, by bringing arterial blood to the acting organ, while by the conjoint action the blood is hastened in its progress through the part.

GENERAL AND LOCALIZED MOVEMENTS.—One of the most potent causes of disease is the habitual employment of the powers of the system in a partial or inharmonious manner. A person who constantly uses his brain to the neglect of his whole body; his senses, rather than his muscles; his hands and arms in preference to his legs; or his legs, and forgets his abdominal muscles, has no right to anticipate the enjoyment of continued good health. It is apparent that in these cases nutrition progresses inordinately in the acting parts, while *other* and as important portions of the frame are suffering for the want of it. The effect after a time—and in individuals of feeble constitutions that period is soon reached—is a total prostration of the general physical energies.

These instances (and they are, alas! too numerous in all communities) illustrate a principle too apt to be ignored by individuals, and neglected by physicians, to wit, that even a moderate use of a part, while other parts are in a state of quiescence, not only stimulates the nutrient actions therein, but also *causes the general current of the circulation to set in toward them to an abnormal extent.* In other words, an undue and continued use of an organ induces a *tendency* to congestion of its tissues. It also generally heightens its nervous sensibility, frequently carrying it to the point of *irritability;* for evidently if an organ be set vigorously at work, while all other parts are at rest, it is made to express the whole available vital force of the system. Any organ may be compelled to do this, and they may all be so compelled in succession by sufficient stimulation. If the organs of the body be employed in union or in proper succession, the current of the circulation thus actively set in motion in them, instead of producing congestion and irritation, only *affords the proper conditions for the high degree of nutrition* necessary for their healthful functional activity. It is only by too long *continued* use, preventing at the same time the healthful employment of other parts, that the most vascular and delicate organs come to be injured.

The state of *congestion*, and the opposite one of *shrunk capillaries*, coexist in different parts of the same body in nearly all cases of chronic disease. The capillaries of some portions, generally situated centrally, are distended and are too weak to push forward their contents, and the stagnant blood soon becomes deteriorated in quality and incapable of affording nutrition; while at the same time other capillaries, generally those belonging to the skin and extremities, do not receive enough of blood to answer the general nutrient purposes of those parts. The rate of the circulation is unequal, for the blood is arrested in the congested organ, whatever may be the state of the pulse. The last cause of the trouble may be a poor quality of blood; but back of this there are causes connected with the blood-making operations of the body, previously described, which the movements are competent to correct.

The removal of *congestion* is one of the important objects of partial movements. The principles concerned in this practice are easily understood. A congested organ is one in which the capillaries have lost their contractility, and are therefore distended with blood, with a tendency to effusion of its serum, to relieve the oppressed walls. Microscopists inform us that gelatinous corpuscles are also present, which must afford further impediment to the onward flow. Most of the local, passive, duplicated movements assist very materially in our efforts to remove this condition. But permanent effects are secured by rousing vital action in, and consequently drawing the congested fluid to, contiguous organs, and even organs remote from the seat of disease, but needing the supply. Thus the affected part is emptied and relieved, and consequently soon acquires a healthy tone again in its capillary circulation; while at the same time the other organs that were suffering from deficient nutrition are supplied in a healthful manner. If tolerable tact be employed in the selection and arrangement of the movements in the prescription, no more efficient means than those here considered are to be found within the limits of the remedial art for relieving congestion, the constant concomitant of all chronic disease.

A similar principle is concerned in the treatment of cases of disordered innervation. If a single organ be the chief medium of nervous action, or even if it be the seat of great pain, other organs are proportionably wanting in sensibility. Nervous power is dependent on the same general conditions of nutritive supply or muscular power, and the nervous equilibrium is restored by agencies that harmonize the general nutrient actions of the body. From these statements, the broad, practical inference may be deduced, that *congestion and morbid innervation may be removed from any locality by employing, in other portions of the system, the materials and actions that are concerned in producing them.*

The attempts to accomplish these objects by ordinary medical means are less successful than by movements, because the control of the circulation thus obtained is less direct and perfect.

It is evident that these principles furnish important, and, indeed, invaluable suggestions for the management of the sick. It is a process of reversing those secret and subtile operations of the system whereby diseases are originally produced. And these principles are capable of the most easy, satisfactory, and beautiful demonstration in every-day practice.

The curative employment of movements is by no means confined to their local application. Those involving the whole body are often used to excellent advantage. Such movements urge the blood into the superficial capillaries, and increase thereby the peripheral circulation. But they need to be employed with much discretion, in order to avoid fatigue and the consequent defeat of the very purposes for which they are applied.

INFLUENCE OF MOVEMENTS IN REGULATING THE FORCES OF THE BODY.—It is already understood that, in accordance with the view of physiology and pathology taken in this work, the *muscles* and the *nerves* are regarded as the two great channels through which the available powers of the system are made to work.

In health, the muscles and nerves exercise co-ordinate functions. The muscles, we know, act only in response to nervous stimuli; but this involves both mental and sensorial action, for the cause or origin of the impulses imparted to the muscles resides in the *intellect* and *sensorium*. The voluntary muscles ordinarily obey only the mandates of the *will* and of the *feelings*. The muscles should be the obedient servants of these higher powers. Indeed, it is the whole aim and end of our corporeal nature to minister to the higher and spiritual; and when it fails to do this, nature fails to accomplish what she undertook in the creation of man.

The laws of nature can not be broken with impunity. Every attempt to work the intellect independently of the forces allied to it, must end in a miserable and disgraceful defeat. But when these are harnessed together and made to draw in concord, there is nothing within the limits of the possible that we do not see men accomplishing and enjoying.

Now in disease, arising from whatever cause, there is a disturbance in the operation of these two classes of powers. Muscular power is partially or wholly suspended, while the sensorial powers are generally increased, frequently to the production of pain. None will dispute this, and most will be ready to admit the truth of the following proposition, to wit, *that if the proper relations between these two sets of powers be habitually disregarded, disease in some form must be the inevitable consequence.* An appeal to common observation would abundantly confirm these statements.

Every one knows how the chronic invalid is tormented with sensations, and often with such as seem to bear but very slight relation to his apparent disease. The imagination in these cases is stimulated to excess; the consciousness is subjugated, and the strongest volition of such an invalid is incapable of resisting the power of feelings and fancies that accumulate with the advancement of the malady and threaten at times utterly to overwhelm their victim.

It is an indisputable fact that much of the disease of our modern civilization has its origin in this partial functional action, which in turn produces partial development, and which is another name for deformity. The nervous system is, in multitudes of cases in civilized life, compelled to act constantly with a force greatly disproportioned to the muscular—and to a degree frequently that renders the healthful nutrition of their organs an utter impossibility. Every physician's practice affords him numerous and lamentable illustrations of this sad truth.

If the constitution is defective from hereditary causes, the proclivity to disease of this kind is proportionally stronger, and the necessity for intelligent training of the system to a condition above the liability to this subjugation to the nerve-power becomes all the more imperative. For if this nervous habit be prolonged, and the muscles continue for any length of time to be deprived of their nutrition, the general nutrient actions throughout the body are enfeebled, and general impairment of the strength results.

Abuse of the nervous system usually operates, as we have hinted, through two channels, the mental and the sensorial. Examples of the latter class are much more numerous than those of the former; indeed, it may be doubted if those of the first often occur uncomplicated with the second. The sensorial faculties, besides being purveyors to the mind, are appointed also to minister to the material welfare and gratification of the body. But whenever the nerves belonging to this class are inordinately stimulated—that is, when stimulated without reference to nutritive ends—they become overstrained, the nutrition of the parts is perverted, their powers debilitated, and their action becomes uncontrollable.

Civilized life furnishes abundant and ingenious devices in the habits of eating, of drinking, and of living generally, eminently calculated to contribute to this end. For this are used spirits, tobacco, condiments, and confections, and the domestic beverages which are said to cheer but not inebriate; and the arts of cookery furnish too often the means of corrupting the taste, while they poison the food.

The habit, so rife with us, of permitting the *emotional* nature to bear undue sway, operates in a similar and hardly less injurious way, and is therefore equally reprehensible. The excitements of extensive or precarious business or of domestic infelicities are well known to produce the effects here pointed out; and not unfrequently the disproportionate degree with which the *feelings* become engaged in questions of politics and of religion bring the same unhappy results to the health. In these cases, bad hygiene and habits sow broadcast the seeds which other influences and circumstances afterward arouse into disastrous and fatal activity.

In all cases of this kind, arising from whatever cause, the use of *movements* furnishes a *direct, safe, powerful,* and *philosophical* means of restoring these interrupted harmonies, and of correcting the ill health that is dependent thereon; provided, of course, that the influence of the causes leading to such results, and which have been here pointed out, are withdrawn.

RELATIONS OF THE ACTION OF THE WILL AND OF THE MUSCLES IN MOVEMENTS.—Much error prevails on this subject. Most persons seem to think that the degree of fatigue one experiences indicates the amount of exercise taken, but it really only shows the amount of exertion put forth, and which depends on the *will*. The degree of fatigue and the amount of exercise do not necessarily bear a direct relation to each other; but the degree of fatigue indicates the greater or less *time* in which a movement was being performed. As evidence that fatigue is inseparably connected with the exercise of the will, it is only necessary to refer to numerous physiological operations that proceed without our attention and without fatigue, some of which, indeed, are capable of being brought by an effort into relation to the will, and thereby immediately become fatiguing. The heart's action, though powerful and incessant, is unaccompanied by any sense of fatigue. The internal organs generally, as the stomach and intestinal canal, are in constant motion, but never grow weary. In itself, the motion of riding by rail-cars or carriages is not fatiguing. Many of the ordinary avocations of life are habitual, and are performed automatically, and without fatigue. In all these movements the volitions are in abeyance, and the actions are carried forward under the control of the *involuntary* or *cerebro-spinal* system of nerves.

The function of *respiration* affords an excellent illustration of the relations of the will and the involuntary nerves in movements. In ordinary respiration there is no fatigue, because it proceeds without consciousness, that is, it is involuntary. But we may *control* this function by the will, and its performance is immediately followed by exhaustion. The reader will infer from this the impropriety, and in some cases the unqualified harmfulness, of employing instruments devised to modify respiration. These contrivances direct the attention to the respiratory act, and thereby embarrass its performance, rendering it no longer involuntary.

A careful analysis of these facts leads us readily to the principle, that *fatigue is in proportion to the amount of mental and nervous, rather than to the amount of muscular action employed.*

Into active movements, the two kinds of action, muscular and nervous, enter in different proportions. And this proportion seems to be determined chiefly by the *time* occupied in executing the movement, the *quick* movement requiring within a given period the greatest expenditure of nervous power. The principle here is analogous to that in mechanics, with which every school-boy is acquainted, viz., that *velocity* is obtained at the expense of *power*.

But if a movement be prolonged, the amount of muscular exercise is *greater* in proportion to the time occupied. This principle is made evident by the physiology of muscular contraction, explained in the second chapter, where it is shown that the longer the action of the muscle is continued, the greater the number of its ultimate elements that participate in the action.

The principle in movements relative to *time* may be stated thus:

Rapid movements necessitate most *nervous* action; slow and sustained movements, the most *muscular* action. If the principle be stated with reference to the limit of the capabilities of these powers, it might be said that the one *exhausts* the most nervous, and the other the most muscular power. If with reference to the effects on nutrition, the statement would be, the one *stimulates* to the most nervous, and the other to the most muscular action and development. These statements will, of course, apply only within certain limits in the healthy state, but which in daily life are being constantly exceeded in respect to the nervous function particularly; so that the proper relation of these two powers is destroyed, and the whole system becomes disordered.

This principle is well illustrated in common experience. If a person *runs* a few rods briskly, he will pant with fatigue; while if he *walk* the same distance, he is refreshed and invigorated, although it is a demonstrated fact that the aggregate amount of mechanical resistance that he has overcome is greater in the latter case than in the former. In the first instance the object was accomplished by means of a greater effort than in the second; but in the second, a larger number of muscle-cells had taken part in the contraction than in the first. In the one case, also, a larger amount of blood was conveyed to the *nerve-centers* to sustain the action; while in the other case, the *muscles* have received the larger quantity to replenish the waste occasioned by their action.

This principle meets also with abundant confirmation in all departments of *pathology*. The paralytic walks with great difficulty, because though the muscles are really unaffected, the *will* is transmitted to them imperfectly and only by great effort on account of the vitiated state of the nerve-conductors.

The effect of poisons whose influence is exerted upon the nerves, presents a pathological state corroborative of this principle. Strychnine produces violent muscular contortion, exhibiting evidence of the excited and rapid action and finally the exhaustion of the nerve-centers; while spirits and most other stimulants produce their deceptive effect by evolving rapidly at first the nerve-power by exciting in the nerve-centers an action which the deluded victim attempts to maintain by repeating the doses. No lasting power is really gained in any of these ways, because the action is essentially of the *destructive*, and not of the constructive kind.

The Movement-Cure makes *direct application* of the general principles here set forth; hence its value as a therapeutic means. It employs *slow* movements in preference to the more rapid, because chronic invalids need to have their nervous powers HUSBANDED, and their general muscular and nutritive powers *increased*. Such invalids have suffered enough already from unnatural and irregular nervous activity. The muscles of such patients not only fail to execute the promptings of the will, but also to control in a proper manner those vegetative actions of the system that so directly depend upon a full supply of nervous energy in the muscular system.

The true principles concerned in the therapeutic application of movements being plain, we only need to be careful that our practice in making remedial application of these principles be made thoroughly to correspond with them. Not only the application of the movements, but the general habits of the body (which, too, are of the nature of movements), must be made to accord with the same principles. The tendency to spasmodic haste, especially, that characterizes the invalid, must be broken up; otherwise this of itself will be likely to perpetuate the troubles under which he labors, in spite of any remedial means he may have been led to institute.

Movements as a Specific Medical Agency.—The single movements only approximate the duplicated movements in importance as a therapeutic means. These latter answer all the distinct purposes indicated in chronic disease. Their effects may be local as well as general, and in this respect they quite equal those of drugs, difficult as some may find it to believe this. The primary impression made by a drug is essentially *pathological;* while that of a *movement* is in the direction of the desired physiological action, and consequently and surely toward health. Movements are also superior to drugs in the extent to which the physiological actions may be influenced by them, especially in the control obtained by their application over the circulation of the blood, and the directness with which respiration and nutrition are influenced; which last results are scarcely expected even as the indirect effect of drugs.

The grand difference between movements and drugs exists in all their relations to the system. The one changes physiological action to pathological, the other carries pathological action toward physiological. The drug accomplishes specific objects by pervading the whole organism, including every structure within it, and leaving thereon its morbid impression. It has no power to encourage or stimulate, *primarily*, the great life-forces of the system.

Movements, on the contrary, secure or restore unity and a just balance to the various functions, and from disorder and discord tend to bring out that blissful order and harmony which it was doubtless the intention of the all-wise and good Creator should characterize the physical nature of his favored children.

MOVEMENTS AS RELIABLE MEANS OF SECURING THE OBJECT OF NUTRITIVE MEDICATION.—Much is said at the present day in regard to supplying, directly to the blood, its deficient saline ingredients. Certain forms of disease are assumed certainly to indicate this want in the blood, and these diseases are supposed to be cured by treatment of this sort. Of the faulty quality of the blood in cases of defective nutrition there can be no doubt; but it is far from being a settled point that its normal quality can be restored to it in this way. It so happens that our ordinary food furnishes an abundance of organizable nutritive matters. The trouble is not in the lack of the material. The power to make use of it is what is wanted chiefly; and this can never be imparted by ever so free an administration of saline, earthy, or ferruginous preparations. It is insisted that the structures require these materials; but the first question to be settled is: *Are these structures in a state of preparation and fitness to receive and appropriate such supplies?* It is contrary to all we know of physiological law to conclude that nutritive actions, or indeed any action, should proceed in the absence of the conditions necessary for the supply of oxygen.

The truth is that the supply of the materials above mentioned is supererogatory. If we examine by chemical tests any proper and wholesome foods, we shall find the saline and earthy matters needed in the system to be present in quantities positively above the demands of the system. These matters are constituents of all common food, and whether they become appropriated or are cast off depends entirely upon the needs of the organism and its appropriating ability. This need exists in direct and uniform ratio to the waste; and though the blood and tissues be ever so deficient in regard to the substances in question, they can never become richer in them in the absence of the imperative and effectual demand created by *action*. *Movements*, it has been found, are the true and reliable means for bringing nutritive materials in general, and the saline elements of the blood in particular, from the cavity of the stomach into the inner chambers of the system, where they are wanted.

But the mode of administering these materials in vogue with our medical friends of the present day is much less satisfactory than the more ancient and natural method. The saline elements of food are in the state of preparation effected by the organs of the plant expressly for nutritive purposes. As here found, they bear an analogy to organic materials, if, indeed, they are not essentially such. The iron, lime, phosphorous, etc., are not in the food as crude substances, but are incorporated with other elements or matters in organic combination, and are thus fitted to accompany them in their errand and mission of good to every needy tissue of the frame.

MOVEMENTS AS RELATED TO NERVE STIMULANTS.—But few persons fully understand the impropriety, in a physiological point of view, of subjecting their nerves to the habitual influence of sedatives and stimulants for the purpose of quieting troublesome sensations, or of allaying unpleasant brain-action. The principles and facts above stated must demonstrate the inutility, to say the least, of such habits. These agents conduce to the act of what is technically termed *retrograde metamorphosis* in the body, in an improper manner. They debase the system, and render its actions habitually vicious, and ultimately overthrow the mental powers. They interfere with the method nature has appointed for the due production of morphological changes in the system.

There is no doubt of the existence of a *real need*, though artificially induced, the consciousness of which impels its subject to resort to these injurious methods of relief. But they do this in ignorance of a simpler and far more trustworthy recourse. A careful study of the principles involved in the Movement-Cure suggests a ready way of securing quietude to the nerves by the simplest of means; for experience has taught us that when irritability or pain exists, the nerves are only demanding to be rescued from the effects of a bad circulation and an irregular distribution of nervous power. It has already been shown that the movements furnish a far more reliable means for attaining these ends than can be mustered in all the drug shops or chemical laboratories on the planet. We believe—and every day see what we believe—that the vexed brain may be relieved by drawing off its surcharged vessels; that the stomach and blood need not be fired by a stimulant in order to warm the skin and excite action in the extremities. We have learned that distressful sensations generally only indicate that dead matter needs to be ejected from the system; that pain, even severe pain, is quieted by employing, in contiguous and even in remote portions of the body, the actions that supply the perverted nerve-power. Destroy thus, by the continuous and thorough use of suitable movements, the hankering (which is seated in the irritable nerve-fiber) for innutritious and inflaming stimulants, and soon the destructive habit will die out, and the sufferer be relieved from a despotism worse than that which merely puts chains upon the body, and has no more that it can do.

MOVEMENTS AS RELATED TO PATHOLOGY.—Pathology wears a greatly changed aspect from the point of view furnished by the Movement-Cure. Disease is no longer hidden to us among inscrutable causes, nor its cure among unintelligible operations or more mysterious mixtures. *Pain* need now no longer be confounded with disease, nor the cure deemed completed when the consciousness has become oblivious to suffering.

On the contrary, disease is proved, beyond dispute, to depend on disturbed physiological action, and it only waits for correct and equable physiological action to be restored, in order that disease shall disappear. The special conditions upon which the symptoms of disease are based are easily and speedily removable when they exist in moderate degree, and often when they exist to a degree quite beyond the reach of ordinary medical art, providing, only, that we are master of the instrumentalities within our reach.

Several of these removable causes or conditions usually co-exist in the same case, but with different degrees of intensity or development. In every effort to remove them, the Movement-Cure seeks to recover the impaired harmony of the system; never, like drugs, develops symptoms of its own worse than the disease; but, by bringing all the forces of the organism into due co-relation, assists the system to glide, naturally, into a state of health, with all its available forces unimpaired, and ready to fulfill the behests of the will.

Those invisible, vito-chemical actions are capable, we see, of producing results that may *agree* or *not* with the standard of health. The *nature* of the product is of but little consequence compared with the productive causes. Morbid materials can never exist without mischievous antecedents. We are not accomplishing much when we apply antidotes to effects, while the causes are busily at work out of sight and out of reach.

The inter-relations of physiological and pathological agencies are so involved, that to look for the first of morbid causes is like seeking the end of a circle, or a needle in a hay-stack. But to the practical inquirer the few essential phenomena that most demand his attention are readily recognized; such as *defective respiration, congestion* or *mal-circulation, imperfect nutrition, morbid innervation.* These are the conditions that chiefly interest us, and to obtain the control over which it is the aim of all our practice and endeavor.

PROVINCE OF MOVEMENTS.—Whether movements are hygienic or remedial in their effects, depends on the character of the case for which they are used. They are hygienic when their influences are such as to maintain the already existing healthy relations of the physiological man—when they give healthy scope to all vital powers in spite of the deteriorating tendencies of sedentary or intellectual occupations; or of such habits

of labor as employ some portions of the body too much
and other portions too little. Movements thus applied
may be called the natural means of counteracting the
evil tendencies of an artificial mode of life, whose name
is legion.

Movements become medical when their effects are
to improve imperfect physiological relations, or break
up pathological states habitually existing; as, for instance, when they permanently increase the circulation
and nutrition of a part previously defective, increase
the respiration, diminish morbid innervation, restrain
morbid discharges, or incite any defective function to a
healthful and satisfactory play.

MORALE OF MOVEMENTS.—Invalids are gaining instruction all the time through their experience in the
daily use of movements in regard to the *causes* of their
troubles, and thus are often enabled to rise superior to
the depressing influences of the disease. As a thorough
system of movements involves a general hygienic treatment, the invalid no longer pursues the preposterous
plan of employing a remedy for difficulties that he is
continually reproducing in himself. Vicious practices
cease to be seductive when he is alive to their probable effects. His faith in the wonderful and reputed
powers of medicine, which forever offers its premium
to vice and folly, collapses, and he, by so doing, resolves to try, at least, to do right.

But the influence of this sentiment does not stop
here. The physiological and the spiritual are co-ordinate departments of our being, sustain relations of
mutual ministry, and conspire to mutual elevation of
function. But the physiological system is anterior in
development, though temporary in function; and its

obvious office and essential purpose is that of *instructor* of the spiritual nature in fundamental truths.

The same law of *development* resulting from the experience of good and evil, pleasure and pain, disobedience and penalty, is common to both departments, but being first apprehended on the physiological plane, meets with a ready transfer to the spiritual. In the body these laws are of temporary application, but applied to the higher life, become fundamental and permanent. Generations of men cast away the weary experiences of life as of no profit, because it has not yet taught their meaning;—even in a physiological sense it has not been comprehended.

Chapter Five.

MOVEMENTS COMPARED WITH GYMNASTICS.

ONE evil has grown out of the recent interest that the Movement-Cure has awakened, and this is the adoption by invalids of those ill-considered and heterogeneous exercises embraced under the general name of *Gymnastics*. The very great danger to the weakly and the invalid from the mistake of confounding the two things, renders it a duty to explain the difference in their effects.

The man who, feeling himself sick, should rush into the first drug-shop in his way and there seize and swallow whatever he might lay hands on, would be considered a madman, whose life would most likely pay the forfeit of his want of consideration. If a physician, who ought to know that drugs are potent substances, should recommend this procedure to his patient, he would be designated by some not very mild term. And yet essentially the same thing is practiced with reference to exercises. Like dosing, exercising, it is assumed, is useful for the sick in a general way, and so the sick are advised to "take exercise," without designating *what, when, where*, or *how*. Upon this loose principle ten thousand doctors are daily prescribing and many more invalids practicing, until aggravating their old complaints, or contracting new, the latter become disgusted with both advice and adviser, and, fancying there can be no help for them, give up to hypochondria, with all its woes. All this comes from not considering that *exercise is a most potent means of affecting the body*, whether for good or for ill, and that it necessarily has *laws*, and must be practiced in obedience thereto, or it will be quite as likely to do harm as good.

The very fact that a person needs exercise distinct from his usual avocations, whatever these may be, implies—as one will see if a moment's thought be given the subject—that he needs it of a particular kind or quality, in particular amount, or affecting particular portions of the body. If one receives it in such parts and of such form as will serve to dissipate the congestion of over-worked or diseased organs, and vivify and set in normal action the parts that are suffering from inaction, he is refreshed, strengthened, and reinstated in health and power. Otherwise, or if the exercise be indiscriminately employed, he has no ground for assurance that undesirable effects will not be produced, that the *congestion*, the *anemia*, the want of power, or whatever the trouble may be, may not be aggravated by the same agency that, scientifically employed, would have produced the happiest results. Such a person, indeed, has reason to become discouraged, and can hardly be blamed for arriving at the conclusion, after such an experience, that exercise is not the thing *he* requires.

The distinction between *Gymnastics* and *Movements* is so plain that it must be readily appreciated if a little consideration be bestowed upon the subject. While the one results mainly in the expenditure of power, both nervous and muscular, indiscriminately, without reference to the particular conditions of the system, either in its original conformation, its idiosyncrasies, its diseases, or its temporary states, the other not only takes all these into full consideration, but also by the aid of a severe, thorough, and systematic analysis of all the modifications of motion applied to the body or produced by it in all its varied conditions, is able to adapt itself nicely to the needs of the individual case. While Gymnastics may be practiced by any one who is accomplished enough to turn a somerset, Movements require the discipline furnished by the schools, by which only can be acquired that knowledge of the nature of diseases, the nicety of tact and quickness of perception which are essential to insure a nice adaptation of the means to the ends contemplated. Movements further require for their greatest success certain mental and moral qualities in the practitioner calculated to gain and keep the confidence of the patient. This is a great point, as might be supposed, *à priori*.

In comparing the effects of *Gymnastics* with the *Movements*, a German writer makes the following sensible remarks:

"It is not denied that gymnastics may serve to develop the parts that execute the movements—muscle, tendon, ligament, and bone; but in doing this they will give a heavy and too concentrated a form, especially to the superior portions of the body. If we examine a gymnast, we find the upper portion of the body much more largely developed than the lower, because it is the general fault of gymnastics that the great proportion of the exercise consists in overcoming either the weight of the body or that of some other object by the *arms*, while the legs only sustain the weight of the trunk, as on ordinary occasions. This effect, of course, is detrimental to the system as a whole. The subject of any special excessive development, instead of being benefited thereby, is absolutely incapacitated by it for the performance of life's ordinary duties to some extent.

Gymnastics, also, in case of the existence of a predisposition to it, are liable to fasten upon themselves a dangerous disease. It is well known that by these violent exercises the veins are rendered full and turgid. This condition is always followed by a general relaxation of the body and mind, a disposition to somnolence, and one can conceive that if this state is frequently reproduced, very injurious physical and moral effects will ensue. If it can be demonstrated that gymnastic exercises produce a predominance of venous blood in the body, it follows, of course, that it is by this means seriously vitiated in all its parts, and we have no need of other facts to assure us that the veins, of which the walls are naturally soft and easily distended, may be readily broken down under the pressure of the accelerated blood, and that there will be a resultant tendency to hemorrhage.

The *circulatory system* is necessarily oftentimes much disordered by gymnastic exercises performed without rule or measure. Gymnastics, we know, can only excite the functions through the medium of the circulation. The irregular flow thus induced is not advantageous, but quite the contrary, to the diseased or enfeebled parts. The common gymnast labors in vain to relieve tendencies to pulmonary disease. For this class of cases all violent exercises are injurious, and for an obvious reason; the passage of blood as well as air is impeded in the lungs; the exercises of the rack and bars force the blood violently into these delicate or diseased structures, causing sometimes a rupture, and frequently congestion therein. And where disease already exists, an aggravation of it must ensue, and the poor invalid, by his rashness, is suddenly put beyond a chance of cure.

It will also be noticed that every violent effort at inspiration not only calls air into the lungs, but exercises an equal power over the return flow of venous blood. The effect, then, of these repeated violent movements of the walls of the chest produced by gymnastic feats, is accumulation of the blood, or *congestion*, in one of the most delicate and fragile portions of the organism, from which not seldom the most serious results have been known to follow.

Whatever of profit may be gotten from these exercises, it is to be feared, is more than balanced by the loss of nervous energy experienced. The invalid feels this, and is soon inclined to desist. Those comparatively well, however, are not apt to notice this declension of nervous force till a serious inroad has been made upon their constitution.

In striking contrast to this are the effects of wisely conducted *movements*. By these exercises, the nervous power is conserved to the greatest possible degree compatible with its continuous development. The *willing* power is husbanded and re-enforced, the superior force of the operator energizing the relaxed system of the patient.

These serious objections that we have raised against gymnastics equally apply to *calisthenics*. This kind of exercise chiefly tasks the nerves, especially the cerebro-spinal axis, upon which all motive power depends. In the practice of this class of exercises, not even the whole weight of the members is to be overcome; but all available power is expended in the production of *celerity* in the motions, an effort that greatly draws upon the nerves. No wonder that feeble ladies, who are directed to use this kind of exercises (for the gymnasium is virtually closed to ladies), experiment with reluctance, and soon give over, conscious of their injurious effect on their already morbidly active nervous systems.

It must be manifest, by this time, to the reader, we think, that there exists an important difference between well-ordered and directed exercise, pursued in accordance with true physiological principles, and that sort which practically ignores all these principles.

THE MUSCLES A MEDIUM OF LANGUAGE, AND OF THE MANIFESTATION OF CHARACTER.—The muscles have other functions besides officiating as agents of the will in the manifestation of mechanical power. They also give expression to the thoughts and emotions of the soul; nature employs them in conducting intercourse between man and man *as their visible sign*. Without this means we can hardly conceive it possible that society could exist, except in the most rudimental and savage way. It is through this agency that not only our transient moods, but our very characters, are represented to others. Not only by the changes that are being incessantly wrought in the lineaments of the face, but in the constantly shifting attitudes of the person involuntarily assumed, are we forever publishing to the world our ever-changing mental and emotional states.

These statements are amply supported by the experience of every living being. We all do involuntarily form judgments as to the characters of the persons we meet, without receiving any other knowledge in regard to them than that derived from this source, and these judgments are proverbially more correct than those

6*

which we subsequently acquire as the result of an analysis of their words and deeds. Deeds often lie, we know; and language is as often used, perhaps, to conceal as to express thought. We are often as much convinced or moved by the glance of the eye, or gesture, or general bearing of a public speaker, as by anything he says, as may be proved by allowing another person to speak or read the discourse that charmed us on its first delivery. We all well enough understand the power of what is sometimes termed silent eloquence in that expression of emotion of fear, for example, or anger, revenge, jealousy, confidence, which is effected in utter silence, and chiefly by muscular play of feature. Indeed, the strongest emotions, we well know, are much more powerfully rendered by facial expressions than by the employment of the most vehement phraseology. Who can not call up in imagination or from memory these representations of fear, disgust, grief, joy, etc?

The accomplished actor, by combinations of attitudes, look, and gesture, is enabled to enhance a thousand-fold the effect of the dramatist's effusions; for by his artistic displays he reaches the mind and heart through avenues that tongue or pen can never travel. One is often more strongly impressed by what he knows to be fiction, when it is empowered in this way, than by absolute truth conveyed by pen or tongue alone. But the feeling conveyed *must really exist, if it only be for the time,* else it can not find expression in the natural language which it is the office of the muscles to furnish. The feeling thus expressed can not be simulated; it must proceed from interior sources. The merit of a public speaker consists mostly in his power to experience, for the occasion, the amount of *intensity of thought and feeling* requisite for the production of the effects he desires. The demagogue, the patriot, and the preacher alike wield these powerful instruments. A gesture, a turn of the head, a lifting of the finger, a grand wave of the arm, has doubtless many a time given that power to a sentence or a sentiment that has decided some great question, perhaps determined the fate of a nation or a soul.

It is because of this universal recognition of a language in the muscular motions and positions of the human figure, that the power exists of giving permanency to these expressions of ideas in marble and on canvas, for the arts of sculpture and painting are nothing more than the art of representing by perspective, color, and form these natural signs, so that the idea, emotion, or event which forms the subject of the work is instantly and forcibly impressed upon the beholder's mind. All muscular action is dependent on the stimulus of the nerves. Destroy the nerves, and muscular power perishes immediately. This stimulus is received directly or indirectly from the *will*, and by will we simply mean mental action.

These effects are similar to those we witness in the cerebro-spinal system. Here, every sensation, though not manifested in the consciousness, is represented by the action of that portion of the muscular system that is associated with the sensitive nerve. So also any emotion pervading the mind is a source of a distinct nervous perception that is immediately reflected upon appropriate muscles. Certain mental states uniformly express themselves through certain nerves, and these, in their turn, being connected with appropriate muscles, a corresponding outward expression is effected. The manner and degree of contraction are the measure of the thought or emotion which is represented by it.

These principles will be admitted as eminently true, so far as regards the muscular apparatus connected with the *face*. The face, indeed, has several muscles for which there is no other known use but that of giving visible expression to thought.

These muscles form—to borrow a phrase from poetry—the dial-plate of the soul, on which all may read its lessons as in a glass. There are faces, to be sure, that are only *masks*, but these are the exceptions.

But muscular expression is by no means confined to the countenance. All the muscles of the body are subservient in various degrees to the same purpose, and the variety of their play gives significance to the *attitudes* and gestures, countless and ever changing, that contribute so much to the effect of conversation, public speaking, and to the charm of the stage.

Thus far the principles I have advanced are those commonly understood and accepted. But it must be borne in mind that the different parts and forces of the body exert a reciprocal action and influence upon each other. Now we say, if mode of mind give character to muscular expression, what, arguing from analogy, so likely as that a careful attention to the healthful and symmetrical development of this wonderful and delicate system of muscles, so intimately associated with the mind, should confer a reflex advantage upon the mind itself, especially when we consider that the body, with all its amazing appliances, was made to answer the ends and contribute to the comfort and welfare of the spiritual resident. The dependence of the mind upon the body it is not necessary that we should prove as a general proposition. All must concede that. *Mens sana in corpore sano*, is the law. A vigorous manhood can not be reached save by a practical obedience to the law that recognizes this mutual dependence of the material and the immaterial elements of our nature. It is said that a person can not assume for an instant the exterior look and action of one in fear without experiencing the emotion. This is but one fact of a thousand pointing to the same principle. One perfectly acquainted with the physiology of the frame and its relations to the soul might, we think, almost be able to infer the character of a man's politics, morality, or religion from his physical habits and manifestations.

If this be so, may it not behoove us to look a little more closely than we are apt to do to the physical condition and habits of those who assume to be our spiritual guides? May we not reasonably inquire whether this dogma, that creed, or the other platform may not possibly result from defective reasoning, itself the result of vicious digestion or a languid circulation —whether the surprising conversion of men to particular forms of faith may not have something directly or indirectly to do with the quality of their nerve-power, or the condition of their livers or mucous membranes?

Chapter Six.

DIRECTIONS FOR PRESCRIBING AND APPLYING MOVEMENTS.

Movements, whether single or duplicated, become remedially valuable only when prescribed with due reference to the condition of the system. The prescription must be based on several principles of physiology, absolute in their nature and direct in their application. If these are not strictly regarded, a given movement becomes of no account, but descends to the level of the ordinary purposeless actions of the body, perhaps harmful; or at best, contributing in but a general and unsatisfactory way to the well-being of the system.

It should be further stated, that the efficiency of movements, *when well prescribed*, depends measurably upon the *tact* and energy of the operator if they be of the *duplicated* kind; and upon the *intelligence*, *patience*, and *strength* of the patient, if *single*.

This treatment regards the system as subject to a continual though invisible growth, and to further and perfect this process is its especial aim and business. And as the pulling-down and repairing operations of the system in health are gradually and unconsciously conducted, so the effects of judicious treatment are gradually and imperceptibly produced. The patient, indeed, ought to arrive at a knowledge of the effects of treatment only by experiencing an abatement of his pains and a restoration of strength and vivacity. Those who expect effects such as follow from the administration of drugs, will be disappointed, although it *may be* stated that many of these effects may be produced indirectly through the agency of movements, but they are not regarded as legitimate or desirable.

TIME CONSIDERED.—If for hygienic purposes, to counteract the effects of sedentary habits, of undue mental application, or the practice of some kind of labor that involves the use of a part of the body only, movements may be taken at any time when this necessity is felt. In cases of positive disease, it is considered desirable that they be taken in the early part of the day, when the system is more plastic, and when, owing to the night's rest, there is most power in store within it: hence, either before breakfast, or a short time after it, the system at this time, owing to the repose of the night, being in condition most favorable for the reception of curative impressions.

In general, a prescription of movements should be practiced no more than once in the day; and in duplicated movements, however moderately used, we must guard against the occurrence of *crises*, headaches, febrile symptoms, etc., which frequently occur after a short term of treatment. Immediately on the occurrence of *crises*, we must change the prescription or leave off treatment altogether, for the effects in such cases are similar to those brought about by the abuse of hydropathy or of drugs.

An auxiliary prescription may sometimes be made for another time in the day, repeating perhaps some portion of the primary one, but only under the direction of a competent physician.

MANNER.—Every movement has two important elements, *mechanical* and a *mental*, or mental and moral, neither of which may properly be neglected for the other. The correct posture must first be taken, carefully adjusting every member. The part to be moved should then be made to pass through the prescribed line until it reaches the indicated limit, which is usually the limit of the contractile capacity of the chief muscles employed; and this last position should then be retained for a few moments, unless the nature of the movement renders it impossible. Generally, the part is returned to its first position with comparatively little muscular effort.

In the mean time, the mind or will is intent on the mechanical execution of the movement, and the nerves, its faithful servants, are busy conveying the needful stimuli to the part, without which we are aware the execution of the movement, if it be a voluntary one, is impossible. The mind is thus engaged in sustaining the vital operations of the moving part. Both the external display of mechanical force, and the internal vito-chemical changes upon which it depends, are the results of mental action. If the movement be duplicated, the mental force of the operator is exclusively employed, while that of the patient is economized. If the movement be inaccurate or faltering; in other words, if to a lack of precision in the prescription there be added a want of intelligent determination and force in the operator, little, if anything, is effected.

RHYTHM.—This is a highly important element of our system, and one that is far too generally overlooked. For the general purposes contemplated by movements, whether hygienic or curative, they should be performed *slowly*, much more slowly than are the habitual motions of the body. Thus the acting part occupies the attention for a considerable time, and the amount of control gained over the changes of the part is consequently and proportionably great, while the energy of will and the expenditure of nerve-power that is required is *small*. The absolute time occupied in a movement should vary with the size, and especially with the *length*, of the acting muscle or muscles, the *short* muscles doing their work in briefer time. The part should retain its extreme position for a short period.

EXERTION.—In duplicated movements the assistant is responsible for the amount of exertion employed by the patient, for it is quite under his control. The effect may be perfectly graduated to suit his judgment, as notes of music respond to the touch of the master-player; indeed, a nicely executed movement has something of the swell and harmonious flow of a musical strain.

The single movements, however, do not admit of this precise control. The resistance is supplied by the weight of the part which is varied as the positions vary, but can be increased only to a limited extent. The amount of exertion possible in any position is dependent upon the degree of mobility of the part concerned.

NUMBER.—The number of movements to be taken at once should be sufficient to engage all parts of the system (there are some exceptions to this rule, as in cases of paralysis and surgical diseases), but not enough to occasion fatigue, or only such moderate fatigue as is quickly recovered from. The number generally required in a prescription ranges from ten to twelve.

ORDER.—This is a very important matter in duplicated movements; so much so that by a re-arrangement of the order quite new effects may often be produced on the invalid. The arrangement should be such that the movements shall support each other, and all work together to the production of the effect. By a vicious arrangement they interfere with and neutralize each other. A proper arrangement is also important in the single movements. Too many in succession applied to the same organ, if enfeebled, would be likely to produce congestion, the usual effect of excessive exercise; if the part is diseased, it would be apt to increase and extend the disease. All the requirements of the system, in any given case, should be considered in the prescription, and the order of their importance. Professor Branting proposes that the following order be generally observed, modifications, of course, being made to meet the needs of particular cases.

1. A respiratory movement.
2. A movement of the lower extremities.
3. Of the upper extremities.
4. Of the abdomen.
5. Of the lower extremities—terminating with
6. A respiratory movement.

The formula, we repeat, is to be varied according to the particular circumstances of each case, the part affected, the temperament, etc. Whatever the order, the movements *should always harmonize with each other;* for it is only from the harmonious union of their separate actions that the best results can proceed.

RELATION TO DISEASED PARTS.—Every formula of movements for persons that have local weakness or disease, will contain both *general* and *special* elements—the latter having particular reference to the disease. But, in general, active movements must *not be applied to organs affected with actual disease.* The diseased part must be approached gradually, beginning at some remote part of the body, arousing it to vital activity, and augmenting its capacity to receive blood. In this way the congestion accompanying the disease is gradually removed, and the vital and nutrient power of the system increased and established, until finally the diseased part is so relieved that it becomes capable of receiving advantageously the direct effects of movement.

The passive kind of duplicated movements are, however, an exception to the above rule. The direct effect of many of the passive movements, such as *vibrations*, etc., is to *move* the blood of the congested capillaries toward the veins. The adherent corpuscles are thus dislodged, and the current arrested by them is allowed again to flow onward. Such movements, in this way, greatly assist in the removal of congestion, and may, with care, be applied to the diseased members or organs.

It is needless to say that the general habits of exercise should be compelled to accord with the tenor of the movement prescription. For instance, as in proportion to the organic disturbance there is always an increase of nervous excitability, and a decrease of physical power, the habitual exercises of the patient should be so ordered as to assist in repressing the excitability and to invigorate the general nutrition of the body. All violent and continued exercises, such as exhaust the powers and induce lasting fatigue, should be avoided. Those that are partly passive, such as riding on horseback or in a carriage, sailing, traveling, etc., are highly appropriate, and may be taken most advantageously in connection with the course prescribed.

REGIONS OF THE BODY.—In their application to the body, movements necessarily have special relations to its individual parts, which I have familiarly termed *regions*. By this term no definite portion of its mass, having distinct boundaries, is intended. The term is very general indeed, and a portion of the body thus designated generally includes a portion or the whole of several anatomical divisions. By thus simplifying our terminology, a knowledge of anatomy on the part of the person making application of movements to himself, is dispensed with; and to such the intelligent and successful use of single movements is rendered practicable.

A *region* generally consists of one or more joints, with the bones, ligaments, muscles, vessels, nerves, areolar tissues, and whatever other elements may be included in the range of the muscles, having their points of origin or insertion within the locality thus designated. Each joint is considered as not only a center of motion of the sound members, but as involving in its motions those invisible physiological or nutritive actions indissolubly connected with the health of the part. If the impulse to motion proceeds from external sources, then the *region* simply indicates the structures thus acted upon.

We are to understand, then, that any portion of the body, however complex in its structure and functions, which may be moved *en masse* and separately from the rest of the framework, constitutes, in the sense here indicated, a *region*. The whole of an extremity, for example, or the whole of the trunk, or even a part of either, may, if included in a movement, be thus denominated.

The reader who is philosophically inclined will remark this difference between the Movement system and the Drug system, in their practical application. In the latter, he will observe, the remedy is primarily applied to the stomach and alimentary canal, which it attacks in full force, while that portion of it which is received into the circulation subsequently spends its power among the vital structures, generally and indiscriminately, wherever the blood circulates, in the well quite as much as in the diseased portions.

In the application of movements, however, the parts demanding succor are pointed out in the prescription, and such portions as do not require the applications are scrupulously avoided. The practical results of this difference are apparent. In the one case there is an unavoidable waste of the forces of the system, while in the other only the conditions for developing power and restoring health are restored. Another object fulfilled by the division of the body into regions is, that the purposes of the movement are rendered distinct. This advantage is in striking contrast with the purposeless and loose method employed in gymnastics.

Chapter Seven.

TERMINOLOGY OF POSITIONS.

IMPORTANCE OF SYSTEM.—When the facts relating to any branch of knowledge become classified according to their mutual relations and importance, they come to constitute a *science*. Any science, to be generally useful, must be capable of being readily communicated. Otherwise it is limited in its influence, however extensive its applicability, or however great the need existing for its diffusion. In order to convey any new truth or system of truth to the mind of the learner, particular forms of expression become necessary; and these acquire a special and philosophic value almost as great as the subject itself of which they treat. This use of language of philosophic accuracy is of the highest importance for the assistance it affords the student in his investigations, and in giving method to his style of thinking with reference to it; so that discovery and classification proceed naturally and properly together; and new truths easily take their proper place in the orderly and symmetrical construction of the system. A *terminology*, indeed, becomes an absolutely necessary instrument in the progress of a science or art of any kind.

No approach was made to a method of designating and classifying the positions and movements of the body for the purposes contemplated in the Movement-Cure, till the time of Ling. In fact, the truths of physiology had first to be so far developed as to clear away some of the rubbish of the old medical science (so called) before such a thing could be even attempted with any chance of success. At the present time the need of this aid is deeply felt by the student, and the writer has thought that an attempt on his part to represent some of the facts of the Movement-Cure by means of a terminology, albeit a crude and imperfect one, would be a labor not altogether useless.

The reader will understand, at the outset, that the writer does not consider the terminology of the positions, as here presented, completely satisfactory and final. Thought and labor will do their work, and perfect, by slow degrees, what is here but a rough sketch of, or, it may be, even but a hint at, the truth.

Though the necessity may be felt of conforming to the order of nature in regard to *when* her storehouses shall be opened to us, yet a regret can not but be expressed that some method has not been known of recording, for our advantage, with the precision necessary for practical purposes, the observations, facts, and experiences of all previous time in relation to this subject. But no such method has ever been employed, if known, in ancient or in modern times, until now.

The reader needs no argument to make him realize the importance of using some method of this kind. In no other way, he must see, can knowledge upon such a subject be disseminated; and a practice, if such a one were possible, not thus reduced to appropriate terms, would die with its possessor. And for *duplicated* movements, in aid of the terminology, it will be seen that it is also necessary, or at least a matter of the greatest convenience, to be able to employ *signs* instead of written words for the purpose of expressing, at a glance of the eye, to the minds of the physician and his assistant, the precise thing indicated.

POSITIONS AND MOVEMENTS.—A movement, by a simple analysis, is resolved into POSITIONS; as, the *commencing*, the *terminating*, and the *intermediate*. Each of these is important, as exercising its share of effect in determining the nature and effect of the movement. The movement, in its execution, consists in the assumption, by the member, of all positions, successively, as it passes through the intermediate space between the commencing and terminating positions. Says Ling:

"To render any movement definite and exact, a point of departure, a point of termination, and the line through which the body or any of its parts must pass, are to be clearly and severally determined, as well as the ryhthm of the action itself."

But the *change of place*, or *motion*, of the member, though it is all that is visible to the eye, is by no means all that is implied by a movement. The muscular contraction and relaxation, with the effects of these actions in the substance of the tissues, and which occur out of sight, are what is chiefly implied by movements. A movement, properly considered, is a *mechanico-organic* effect, the result of the contractile power of the muscle, or muscles, and may be effected while the member is resting as well as when it is in motion. The character of a movement, in this sense, is determined by the *resistance* which the muscular contraction tries to overcome, which may consist of *gravity*, the opposing force of antagonizing muscles, or that which is exerted by another person. This last may be exactly graduated to the amount of effect it is desirable to secure.

In applying a movement, the commencing and terminating positions must first be determined in the mind of the operator; and without *intention*, on his part, no proper movement can take place. Sometimes the terminating position coincides with the commencing position, and no visible change of place occurs. Such a movement is called *holding*, and consists simply in maintaining, for a certain time, one position.

COMMENCING POSITIONS.—These relate, first, to the *trunk;* secondly, to the *upper extremities;* thirdly, to the *lower extremities;* fourthly, to the *head*. In describing positions, the head is generally neglected, as it is assumed to be erect. They are divided into *principal* and *derivative*, or *sub*-positions.

PRINCIPAL POSITIONS OF THE TRUNK.

These are five, viz., *standing, kneeling, sitting, lying, hanging*. The names of these principal positions are sufficiently descriptive of their character, and it is unnecessary to refer to illustrations.

Each of these positions admits of several variations.

I.—STANDING POSITIONS.

1. STANDING, OR ERECT-STANDING.—In this important position the body is straight and perpendicular, the arms hanging from the shoulders, the legs parallel, the heels in contact, the toes about twelve inches asunder.

The derivative positions are—

2. FALL-STANDING.—The whole body inclines at an angle greater or less from the perpendicular; all of the members, in the mean time, retaining their natural relative positions. The body in this position must be supported at some point by a firm object. An illustration of fall-standing may be seen in fig. 19. A slight

7

deviation forward is called *inclining;* backward, *reclining.*

The body may *greatly* deviate from the perpendicular, and the position is then called *low* fall-standing; or but slightly, and then it is *high* fall-standing.

It may deviate in any direction; as *forward, right* or *left sidewise,* or *backward;* and at various points in these directions. The position is described with sufficient accuracy by designating the two cardinal positions between which the body falls, as *forward-sidewise, right* or *left,* and *backward-sidewise, right* or *left.*

3. BENT-STANDING.—This indicates that the trunk is bent in its middle portion. *Deep-bent,* means bent to the utmost extent. The *bending* may be either forward, sidewise, or backward, to any degree.

II.—KNEELING POSITIONS.

1. KNEELING, OR ERECT-KNEELING.—The trunk rests on the knees instead of on the feet. A soft cushion must be placed under the knees.

2. FALL-KNEELING.—The trunk may assume the falling position while kneeling, corresponding with this form of the standing position.

III.—SITTING POSITIONS.

The derivatives of this position relate to the disposition of the legs as well as of the trunk.

1. SITTING.—The trunk rests upon the seat, the legs at right angles both at the hips and knees, the feet resting upon the floor.

2. SHORT-SITTING.—The seat rests upon the edge of the chair, occupying as little of it as possible, to maintain its posture.

3. LONG-SITTING.—The legs are extended horizon-

tally in the same plane with the seat, while the trunk is erect. See fig. 10.

4. LIE-SITTING, OR HALF-LYING.—In this position the trunk reclines, and is supported by cushions or by a movable seat constructed for this purpose.

5. FALL-SITTING.—The trunk deviates from the perpendicular at a certain angle, greater or less; thus it may be *falling, inclining,* or *deep-falling.*

Fall-sitting may also be *forward, sidewise, backward,* or at any intermediate point.

6. STRIDE-SITTING.—This indicates that the legs are placed at right angles apart, and also that the feet are widely separated, so as to afford as broad a base as possible.

IV.—LYING POSITIONS.

In this position the whole body is horizontal. This position is to be varied by changing the points of support.

1. FORWARD-LYING.—In this position the face is down, the body extended on a cushion, its anterior surface in contact therewith.

2. BACKWARD-LYING.—Lying extended upon the back.

3. SIDEWISE-LYING.—Lying upon the right or left side.

4. TRUNK-LYING.—In this position the trunk only is supported, while the legs project beyond the supporting surface, and are sustained by the force of the muscles. The derivatives are—

(*a*) *Trunk-forward-lying;*
(*b*) *Trunk-backward-lying;* and—
(*c*) *Trunk-sidewise-lying.*

5. LEG-LYING.—In this position the legs only rest upon a suitable couch or seat, while the trunk projects,

sustained only by the action of the muscles. It admits of the same variations as *trunk-lying*.

In *leg-lying* it is always necessary to employ some device, as the weight of another person, or some suitable fixture, to counterbalance the superior weight of the trunk.

This position admits of the same modifications as the preceding.

6. HEAD-AND-HEELS-LYING. — In this position the head and heels are supported by a cushioned stool, while the body is extended horizontally between them, back down, sustained by the muscles. Fig. 0 represents the position.

7. ELBOWS-AND-TOES-LYING.—In this position the body is sustained only by the elbows and toes. See fig. 0.

8. SIDEWISE-LYING.—This also admits of several varieties. as *plain*, *elbow*, and *foot*, *right*, *left*, etc.

9. BALANCE-LYING.—In this position, the support of the body is under the center of the trunk. It may be *backward*, *forward*, or *sidewise*.

V.—HANGING.

In this position the body is perpendicular, as in standing, but the weight is sustained by the hands, instead of the feet, by grasping a transverse pole, or something of the sort, overhead.

SWIM-HANGING is when the body is made to deviate from the perpendicular position, through the instrumentality of another person.

POSITIONS OF THE ARMS AND LEGS.

In each of the above postures of the body, the arms and legs may assume all the various positions that are consistent with the anatomical arrangement of the parts concerned. These variations of position are dependent upon the nature of the joints which connect these extremities with the trunk.

These joints are of the *ball-and-socket* kind, which permit the greatest degree of freedom of motion. The arms are capable of describing an entire circle, of which the shoulder is the center. The mobility of the leg is considerably less, its motion in an upward direction being prevented by ligaments and osseous projections at the upper edge of the acetabulum.

The other two joints of the limbs—viz., the elbow and knee joints, act on the hinge principle, permitting motion of those portions of the extremities beyond the joint only in *one* direction.

In studying the positions of the extremities we must keep distinctly in mind not only the difference of these two kinds of joints, but also the fact that the position resulting from the flexure of the one joint is to be regarded as entirely distinct and different from that resulting from a flexure of the other. Thus, for example, the upper arm is capable of bending at the shoulder, in many directions, and it makes no difference in regard to that motion whether the elbow joint is bent at the time or not. If we keep this simple fact in view, it will greatly simplify our study of the positions of the arms and legs.

The arms and legs, whether bent at the elbow and knee joints or not, may be considered as forming the *radii* of a multitude of circles, of which the shoulder and hip joints form the centers, so that the hands and the feet, when the limbs to which they belong move freely, describe arcs of circles, not only parallel with the antero-posterior diameter of the body, but also at every conceivable angle with this diameter.

Of course, it is impossible to invent a nomenclature that shall define with accuracy, through this great range of possibility, all the positions the members may assume; but for the ends demanded in the practice of *movements*, both as a hygienic and as a remedial art, a description sufficiently accurate to fulfill all purposes of practical utility, becomes quite easy.

We reduce the description of the positions of these members to the utmost simplicity, bringing them down to a few cardinal points easily remembered. Thus, we may refer all the positions of the arms to the *perpendicular*, the *anterio-posterior*, and the *transverse* diameters of the body. Every direction in which the arm can be extended will either correspond with these planes, or be related to them more or less nearly, so that they may be described or designated accordingly.

ARM POSITIONS SEEN IN A FRONT VIEW OF THE BODY.—These positions of the arms will be understood by reference to the following diagram.

In this diagram, the positions of the arms are represented in the plane of the transverse diameter of the body. The left side of the diagram represents the chief positions of the arms in that plane. A is the shoulder joint, representing the center of the circle of which the arm is the radius. The names of these positions are as follows:

Stretch, or *upward-stretch*, A *a*.
Side-stretch, or *yard*, A *c*.
High-side-stretch, or *high-yard*, A *b*.
Low-side-stretch, or *low-yard*, A *d*.
Downward-stretch, or *natural position*, A *e*.

The *right* side of the diagram represents the same

TERMINOLOGY OF POSITIONS. 151

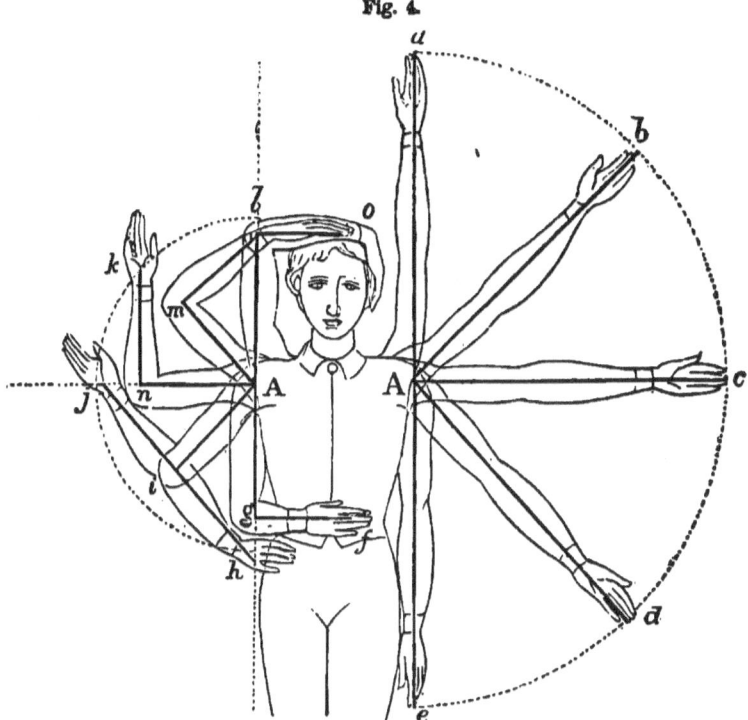

Fig. 4.

FRONT VIEW, SHOWING THE ARM POSITIONS.

positions, but with the *elbow-bent* at a right angle, the shoulder being at A.

Each of these positions might receive the same name as the corresponding ones of the opposite side, with the addition of the term *elbow-bent*, to denote the variation of the forearm from a straight line with the upper arm. Thus, A *l o* is *stretch elbow-bent;* A *m l* is *high side-stretch elbow-bent;* and so of all the other positions with the elbow bent, corresponding with the positions on the opposite of the diagram, in which the elbow is straight.

But as this would be a rather cumbrous mode of expression, and as it is easier to remember shorter specific names for these positions, the following terms are used for convenience:

Curve, A *l o*, indicates that the arm is placed in close contact with the head, both the elbow and wrist joints being bent so as to bring the member in close contact with the head. This is otherwise expressed as *stretch, elbow,* and *wrist-bent rest.*

Shelter, A *m l*, is equivalent to *high side-stretch,* or *yard, elbow-bent rest.*

Heave, A *n k*, is the same as *yard elbow-bent.*

Angle, A *i j*, is *low-yard elbow upward-bent.*

Wing, A *i h*, is *low-yard elbow downward-bent rest.*

Cover, A *g f*, is *down-stretch elbow-bent rest.*

The above comprises all the arm positions that it is necessary to describe in the transverse plane of the body. It is obvious that the same kinds and the same number of positions, with slight variations, may be had in any other plane as in this, and they admit of an analogous mode of description.

ARM POSITIONS SEEN IN A SIDE VIEW OF THE BODY.—The accompanying diagram represents the positions of the arms in the plane corresponding with the antero-posterior diameter of the body. It will be seen at once that the shoulder being the center, the arm may describe the greater part of the circle of which it is the radius, a small arc posteriorly being excepted.

It will also be seen that when the arm is extended perpendicularly, either *up* or *down*, it is in exactly the position it occupies on the plane of the previous diagram, which plane, it will be noticed, cuts the one represented in this diagram at right angles. The positions of the arms shown in this view are as follows, viz.:

Stretch, arm upward.

TERMINOLOGY OF POSITIONS. 153

Fig. 5.

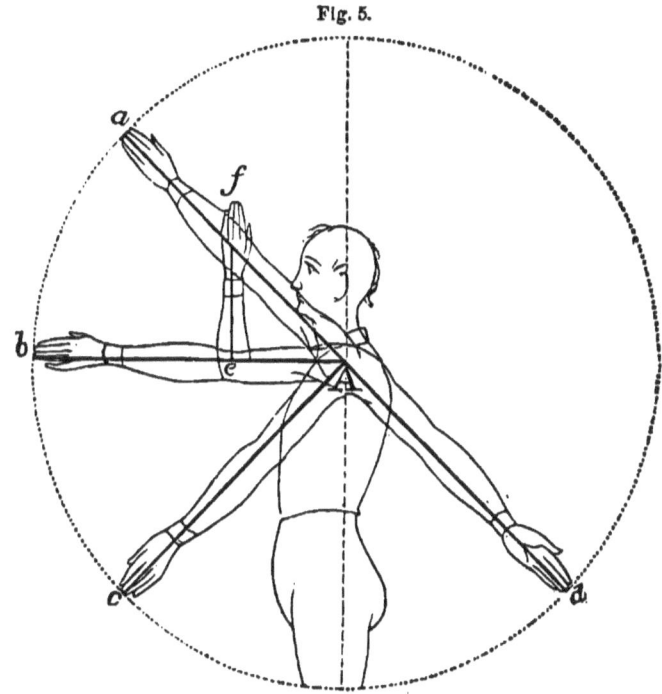

SIDE VIEW OF ARM POSITIONS.

Rack, A *b*, or *forward-stretch*.
High-rack, A *a*, or *high-forward-stretch*.
Low-rack, A *c*, or *low-forward-stretch*.
Backward-stretch, A *d*.

The chief variation of the positions in this plane, produced by bending the elbow joint, is *flight*, A *e f*.

The positions intermediate to those represented in the above diagram, which represent the positions seen in the front and side views of the body, are named from these. Thus the position between *rack* and *yard*, is *forward-side-stretch;* the position between this and stretch, in the same plane, is *high-forward side-stretch*, etc., etc. The only one of the intermediate positions that has received a name is *low-forward sidewise-stretch*, which is termed, briefly, *speak* position.

Beside the extensive rotary motion technically termed *bending*, of which the shoulder joint is capable, it may also be considerably *twisted* to the right or left, in nearly every position of the upper arm that has been above described. Hence the term *twist*, or *right-twist*, or *left-twist*, prefixed to the names of these several positions.

LEG POSITIONS.

The leg positions are produced by the bending of the hip and knee joints, except in standing, lying, etc., when the lower extremities are parallel with the trunk. The mobility of the hip joint is not quite so great as that of the shoulder joint, since it is limited in its motion upward, but in general it may be said that the positions of the legs may be made to correspond with those of the arms.

The general appellation given to any deviation of the leg from the perpendicular produced by bending the

Fig. 6.

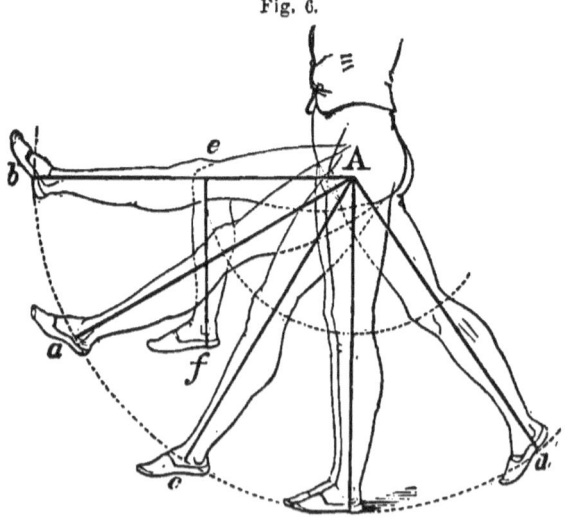

hip joint, is (one less graceful than expressive, perhaps) *kick*.

Forward-kick, the leg carried forward and raised to an angle of about forty-five degrees.

High-forward-kick is between forward-kick and the horizontal.

Low-forward-kick is between forward-kick and the perpendicular.

Sidewise-kick, the leg extended sidewise.

Backward-kick, the leg extended backward.

There are also intermediate positions, as—

Forward-sidewise-kick, high and low.

Backward-sidewise, high and low.

LOWER LEG POSITIONS.

These positions are designated by the term *knee-bent* prefixed to the names of positions resulting from flexure of the thigh joint.

A number of the positions of the legs, as in the case of the arms, are better expressed by distinct terms, as follows:

1. STRIDE.—In this position the legs are set apart, on each side of the perpendicular, distant about two or two and a half feet; whether sitting, standing, or lying.

2. WALK.—One leg is placed before the other, the trunk perpendicularly between them, as in ordinary walking.

3. STEP-STANDING.—One foot rests upon a step or stool, eight to twelve inches high; the knee and thigh joints are bent, to permit the foot to be thus raised, and the leg may be extended either forward or sidewise.

4. FOOT-SUPPORT-STANDING indicates a similar position. When this term is used, the position of the leg

must also be designated; a matter often neglected in *step-standing*. Thus, *forward-kick, foot-support, half-standing*, indicate that while the body rests upon one leg, the other is raised in forward-kick position, and that the foot rests upon some object that elevates it from the floor.

5. SQUAT-POSITION.—This is when both thigh and knee are bent at right angles.

6. LEG-ANGLE is a term indicating the bending of both thigh and knee, without precision as to degree.

In describing positions, the word *half* denotes that but one side is concerned, whether in reference to the arms or legs.

PART II.

EXAMPLES OF SINGLE MOVEMENTS.

Chapter Eight.

REGION OF THE FEET.

REMARKS ON MOVEMENTS OF THE FEET.—A large number of small bones enter into the composition of the feet, and are firmly bound together by ligaments and tendons. Some of the muscles of this region are confined to the feet, while others extend beyond them and are attached to the bones of the leg, nearly as high as the knee. Motion of the feet is produced by the action of these muscles, the chief bulk of which are situated in the lower leg, which member is, in consequence, affected by most of the movements of the feet, so that these muscles are properly included in this region. The feet are so constructed as to be very elastic, and at the same time very compact and strong, and little liable to injury from accidents to which they may be subjected.

The strength of the muscles and tendons of the feet is necessarily subjected to much more constant and severe trials than that of almost any other portion of the body. This results from their location, which obliges them not only to sustain the weight of the entire superior portion of the body, but also any additional weight that the person may carry. It is plain, too, that whatever power the muscles of the superior portions of the body may exert, must necessarily be continued to the ground or floor upon which the feet rest; because, through them, the feet not only sustain the body, but must sustain, as well, the effects of all the forces brought to bear upon it. Thus we brace ourselves with the feet in performing any action by means of the upper extremities—as in lifting a weight, pushing, pulling, etc.

To maintain the ordinary perpendicular position of the body upon the narrow base furnished it, it requires a stronger action of the muscles of the lower extremities than of those of any other part of the body. In inferior animals the weight is shared by four legs, which gives a base so broad as to render any such concentration of muscular power unnecessary.

This arrangement in the human framework may seem, at first sight, to be unwise, but a little reflection will show that it is a very wise and gracious provision of nature. We find, indeed, throughout nature, a law of compensation and balance, and in the present instance we see it most beautifully illustrated. At the superior extremity of the body is the head, containing those intellectual organs which, *par excellence*, distinguish man from the unthinking beasts. The functions of this part of the body require much nutrition, for which it draws largely upon the common reservoir. Now, to maintain an equilibrium of the circulation, it is needful that the *inferior* extremity of the body should be subjected to such habitual and vigorous action as to make an equally great counter demand upon the circulation. This is secured by the arrangement that we have just noticed, in which the lower extremities may be considered as the grand functional counterpoise of the brain. If this view be correct, it seems plain enough that when the health suffers from excessive cerebral action, the true remedy will consist in instituting strong action of the lower part of the body, especially at the feet, which must conduce to an equilibrium of the circulation by creating a counter flow in the direction of these members. And, in fact, in proportion as the demand for nutrition in those regions is responded to, *will the cerebral symptoms abate.* This principle is popularly understood and practiced upon in the application of irritants to the feet—every old nurse understands it; it holds equally true when the effect is realized by the natural method of exercise. In the technical language of the doctors, the effect here spoken of is termed *derivative.*

Thus we see that *movements* of the lower extremities supply a ready and efficient means of counteracting the effects of excessive stimulation in the superior portions of the body, consequent on the mental labor and anxieties inseparable from cultivated and busy life. They are also an efficient auxiliary means in the treatment of many cases of chronic disease.

We may remark here, that the feet sustain precisely the same relation to *temperature* as to motion. That is, by contact with the earth, which is cooler and damper than the air, they part more rapidly with their heat than do other portions of the body. And to supply this loss it is necessary to urge forward the heat-making process in the feet in proportion to the necessity thus produced, and thereby to cause the blood to flow into the extremities in suitable measure.

We will now enter upon a description of particular movements, charging the reader to bear in mind that he must not depend upon them for any curative or recuperative effects unless he is willing to practice them in conformity to the directions and principles laid down. To accomplish any good, they must be performed very slowly and with the utmost precision.

EXAMPLES OF MOVEMENTS OF THE REGION OF THE FEET.

1.—STANDING, FEET-EXTENDING.

Position.—To execute this movement, one should stand in the erect posture, with one hand extended so as to preserve the balance of the body by touching a wall, chair, or other object.

Action.—1. The feet should stretch at the ankle joint in such a way as to slowly raise the whole body, which they support, as high as possible, bringing it at length into the *tip-toe* position, in which it must be sustained for a few moments. 2. Relaxation of the stretched muscles should be allowed slowly to take place, till the heel reaches the floor, and the feet and trunk have recovered their original position. The cut shows the position after the extension is completed—in other words, the terminating position of the movement. This action should be repeated from six to ten times, slowly, as at first, with a slight interval between. If a more strenuous exercise of the muscles is desired, the movement may be performed with *one* foot only, the knee of the opposite leg being slightly bent, to clear the floor. After performing it with one foot, change to the other, and repeat the

Fig. 7.

movement in the same manner as it was performed at first.

EFFECT.—In this movement the muscles of the bottoms of the feet, also those of the posterior parts of the legs below the knee, are brought into powerful action. By this process they are strengthened, that is, their nutrition is increased, owing to the blood being attracted to the parts that have acted *away* from other organs. Hence the term *derivative* applied to such actions.

2.—TOE-SUPPORT, HALF-STANDING, HEEL-PRESSING.

POSITION.—One knee is bent, the foot lifted, its upper surface resting upon a cushioned seat or chair, while the weight of the body falls upon the other leg, standing in the erect position; the hand on the side of the raised foot is placed upon it, requiring the body to be slightly turned that way.

Fig. 8.

ACTION.—1. The hand placed upon the heel of the foot strongly pressed upon it, stretching the muscles and forcing the upper surface of the foot into a line with the leg, where it remains a short time. 2. The ankle bends, raising the heel against the pressure of the hand, till the foot is at right angles with the leg. The dotted lines of the cut show the terminating position. This action is to be repeated six or eight times with each foot.

EFFECT.—This movement renders the ankle joint supple, warms the feet, and is powerfully derivative. The muscles of the top of the foot and of the sides of the lower leg are chiefly affected.

3.—WING-WALK, TOE WALL-STANDING, FOOT-BENDING.

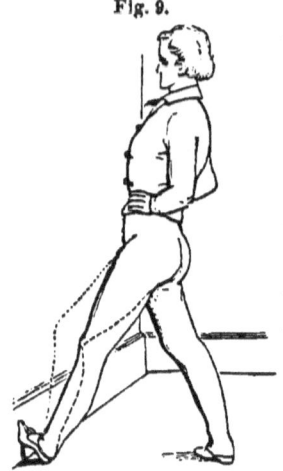

Fig. 9.

POSITION.—The hands should be placed upon the hips, one foot advanced a yard or so beyond the other, in *walking* position, but with the ankle of the forward leg a good deal bent, and the toe against the wall, with the heel as near the wall as possible.

ACTION.—1. The knee of the forward leg should bend, causing the instep to form a more acute angle with the leg; this position to be maintained for a short time. 2. The bent knee should now be extended, and the ankle and foot made to resume their former position. The cut shows the posture, the dotted outline indicating the position at the end of the first part of the movement. This should be repeated five or six times with each foot.

EFFECT.—The calf of the leg is very strongly acted upon, as well as the sole of the foot, producing a derivative effect, and rendering the ankle supple, and the calf strong, elastic, and voluminous.

In each of the preceding movements the weight of the body is the chief resistance that the acting muscles are compelled to overcome.

4.—LONG-SITTING, FEET SIDEWISE-BENDING.

POSITION.—Sitting in an easy posture in a chair, the hands placed upon the hips, and legs extended horizontally across, and supported by another chair that is placed immediately in front of the one occupied by the body. The feet should extend quite beyond the chair supporting the legs, and should remain quite free.

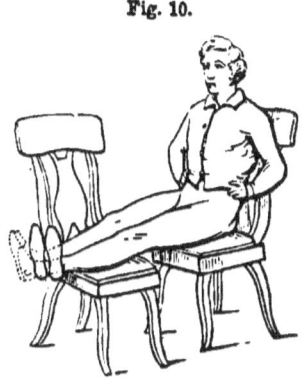

Fig. 10.

ACTION.—1. The feet should be turned to one side slowly, as far as they will go, being kept in the mean time in close contact; they should so remain for a short period. 2. They should then be turned in the opposite direction, in the same manner. This action should be repeated ten or twelve times. The cut shows the position; the dotted outline indicates the extent of the motion.

EFFECT.—This motion is produced chiefly by the muscles of the lower leg, and it strengthens these parts, and is derivative. If the ankle be weak, so that it is inclined to bend too easily in one direction, the movement should be directed to that side. Slight deformities of the ankle may be corrected by persevering in this discipline of the faulty muscles.

Fig. 11.

5.—LONG-SITTING, FEET-ROTATION.

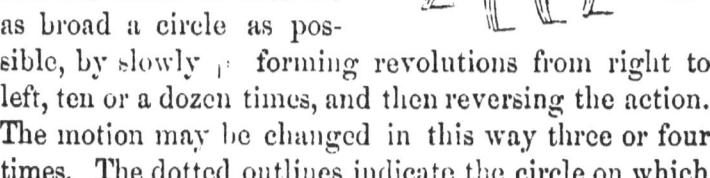

POSITION.—This is the same as in the preceding movement.

ACTION.—The toes of both feet are made to describe as broad a circle as possible, by slowly performing revolutions from right to left, ten or a dozen times, and then reversing the action. The motion may be changed in this way three or four times. The dotted outlines indicate the circle on which the toes revolve, which, it will be seen, represents the base of a cone, of which the heels are the apex. The two feet are to be kept close together during the execution of the movement, and the legs and body must maintain a uniform position.

EFFECT.—In this movement *all* the muscles of the feet and lower leg are put in vigorous action, and all the motion of which the ankle joint is capable is effected at each revolution. The movement is strongly derivative, and especially useful to the joint when in a weak state.

6.—FOOT-PERCUSSION.

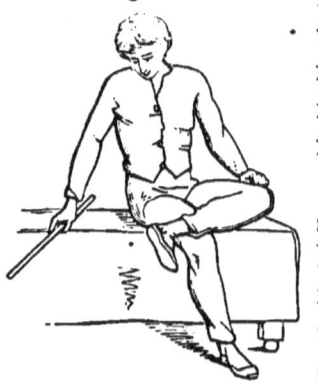
Fig. 12.

POSITION.—Sitting in a chair with one of the lower legs supported by the thigh of the other, near the knee, the foot projecting a little beyond it, while the other foot rests firmly upon the floor.

ACTION.—The hand of the side next to the raised foot holds a ruler or stick fifteen inches long and half an inch thick, by which a rapid succession of light blows, amounting to thirty or forty, are dealt upon the sole of the uplifted foot. The sole of the foot thus treated should be protected by a shoe or slipper. The cut shows the position, and suggests the mode of the action. Both feet are to be acted upon in this way alternately. This is what is called a passive movement, because the effect derived is not produced by inducing muscular contraction of the part.

EFFECT.—The benefit derived chiefly belongs to the

capillaries and nerves of the part. In the capillaries the clogged vessels have their blood renewed thereby, while the arteries, through the increased action of the nerves supplying them, are made to contract more vigorously. If there is congestion of the capillaries, as in *chilblains*, it is quickly scattered, and the normal condition restored. The movement is derivative, and warms the feet. The cure of chilblains by this method is speedy and permanent.

7.—FOOT-ROTATION (PASSIVE).

POSITION.—The same as shown in the preceding cut, except that the hand, instead of holding a stick, grasps the toe of the foot.

ACTION.—The toe of the foot thus grasped is made by means of the action of the hand thus grasping it to describe as broad a circle as the ankle joint will allow, the foot itself remaining in the mean time quite passive, that is, offering no resistance by means of its muscles. The motion is wholly effected by means of the hand thus applied to it. The foot should make about six revolutions in one direction, and then as many in the opposite. This change should be repeated five or six times. The movement should be applied to both feet.

EFFECT.—The foot may be turned farther in each direction in this manner than by its own muscles, and the movement is made with less effort and with more grateful effect; otherwise the general effects flowing from it are similar to those of the preceding movements.

8.—SUPPORT HALF-STANDING, LEG-SWINGING.

POSITION.—Standing with one foot resting upon a stool, one hand is extended and touching a wall, and

Fig. 13.

supported by it, one leg free.

ACTION.—The free leg is caused to *swing* by bending at the hip joint, in a plane parallel with the antero-posterior diameter of the body, the foot describing an arc of a circle, to be repeated fifteen or twenty times on each side.

EFFECT.—This motion assists the flow of the arterial blood toward the feet, while it retards the venous flow in the contrary direction, and thereby causes the blood to accumulate in the lower extremities. It warms the feet, and induces a pleasant sensation in the limbs.

All the above movements tend, if repeated at regular intervals, and in a proper manner, to increase the healthful flow of arterial fluid toward and into the lower leg and feet, while at the same time the venous blood is abundantly removed. They augment the bulk and energy of the parts thus brought into special action, warm the extremities, derive from the head and superior organs, and so bring great relief to a system suffering from oppression, congestion, or fatigue in its superior portions.

Chapter Nine.

REGION OF THE LEGS.

REMARKS ON MOVEMENTS OF THE LEGS.—The legs are endowed with very large masses of muscle, and it is necessary to employ them freely in movements, in order to secure the objects contemplated in our prescriptions for diseases. They are used as means of modifying the circulation of the blood, and by the auxiliary power thus derived, of securing the more special and desired effects of movements for other regions of the body. When a derivative effect is desired from movements of the region of the feet, it is best secured by employing the auxiliary influence of movements of this region; for the effect of these is strongly derivative also, and the whole result then produced is greater on account of the larger mass of muscle belonging to this region. It will be borne in mind that every part of the body is charged with the duty of perfecting the circulation of the blood in itself, and also of aiding its passage in the blood-vessels both *to* and *from* other parts more remote, for which it necessarily furnishes a channel.

WALKING.—This most common and most useful species of exercise is performed chiefly, though not entirely, by the muscles of the legs, and the act of walking constitutes a movement that deserves attention, as it enters not only as an element into many of the Movement-Cure prescriptions, but is very generally prescribed by physicians of every class and creed. We will briefly consider the special purposes it is supposed to answer, and its mechanism. Walker gives the following analysis of the actions concerned in walking:

"For the purpose of walking, we first bear upon one leg the weight of the body, which presses equally upon both. The other leg is then raised, and the foot quits the ground by rising from the heel to the point. For this purpose, the leg must be bent upon the thigh, and the thigh upon the pelvis; the foot is then carried straight forward at a sufficient height to clear the ground without grazing it. To render it possible, however, to move the foot, the haunch, which rested with its weight upon the thigh, must turn forward and outward. As soon as by this movement this foot has passed the other, it must be extended on the leg, and the leg upon the thigh, and in this manner, by the lengthening of the whole member, and without being drawn back, it reaches the ground at a distance in advance of the other foot, which is more or less considerable according to the length of the step, and it is placed so gently on the ground as not to jerk or shake the body in the slightest degree. As soon as the foot which has been placed on the ground becomes firm, the weight of the body is transferred to the limb on that side, and the other foot, by a similar series of actions, is brought forward in its turn. In all walking, the most important circumstance is, that the body incline forward, and that the movement of the leg and thigh spring from the haunch, and be free and natural. Viewed in this way, the feet have been well compared to the spokes of a wheel, the weight of the body falling upon them alternately."

The exercise of walking is extremely gentle, and it becomes fatiguing only by being unduly prolonged. The leg is raised, not by a direct *lifting*, but by causing the limb to deviate from a straight line by simply bending the thigh and knee joints. This action shortens the distance between the hip and foot, and thus the foot is elevated from the ground. The act requires comparatively little muscular power. Then the leg is brought forward, not by projecting it by means of sheer muscular force, but by an easy swinging motion, like that of a pendulum; its own momentum is made to assist the action. The progress of the trunk, in the forward direction, renders the swinging of the leg necessary and easy.

In walking, all the muscles of the legs and feet are moderately exercised, as also those of the back and shoulders. By these latter the body is kept upright, while the arms gently swing with a motion opposite that of the legs, so as to preserve the center of gravity over the changing base. If the pace be quickened, the muscles of the feet and legs enter upon a more vigorous action, whereby the body is projected more rapidly forward at the same time. This great expenditure of muscular power calls for a more rapid and profound respiration, and the respiratory muscles respond energetically to the demand, the chest dilates, and air passes into the farthest cells of the lungs.

In consequence of these actions, a surplus amount of heat is developed; more water, carbonic acid, and urea are produced, and these soon show themselves at the different outlets; perspiration appears upon the surface of the whole skin, and there are more frequent calls for urination, while the volume of vapor discharged by the lungs is greatly augmented.

Walking is doubtless superior to any other single exercise that a person can take, yet it fails to answer all the ends of exercise. As there are many other exercises involved in many kinds of *work* better adapted to preserve the health and power of all the organs of the well man, so there are others better adapted to certain morbid conditions. Though these should be employed in connection with a suitable amount of this exercise, walking, alone, fails to bring the abdominal organs into sufficient activity. On the contrary, these organs are simply carried, and are, until the respiration becomes accelerated, nearly as inactive as in sitting. Hence weakly persons, especially females, complain of a dragging sensation in walking, in this condition of the system; and without some other movement to invigorate the enfeebled parts, walking may be considered not only useless, but even injurious to the health. In these cases, certain movements of the trunk and abdomen are absolutely required to render walking proper and useful.

EXAMPLES OF MOVEMENTS OF THE LEGS.
9.—WING-STRIDE-STANDING, CURTSEYING.

Fig. 14.

POSITION.—The hands are fixed upon the hips, in the standing posture, with the back in contact with a smooth wall, the heels two or two and a half feet apart, and five or six inches from the wall, against which the trunk is slightly supported, the toes turned outward.

ACTION.—1. The feet stretch (as in No. 1). 2. The knees bend forward and outward, while the trunk sinks quite down. 3. The knees stretch, raising the body to its utmost height. 4. The heels sink and rest again upon the floor. At each stage the movement should be performed very slowly, observing a few moments' pause between its distinct portions. The cut shows the position at the stage of the movement when the body begins to descend, also by the dotted outlines, the position at the extreme limit of motion. The movement may be repeated four or five times.

EFFECT.—The action is felt at the bottoms of the feet, in the calves of the legs, and, after the knees bend, strongly in the muscles of the legs. The effect increases in proportion as the knees deviate from the perpendicular by the bending of the knee joints. The muscles of the perineum, and even of the rectum, in the extreme position, are strongly affected.

10.—HALF-STANDING, CURTSEYING.

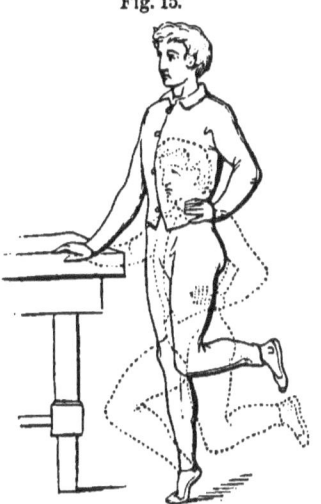

Fig. 15.

POSITION.—One hand is placed upon the hips, the other rests on some object to steady the body; the trunk erect, one leg straight, and the foot resting on the floor, the other leg bent at the knee at right angles.

ACTION.—1. The foot on the floor is bent so that the weight rests upon the toes. 2. The knee slowly bends, and the trunk sinks as low as the leg is able to support it. 3. It is again stretched till the trunk rises to its erect position, when, 4, the heel sinks to the floor. The cut shows the position, and the dotted outline the extreme position. This action should be repeated three or four times with each leg.

EFFECT.—This is similar to that of movement No. 8; but as the whole weight of the body is supported by one leg, the movement is thereby made much more positive.

11.—BALANCE-STANDING, CURTSEYING.

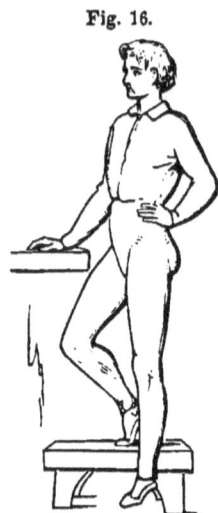

Fig. 16.

POSITION.—One hand is placed in contact with some firm object to steady the body; the other is placed upon the side; the trunk erect, and its weight is borne by one foot resting upon a stool about eighteen inches high, while the other is free.

ACTION.—1. The knee slowly bends, and the trunk with the suspended leg falls, but it does not touch the floor. 2. The bent knee is slowly extended till the body is in the first position. The cut shows the position after the knee is bent. Repeat the action five or six times with each side.

Fig. 17.

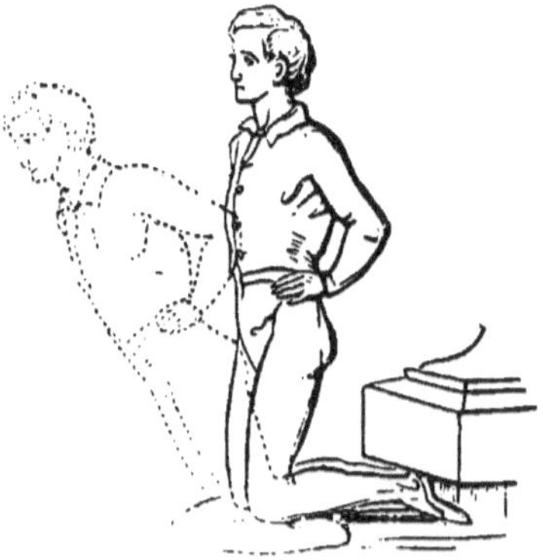

EFFECT.—This movement is only a modification of the previous one, and the effect is much the same.

12.—WING-KNEELING, KNEE-STRETCHING.

POSITION.—The hands are placed upon the hips, trunk, or kneeling position, with a cushion under the knees, and the heels prevented from rising by being forced down by some firm object, as the frame of a sofa.

ACTION.—1. The trunk inclines gently and slowly forward, without bending at the hips or in the back, the knee only being slightly straightened or stretched. 2. It rises upward and backward till it regains its erect position. The cut shows the commencing, and the dotted outline the extreme position of the movement. This movement should be repeated five or six times.

EFFECT.—This movement powerfully affects the muscles and fascia of the thigh, its influence extending to the hips and back, also to the calves of the legs. It is derivative, and counteracts the ill effects of too much exercise of the muscles of the anterior portion of the thigh.

13.—HALF-STANDING, ALTERNATE LEG-TWISTING.

POSITION.—The hands being fixed upon the hips, the trunk rests upon one foot, while the other foot is placed upon a slight elevation, about two feet distant, in a direction diagonal to the front of the body.

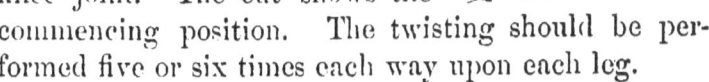

Fig. 18.

ACTION.—By a slight effort of the body and of the leg upon which it rests, the trunk turns horizontally upon the axis of the leg, right and left, alternately. Care should be used not to twist too strongly, so as to over-tax the knee joint. The cut shows the commencing position. The twisting should be performed five or six times each way upon each leg.

EFFECT.—The amount of contraction of the muscles of the leg in this movement is comparatively small; all the muscles, however, together with all the other structures of the part, are strongly affected by it. The muscles, nerves, areolar structures, vessels, etc., are subjected to an unusual agitation, that induces peculiar sensations and marked effects.

14.—WING-WALK, FORWARD-FALL-STANDING, KNEE-BENDING

Fig. 19.

POSITION.—The hands being fixed upon the hips, one foot is placed about two and a half feet before the other in walking position; the posterior foot is at right angles with the anterior.

ACTION.—1. The heel of the forward foot rises at the same time that the knee slowly bends; and since this action shortens the forward leg, the body is inclined forward, throwing its weight upon it. 2. The bent knee slowly extends, the leg becoming straight, until the heel reaches the floor, and the trunk is raised to the commencing position. The cut shows the movement in one stage of it. This action may be repeated five or six times with each leg.

EFFECT.—This movement very strongly affects all the muscles of the legs, and it proves derivative in cases of cold feet or rush of blood to the head.

15.—LEG-ANGLE HALF-STANDING, LEG-CLAPPING.

POSITION.—The knee and thigh of one leg are bent so as to raise the foot, which is placed on a chair or stool, while the trunk rests upon the other leg in the erect or gently inclining posture.

ACTION.—Both hands, with the palms open and fingers outstretched, are employed to *clap*, from the hip to the ankle, the whole of the leg thus brought within their reach. The *clapping* consists of rapid but light strokes of the palms of the hands. Each leg may be thus clapped throughout its length five or six times. The clapping is a passive movement for the legs, although the arms are active, of course, in applying it.

Fig. 20.

EFFECT.—This action imparts a high degree of nervous sensibility to the legs thus operated upon, and greatly increases the vascularity and warmth of the skin. It is derivative for the superior organs, and also for the interior vessels of the parts subjected to the action. This operation will also be found an excellent means of warming cold hands and of increasing the circulation in the arms.

REGION OF THE HIPS.

REMARKS ON THE REGION OF THE HIPS.—This region includes the pelvis, its contents, and its connections. In debility from any cause, this region frequently presents some severe symptoms, and is often afflicted with grave disease, such as *constipation, prolapsus of the womb and rectum, uterine congestion, ovaritis, amenorrhea, leucorrhea,* diseases of the prostate, bladder, and sexual organs.

The movements applicable to this region are numerous and important, affording us the means of controlling the circulation and nutrition of these parts, and if well selected and applied in proper connection with others that may be indicated, such movements prove an invaluable means for maintaining or destroying the health.

The utility of these movements will be realized when it is noticed that after childhood the class of persons afflicted with the diseases referred to, seldom make use of much *variety* in their exercises, but are in the habit of carrying themselves stiffly about, employing as few muscles as possible. Most of the following movements necessarily affect the thigh, back, and abdomen, because the muscles acting have their attachments at one extremity in one or the other of these regions. Many of them affect the legs equally with the pelvis.

16.—WING-STRIDE, SHORT-SITTING, LEG OUTWARD-STRETCHING.

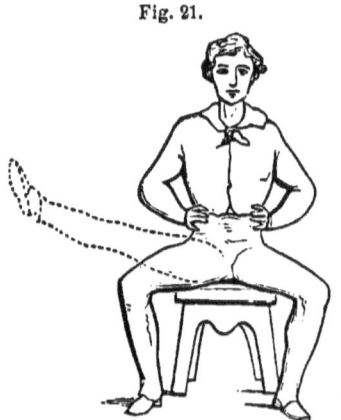

Fig. 21.

POSITION.—The hands are fixed on the hips, the body erect, in the sitting posture, upon the edge of a chair or stool, with the thighs separated at right angles, feet resting on the floor.

ACTION.—1. The foot of one side is raised a few inches from the floor. 2. The knee is slowly stretched, till the legs are quite straight, and in a horizontal position, and pointing forward-sidewise. 3. The knee bends and returns to its first position. This movement may be repeated five or six times with each limb. The cut shows the position, and the dotted line indicates the extreme position of the movement.

EFFECT.—This movement requires strong action of the internal muscles of the pelvis, and of the muscles of the abdomen and upper portion of the leg, and causes the blood to circulate toward the feet. It strengthens the pelvis, and is derivative in congestion of its organs.

17.—LEG-ANGLE HALF-STANDING, KNEE-STRETCHING.

POSITION.—With one hand extended, and grasping some firm object, and the other upon the hip, the body stands erect upon one foot—namely, that on the supported side; the other leg is bent at both knee and hip, the thigh being horizontal.

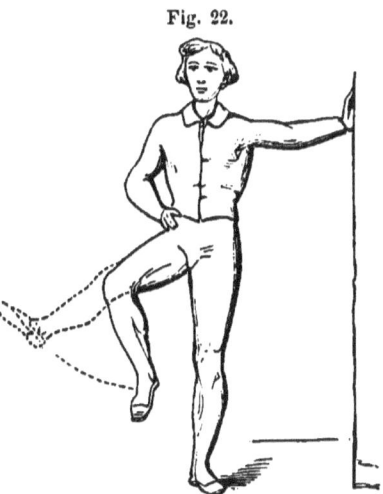

Fig. 22.

ACTION.—1. The knee is slowly stretched until the leg is straight. 2. The knee bends, and the leg assumes the first position. This action may be repeated three or four times with each side. The cut shows the position, and the dotted line indicates the terminating position.

EFFECT.—The action in the movement is like that of the preceding, though somewhat more energetic, and more difficult to perform, and it produces similar effects.

18.—WING-RECLINE, SUPPORT-SITTING, KNEES-RAISING.

POSITION.—The hands are placed upon the hips, the trunk sustained in a chair, in reclining posture, or on

8*

a couch with the shoulders a good deal elevated; the feet resting upon the floor, and the knees bent at right angles.

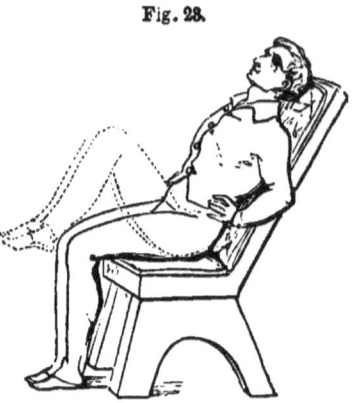

Fig. 23.

ACTION.—1. The knees are slowly raised as high as possible, the lower leg remaining in the same relative position. 2. The legs slowly return to the first position. This action may be repeated five or six times. The cut shows the first position, and the dotted outlines the direction and the extent of the movement.

EFFECT.—In this action the lower abdominal muscles and the internal pelvic muscles are strongly affected. The movement strengthens the part, and removes internal congestion of the pelvic organs.

19.—HALF-STANDING, LEG FORWARD-RAISING.

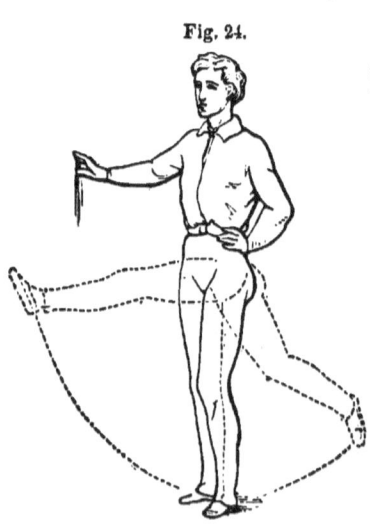

Fig. 24.

POSITION.—The body is steadied by extending one hand for this purpose, while the other is placed upon the hip, the body in standing position, resting its weight upon one leg.

ACTION.—1. The leg of the side opposite the support is slowly raised forward till it nearly reaches the horizontal position. 2. It then slowly returns to its first position. This action may be repeated four or five times with each leg. The dotted line of the cut indicates the direction and the extent of the movement.

EFFECT.—This is similar to that of the preceding movement.

20.—HALF-STANDING, LEG BACKWARD-RAISING.

POSITION.—This is precisely like that in movement No. 19, to which the reader is referred.

ACTION.—1. The leg is extended *slowly* backward, and raised as high as possible. 2. It returns slowly to its first position. The cut (fig. 24) shows this movement, the dotted outline extending backward indicating the limit of the backward motion.

EFFECT.—In this movement the muscles of the seat, the lower portion of the back, and those of the pelvis are strongly affected. It is useful to strengthen these parts, and to remove internal weakness and congestion. The action of the muscles in the direction in which the leg moves is *concentric*, while that of the anterior and internal muscles is *eccentric*.

21.—HALF-STANDING, LEG SIDEWISE-RAISING.

POSITION.—For this the reader is also referred to movement No. 19, fig. 24.

ACTION.—1. The leg is separated from the standing one, and slowly raised sidewise as far as possible. 2. It then falls slowly to its first position. The plane in which the leg moves is represented by the perpendicular dotted line.

EFFECT.—Similar to that of the preceding, except that the muscles of the thigh and hip on the side moved, are brought into strong action.

Each of the above four movements acts upon the muscles of the thigh and leg in a very powerful manner, especially if the extremity be maintained for a few moments at the extreme limit of the movement; and since not only the muscles of the hips and thighs, but also those of the leg enter into these actions, they are all strongly derivative in their effects.

22.—FORWARD-FALL, HEAD-SUPPORT-STANDING, LEG-RAISING.

POSITION.—The head rests upon the folded arms placed upon some object of convenient height, as a table or mantle-piece; the feet resting on the floor, so far back from the perpendicular as to cause the body (which is in a nearly straight line) to form an angle with the floor of about forty-five degrees.

ACTION.—1. The leg is slowly raised as high as possible, where it remains for a few moments. 2. It then slowly returns to its first position. The dotted outline of the accompanying cut indicates the direction and extent of the movement. This action may be repeated four or five times with each leg.

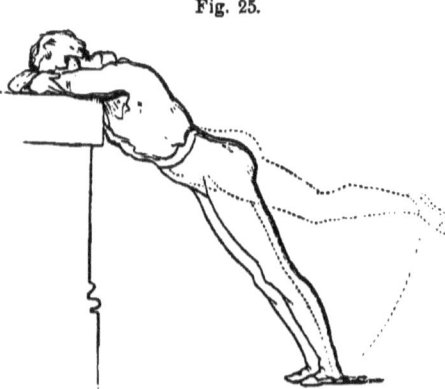

Fig. 25.

EFFECT.—The muscles of the thigh, leg, seat, perineum, and back are strongly affected, and also those of the anterior surface of the body. This movement is especially valuable for sedentary people whose legs have become weak from disuse.

23.—HALF-STANDING, LEG-ROTATION.

Fig. 26.

POSITION.—One hand extended steadies the body by leaning against a wall or some firm object; the other hand being fixed upon the hip. Body erect, and resting upon the leg nearest the supporting hand.

ACTION.—The free leg is made to rotate so that the foot shall describe the broadest possible circle, of which the inner edge is near the supporting foot. This motion is produced by the alternate gentle action of the muscles attached to the hips. The rotation may be performed six or eight times in one direction, when it is reversed, and performed in the opposite direction. In the cut, the dotted outline indicates the action.

EFFECT.—This movement gently affects all the muscles of the thigh, and by the centrifugal effect that results from the motion in a circle, restrains the return of the venous circulation for a moment, whereby the circulation of the leg is subsequently quickened, and the leg warmed.

24.—WING-SITTING, DOUBLE LEG-TWISTING.

POSITION.—The hands are upon the hips, the trunk sustained by a chair, or lying upon a couch with the shoulders raised high; the legs are extended across another chair, the feet projecting freely, and placed so far apart that the toes will barely touch in the movement.

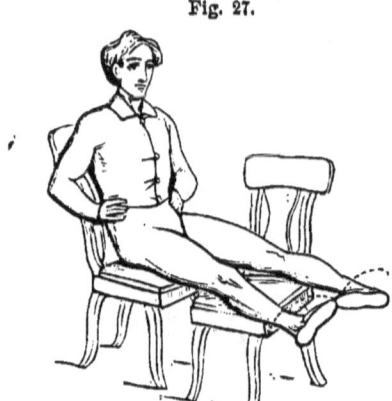

Fig. 27.

ACTION.—1. The legs slowly rotate, the toes turning *outward*, the rotation being effected at the upper extremity of the thigh. 2. They then rotate *inward*, till the toes touch in a nearly horizontal position. This action is repeated five or six times, each time in both directions. In the cut, the dotted curved line indicates the direction of the movement. Care should be taken that the limbs turn on their own axis, without bending at the knees, stretching at the ankles, or in any other way deviating from the first position of the legs.

EFFECT.—This movement is chiefly effected by small muscles about the head of the thigh bone, some of which are intimately related to the cavity of the pelvis, though many others assist in the movement. It circulates the blood in the legs, strengthens the hips, and removes congestion of the organs contained in the pelvic cavity.

25.—LEGS-ANGLE, LIE-SITTING, KNEES-STRETCHING.

POSITION.—The hands are placed upon the hips, the trunk reclining on a couch with the shoulders raised, the legs bent both at the thigh and knee joints so that the feet may rest upon the couch near the seat, the legs being in *angle* position.

ACTION.—1. The knees are slowly stretched, the feet being raised and the lower legs being brought into a line with the thighs, the thigh in the mean time remaining at an angle of about forty-five degrees with the body, which position is maintained for a few moments. 2. The knees slowly bend, bringing the feet back to their original position, resting on the couch. This action may be repeated six or eight times.

EFFECT.—If the extreme position of the legs be maintained, the action at the lower portion of the abdomen and in the pelvis is powerful, and in character concentric. The anterior part of the leg is also affected.

26.—SHELTER TRUNK-BACKWARD-LYING, LEGS-RAISING.

POSITION.—The hands are placed upon the crown of the head, the trunk lying backward upon a couch, the legs, from the hips, projecting beyond the edge, their weight causing them to descend considerably below its level.

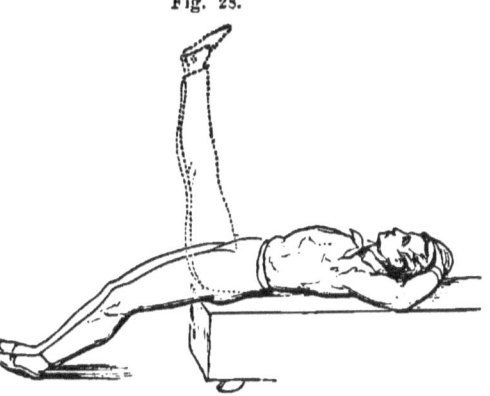

Fig. 23.

ACTION.—1. The legs are slowly raised till they are in a position approaching right angles with the trunk, and are held there for a few moments. 2. They are permitted slowly to fall back to their original position. This action may be repeated five or six times. The dotted outline in the cut shows the position reached at the limit of motion.

EFFECT.—This movement acts upon the abdominal coverings and the muscles of the pelvis, presses upward the pelvic and abdominal contents, and affects eccentrically the muscles of the chine and hips.

27.—KICK BACKWARD-LYING, LEGS-SEPARATION.

POSITION.—The hands are placed upon the hips, the head slightly elevated, the trunk lying on the back, and the legs raised nearly to the position shown in fig. 31.

ACTION.—1. The legs are allowed slowly to separate, as far as possible, being carried apart laterally by their own weight. 2. Are slowly brought together again. This action may be repeated five or six times.

EFFECT.—The insides of the legs, the perineum, the pelvis, and the lower portion of the abdomen are affected by this movement.

28.—SIDEWISE-LYING, LEG-RAISING.

POSITION.—The body lies upon one side in a horizontal and straight position, the head being pillowed upon

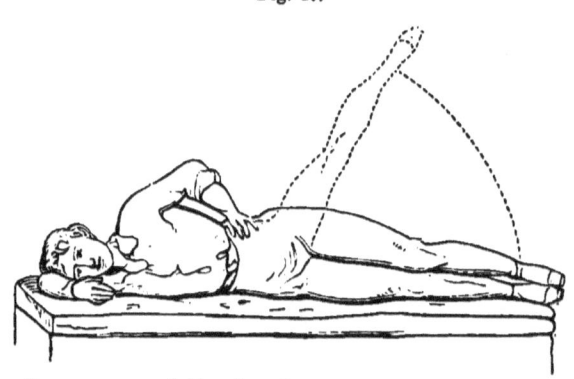

Fig. 29.

the under arm, while the hand of the other is placed upon the hip.

ACTION.—1. The leg slowly rises in the perpendicular plane of the body as far as it may, where it remains for a few moments. 2. It then slowly falls back to its first position. This action may be repeated six or eight times with each side. The dotted outline of the cut indicates the point to which the leg rises, and the direction of the movement.

EFFECT.—The sides, the outsides of the legs and hips, and the perineum, are brought into action in this movement.

29.—BACKWARD-LYING, LEGS-ROTATION.

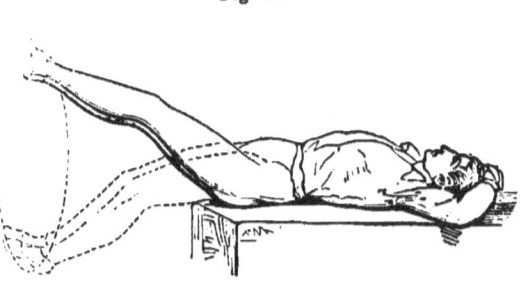

Fig. 30.

POSITION.— The commencing position is exactly like that of No. 28.

ACTION.—1. The legs are carried to one side by bending at the hips. 2. The feet are then made to revolve in as wide a circle as possible while the legs are kept in contact. 3. The direction of the rotation is then reversed. This change is repeated three or four times. The dotted outline of the cut shows the circle traversed by the feet.

EFFECT.—This movement acts upon all the muscles of the thighs and hips, the lower portion of the abdomen and back in turn, also the rectum, uterus, bladder and lower portion of the spinal cord.

30.—WING LEG-ANGLE HALF-LYING, KNEE-STRETCHING.

POSITION.—The arms are in wing position, trunk lying with the shoulders much elevated, the legs bent at both thigh and knee joints at right angles, the feet resting on the same horizontal level with the body.

ACTION.—1. The knees slowly stretch, without changing the position of the thighs, until the legs are straight,

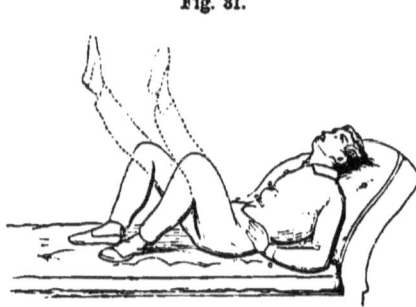

Fig. 31.

the feet being elevated. 2. The knees slowly bend, and the feet take the position from which they started, *i.e.*, the commencing position. This action may be repeated five or six times. The dotted outline of the cut shows the position at the end of the first part of the movement.

EFFECT.—This movement brings into action all the anterior muscles of the leg, as well as those of the lower abdominal and pelvic regions, and affects the internal organs of these parts. It also warms the feet.

31.—THIGH-ROTATION.

POSITION.—The hands are placed upon the hips, the trunk is lying backward, with the shoulders and head elevated, the thighs bent strongly upon the abdomen; the knees also are bent to their acutest angle.

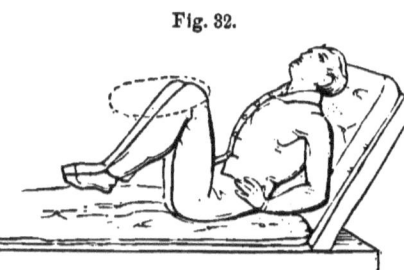

Fig. 32.

ACTION.—The knees are caused to revolve five or six times in a circle as broad as possible, the inner part of which is close to the body. The direction of the motion should change four or five times, as in No. 31.

EFFECT.—This movement excites the rectum, lower intestines, and abdominal contents generally, and also strengthens the muscles about the hips, and all the organs depending for their innervation on the lower part of the spinal cord.

32.—CHINE KNOCKING.

POSITION.—One hand is extended so as to brace and steady the body by its contact with some firm object; the trunk leans forward, the body in the standing position.

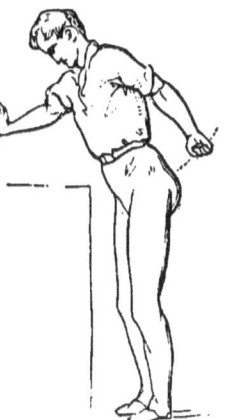

Fig. 33.

ACTION.—The free arm and hand, strongly clenched, is used to deal a number (twenty or thirty) of smart blows upon the lower portion of the chine.

EFFECT.—This movement makes a vibratory impression upon the sacral bone, its contained nerves — the lower portion of the spinal cord and branches. The effect is also communicated to all the pelvic organs, as the rectum, uterus, bladder, etc., both directly, and as a result of the excitement produced in the part of the spinal cord supplying the affected region with nerves. The movement is highly useful in many cases, but should be omitted in others. The question of its appropriateness may generally be decided by the sensations produced. If it is intended to stimulate the action of the rectum, the knocking should be applied to the lower extremity of the sacral bone.

Chapter Ten.

REGION OF THE TRUNK.

THE trunk of the body consists of external walls, with the included space, which is filled with the organs of digestion and respiration, and their appendages. This space is divided by the diaphragm into two parts or chambers; the one below the diaphragm containing the apparatus for the digestion of food and the preparation of nutritive material, that above it being devoted to the aeration and circulation of the blood.

In the light afforded by the Movement-Cure, there is seen to be an intimate connection between these two sets of functions, whether physiologically or pathologically considered. The therapeutical indications also relate to *both* sets of organs and their functions— even though the *symptoms* of which the invalid chiefly complain relate more especially to *one* or the *other*. There can be no good digestion with imperfect respiration, and no efficient respiration while the blood is overwhelmed with the crude materials derived from imperfect digestion. The location of these organs very much favor their associative treatment. These organs are the media through which the materials destined for vital service are brought into those peculiarly intimate relations with each other that are required.

By digestion, food is reduced to a fluid state; it then passes the digestive boundaries into the blood. The circulation carries the materials in this condition to the lungs, where they become associated with the oxygen of respiration, and the products of this association are then applied to all the nutritive purposes of the body; oxygen or the blood-plasma being yielded up to the tissues according to the various vital requirements.

It has been already shown that the quality of the vital manifestations depends upon the manner in which these preparatory processes are performed. The modes of attempting to control these processes are as numerous as the devices of medicine; for it is to gain this control that the remedial art is exercised everywhere. But to accomplish this grand object successfully, we must make use of the appliances furnished us in the Movement-Cure.

MOVEMENTS OF THE DIGESTIVE ORGANS.—It has already been shown, pp. 88, 90, how necessary are movements to further the different stages of the digestive processes; to set the blood in healthful motion; to rouse to activity the secretory functions, etc., etc. But their applicability in disease would seem, at first view, not to be demonstrated by these facts. That they are so, however, one is convinced from attending to the essential nature of many pathological conditions, as revealed to us by the Movement-Cure, and by a consideration of the advantages that these organs are constantly receiving from those natural and constant movements to which they are subjected while in a state of health.

1. In the alimentary canal we have a tube more than twenty-five feet in length, variously convoluted and folded upon itself, but the greatest portion of which is quite *free to move* when acted upon by causes external to itself. It is fixed to the abdominal wall by few and movable attachments, so that it readily yields in all its

parts to the least mechanical force exerted upon it. The tendency of the several portions of the canal to glide upon each other is highly favored by the exceedingly smooth and polished surface they present, and by the fine, glairy secretions with which they are lubricated. These surfaces glide and play upon each other with every change of posture, and with the muscular exertion put forth in nearly every part of the body. These mechanical displacements, caused by impressions received from external sources, afford to the intestines the stimulus necessary to induce their own worm-like motion, which is effected by means of the circular muscular fibers that enter into the structure of the tube itself. It is by this motion that the contents of the canal are carried forward and the condition supplied for absorption of the fluid portions and for the passage of the portal blood in the direction of the liver.

It is a curious and most interesting fact, that children and young animals, whose desire for motion is inherent in their constitutions, are inclined chiefly to those kinds of exercise, and to assume those positions, that necessarily affect the abdominal contents in the way above described. It is in such exercises as *climbing*, *rolling*, *crawling*, *jumping*, and *playing* generally, that these contents are most disturbed; but we never hear that these movements, though often violent, are attended with harmful consequences. On the contrary, we are convinced that these are the very means that nature prescribes to secure healthful development and power in these most essential parts of the body.

2. And, as if to insure these healthful effects, nature *has* ordained that by *respiration*, as an efficient and constant means, these motions shall be secured to the alimentary canal. The abdominal contents may be

considered as located between two great muscular organs, the diaphragm and the abdominal walls. These muscles act conjointly *simultaneously*, and upon all the included parts, causing them to play incessantly upon each other, and subjecting them to a constant and gentle pressure.

Fig. 34.

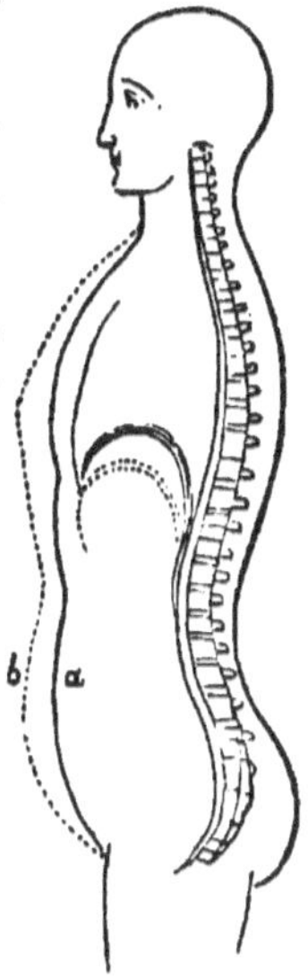

Diagram illustrating the movements of the abdominal walls and contents under the influence of respiration; *a*, position after expiration; *b*, position after inspiration. The diaphragm is shown to be much more concave after expiration.

The accompanying diagram shows how the diaphragm and walls of the abdomen are moved and acted upon by the included organs at each respiration. And as these respiratory acts are at the rate of about eighteen per minute, we see these organs must undergo a pretty thorough churning.

Any cause operating to deteriorate the health, diminishes the amount of this motion, for the simple reason that the respiration, in chronic disease of every kind, is *less vigorous* than in health. In disease, also, these natural movements are not only less in extent, but faulty in kind; for we frequently find that, to afford play to the lungs, some other part of the walls of the body take on motion that compensates for the lack of it in the parts originally intended for the performance of that function. In this way the advantage of the respiratory movements to the abdominal contents is partially lost. The common causes operating to produce these injurious results are too long continuance of the fixed positions of standing or sitting, at work or study. The prevalent style of *dress*, too, by limiting the movements of the chest and abdomen, and compressing and weakening the muscles, has much to do in the production of these disastrous consequences.

3. One prime effect of exercise is the increase of the substance and the contractility of the abdominal muscular coverings. The walls of the abdomen become, in the absence of proper exercise, weak, flabby, and unnaturally distended. When this occurs, the abdominal contents necessarily obey the laws of gravity, become dislocated, and their function consequently impeded. Well-directed movements restore the power of these walls; the sinking organs are reinstated in their original position, and their function is recovered.

4. The *action* of these muscles necessarily calls blood into them to supply their nutrient wants. The advantage of this does not stop with the maintaining of the powers of these muscles. An equal benefit is derived in the scattering of the visceral congestion, which will necessarily occur when the blood is not employed in external parts. Congestion of the mucous surfaces, or of some portion of the contained glandular apparatus, is quite sure to accompany the weaknesses above mentioned.

The reader will now be able to understand the morbid conditions that coexist in nearly all forms of dyspepsia, constipation, bronchial, laryngeal, and liver affections, that so extensively prevail in the community. There is insufficiency of respiration, and consequently of the natural movements of the digestive organs; these functions are hence impeded, and the well-known *symptoms* are manifested that are so freely *doctored* instead of the diseases themselves. And the reader will also readily infer that, in order to correct all the above-mentioned difficulties, it is only necessary to employ movements with due reference to the exact pathology of the case, and with a rational understanding of the limits of their ability to correct physiological aberrations. Otherwise employed, movements are quite as competent, and as likely, in fact, to do injury as good. In congestion of the liver, for instance, it is highly improper to employ such movements as would tend to promote that condition in a healthy person. Ignorance will not shield one from the consequences resulting from such foolish practice. That an aggravation of disease frequently follows the use of heterogeneous exercises, is only a proof of their power to do good when properly directed. The beginner can not observe too much caution in prescribing for himself.

Movements of the Respiratory Organs.—The function of aerating the blood would seem to be more important than any other of the system. Every function may suffer a temporary suspense except this, and those intimately connected with it, as the action of the heart; but life shortly ceases when respiration is from any cause too long suspended. When, also, respiration becomes defective or inefficient, whether from external or internal causes, all the other functions speedily fail. This fact shows the direct dependence of all other functions upon this. All changes in the system, whether for the purpose of evolving sensorial, intellectual, or muscular power, require in the blood the presence of oxygen obtained from the air of respiration. It is by means of oxygen that the compounds into which the wasting organs are resolved, are reduced to the still simpler and less noxious forms in which they are dismissed from the body. It is the abundant supply of this element, secured by wholesome avocations, or, in the absence of labor, by special exercises, that secures to the system that elasticity and vigorous tone, which is health. Withdraw this element, by contracting the respiratory capacity, and important vital changes are interrupted, and the forces of the system begin at once to fail—the bow has lost its spring, the eye ceases to sparkle, the rose fades on the cheek, and that form that once no trouble could bend, now bows under grasshopper burdens.

The need of a supply of oxygen to the system is general; all parts are equally liable to suffer without it. Hence all the organs and tissues, including the nerves and muscles, unite in a common effort to secure it, and to perfect the respiratory process. That such is the case is proved by many symptoms in acute disease. In these cases the efficiency of the respiratory process is first diminished by a deterioration of the quality of the blood, whose attraction for oxygen is thereby lessened.* The whole system is then aroused, and the respiratory and circulatory actions excited to a high degree in the *effort to attain more air* by means of which to reduce its noxious principles to the more neutral and bland state of *carbonic acid, water*, and *urea*, which are the ultimate products of the oxydation attending these vital operations.

There are two principal circumstances that control the amount of oxygen received into the system. One is the affinity of the blood and tissues for this element, which, there is reason to believe, varies with the health, habits, diet, etc. The other is, the capacity of the chest in cubic measure, and the *degree of the mobility of its walls*. In complete health there is, of course, a com-

---

* There is no disease characterized by an increase of the products of respiration. —*Lehmann.*

plete harmony between the chemical and the mechanical conditions of supply and the general needs of the system for oxygen. But it is also necessary that in health there should be a large funded capacity, beyond the ordinary needs of supply, to meet the emergencies into which the system may be thrown; for instance, the extra breathing made necessary during temporary forced labor or excessive cold. The powers of the system soon succumb under hardships, if this reserve capacity for respiration is limited or deficient, as in pulmonary affections.

That the walls of the chest are very mobile and well adapted to contain and to charge different quantities of air according to circumstances, is apparent from anatomical considerations. This cavity is bounded below by a thin muscle, the diaphragm, which is convex upward during respiration, but which by contracting is flattened, leaving much space above it to be filled by the air which simultaneously rushes in to supply the vacuum thus produced.

The sides of the chest are formed by the ribs, and their tendonous and muscular attachments. The ribs extend downward and forward from the spinal column, are connected with the sternum in front by long elastic cartilages, except the two lower ones of each side, whose anterior extremities are entirely free. Simultaneously with the contraction of the diaphragm, the external muscles of respiration also contract. This action elevates the forward extremities of the ribs, causing them to include a larger space; and it also turns them slightly outward, thus contributing to the same result. The extent of this effect is precisely in proportion to the degree of the muscular action. The diagram, fig. 34, page 191, illustrates the motions of the inferior and lateral walls of the chest. It may not only be inferred that the amount of air revivified in respiration depends on the amount of the motion of the walls of the chest, but also that the amount of air habitually resident in the lungs depends on the tone of these muscular walls.

Habitual immobility of the walls of the chest is a characteristic of all chronic diseases. The capacity of the chest has become restricted, the power of the muscles lessened, most likely from habitual disuse; for in these cases the occupations and habits of life have not enforced that abundant exercise that the requirements of the system demand. In most cases, the evil is not lack of exercise in general, but lack of the particular kinds that are calculated to serve the wants of the particular function in question. The kinds of exercise that the weakly and sedentary are most inclined to engage in do not, it is admitted, sufficiently affect the respiratory apparatus. Just here, often, is the true disease, while the invalid is suffering from symptoms that have not yet suggested to him their origin.

The important part played by respiration in the animal economy is not doubted, but we fail to recognize the practical inference deducible from this consideration bearing upon the restoration of the invalid. We also fail to consider that one is running in the direction of disease whenever the efficiency of this function is from any cause abated. When these facts are well considered, and not till then, will the importance of special means adapted to counteract the effects above indicated be appreciated.

All exertion of the voluntary powers, we have said, causes an increase of respiration. Profound thought or study, all may have noticed, demands frequent and profound inspiratory efforts; while preliminary to any very strong muscular efforts there is invariably an involuntary preparation made by a deep inspiration. The inspired air, at such times, is frequently *held*, and subjected to all the pressure that the chest can exert upon it, apparently to accelerate and increase the solution of the oxygen brought in this way into contact with the blood. Thus we see that exercise not only increases the expansibility of the chest, but probably, after the manner here noticed, deprives the respired air of a larger proportion of its oxygen.

Great caution, let it be remarked here, is indispensable in prescribing movements designed to enlarge the chest, for great injury is easily done in this direction. Persons of feeble habits we would caution earnestly against indiscriminate, random movements. Let it be understood, and always borne in mind, that movements of this region tend more decidedly than those of any other to produce congestion; while the production of this condition ought specially to be avoided, and the movements should be so prescribed as to overcome it if it already exists.

It is to be borne in mind, too, that the same act that causes the chest to become filled with air, assists also the flow of venous blood to the same locality. Hence, movements of this region should always be given in such connection and order as to counteract, or render impossible, these pernicious effects. By inattention to this caution, not only may congestion be produced, and alarming disease promoted, but even serious hemorrhages may occur that may threaten life, especially if there be previous disease of the pulmonary organs. These accidents need never occur in the most delicate or in the worst cases of disease, but the capacity and power of the chest may be greatly but surely improved in nearly all of them.

33.—STRETCH-STRIDE SHORT-SITTING, TRUNK FORWARD-SIDEWISE FALLING.

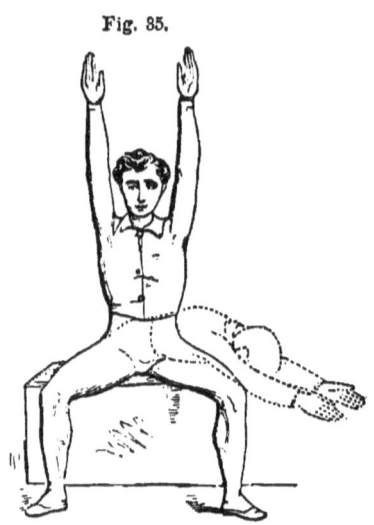

Fig. 85.

POSITION.—The arms are brought up nearly in contact with the ears, and parallel to each other; the trunk erect, supported upon the edge of a chair or other convenient seat; the thighs at right angles apart; feet so extended upon the floor as to form a large base.

ACTION.—1. The trunk falls slowly, diagonally forward, that is, in a line directly over one thigh, bringing the breast in close contact with the knee. 2. It then slowly resumes the first position. This action may be repeated five or six times on each side. In the cut, the dotted outline indicates the direction and the extent of the falling.

If it is deemed advisable that less effort be expended in this movement, the arms may be put in *wing* position instead of stretch; when considerable effort is demanded, the stretch position may be used. In this case the hands should grasp some weighty object, as a pair of dumb-bells, and the movement be performed as before.

EFFECT.—This movement affects the region of the loins, and if weights are used, also the back and arms.

34.—STRETCH-STRIDE SHORT-SITTING, TRUNK BACKWARD-SIDE-WISE-FALLING

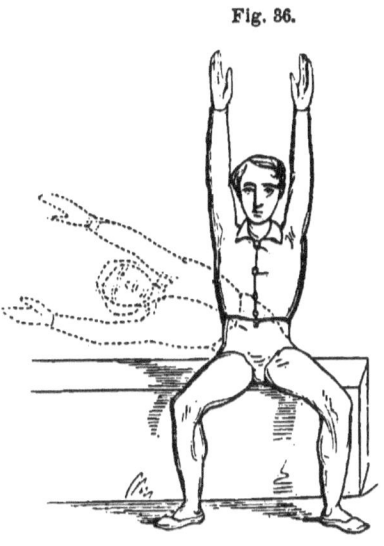

Fig. 86.

Position.—This is precisely like that represented in No. 33, except that it may be necessary to secure the feet by placing them under some firm object, or they may be held to the floor by another person, as may be most convenient.

Action.—1. The trunk to be twisted a little toward the knee of one side. 2. It must now be allowed to fall slowly backward till it reaches a position approximating the horizontal, where it remains for a few moments. 3. Then rises slowly again to the commencing position. This action may be repeated three or four times with each side. In the cut, the dotted outline indicates the direction and the extent of the movement.

Effect.—This movement calls powerfully into action the muscles of the abdomen upon either side, and strengthens them as well as the fasciæ of the groin and leg, especially in the region liable to rupture. It also presses the bowels, and is derivative in respect to the visceral organs.

35.—STRETCH-SITTING, TRUNK BACKWARD-FALLING.

Position.—This is the same as in No. 34, including the support necessary for the feet.

Action.—1. The trunk falls directly but slowly backward till it reaches a position nearly horizontal.

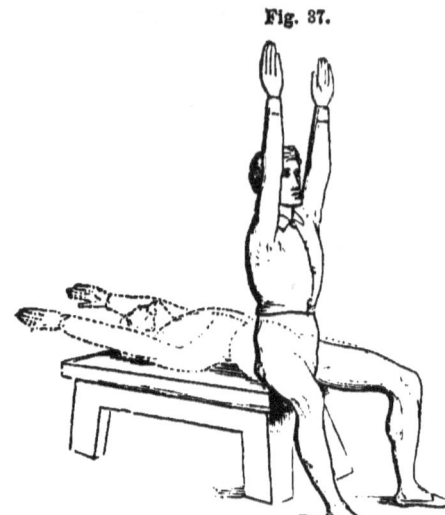

Fig. 37.

2. It then rises slowly till it regains the commencing position. This action may be repeated four or five times. In the cut, the dotted outline indicates the direction and extent of the movement.

EFFECT.—This is a very useful movement to increase the nutrition of the abdominal coverings, especially the lower portion of the walls of the abdomen. It also produces strong derivative effects, and consequently tends to remove visceral congestion, and to restore the contained organs to their natural situation in the abdominal cavity. If the arms be in wing position, the movement will be easier; if weights be held, it will be more positive in its effects.

36.—HALF-STRETCH, HALF-WING, STRIDE SHORT-SITTING, TRUNK SIDEWISE-BENDING.

POSITION.—One hand is placed upon the hips; the arm of the other is stretched perpendicularly upward; trunk erect, sitting; thighs at right angles; feet extended and braced against the floor.

ACTION.—1. The trunk gently bends in the lumbar region in the direction of the hip, on which the hand is fixed, while the stretched arm retains the position relative to the head, in which the movement commenced. The trunk falls as far as it can without raising the seat at the opposite side. 2. It then slowly rises to its original position. This action may be repeated three or four times upon each side. The perpendicular dotted line and the arrow indicate in the cut the direction of the movement. The *extent* of the movement will increase after a little practice. If the action needs to be stronger, a weight may be held in the upright hand. The action may be repeated four or five times with each side.

Fig. 38.

EFFECT.—This movement strongly affects the side of the body, and the effect is extended to the liver, spleen, and other visceral organs.

37.—HALF-STRETCH, HALF-WING STRIDE-SITTING, TRUNK-TWISTING.

POSITION.—This is the same as in No. 36.

Fig. 39.

ACTION.—1. The trunk remains perpendicular, neither bending nor swaying in any direction, but *twists* on its own axis, while the seat remains immovable on the chair or stool. In *twisting*, the side of the raised arm moves forward, while the opposite side moves to an equal extent backward, performing the twisting to the extent of about a quarter of a circle, there remaining for a few moments. 2. The trunk then moves on its axis in the opposite direction; or, in simpler phrase, it *untwists*, bringing the anterior part of the body forward to the commencing position. This action may be repeated four or five times with each side.

EFFECT.—Although in twisting movements the limit of the power of motion is soon reached, on account of the confined condition of the muscles, yet this class of movements are potent, especially in their effect on the circulation, since nearly all the muscles of the part are put in action—some concentrically, others eccentrically. The muscles are thus nearly all rendered very tense, producing much pressure upon the blood-vessels and nerves, followed by increased flow of blood into, and nutrition of, the parts subjected to this action. Twisting also tends to contract the diameter of the cavity of the trunk, and hence produces slight pressure upon the contained organs. This class of movements are derivative.

38.—SHELTER STRIDE-SITTING, CHANGE-TWISTING.

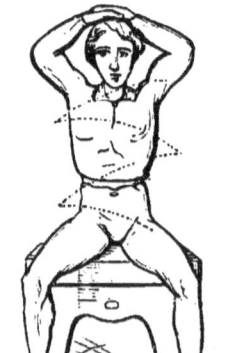

Fig. 40.

POSITION.—The hands are locked upon the top of the head; in all other respects the position is identical with that in the last four examples.

ACTION.—The trunk turns on its axis with moderate rapidity as far as it will turn, and then in the opposite direction for the same distance. This action may properly be repeated fifteen or twenty times successively. The cut shows the position, which is not varied, except by the twist motion during the movement.

EFFECT.—This movement, for the great majority of the parts affected, is nearly *passive*, only a few muscles, comparatively, being employed to give the motion, while all the organs contained in the cavity of the body are agreeably stimulated by the agitation imparted to them. The movement is tranquilizing for the nerves, and equalizing in its effect on the circulation, while certain muscles in different portions of the body are performing active service.

39.—YARD-SITTING, SWAYING.

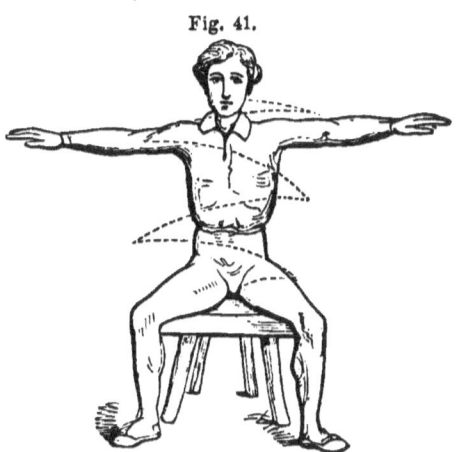

Fig. 41.

POSITION.—The arms are extended horizontally until they are both in the same line; trunk sitting, legs stride, and feet well braced.

ACTION.—The trunk turns on its axis, as in No. 38; but on account of the position of the arms, much more deliberately. It first turns as far as it can to the right, and then in the same way to the left, allowing the extended arms to acquire considerable momentum, and, by the consequent reaction, increasing the effect of the movement upon the loins. This twisting may be repeated ten or fifteen times each way.

EFFECT.—The muscles of the top of the shoulders, and nearly all those of the arms, and those of the sides, are strongly affected. The centrifugal effect upon the circulation of the blood in the arms is to detain and then quicken the circulation, and warm the hands. The movement acts derivatively for the chest.

40.—STRETCH STRIDE-KNEELING, TRUNK BACKWARD-BENDING.

Fig. 42.

POSITION.—The arms are stretched upward parallel with each other, and with the head; the trunk erect, kneeling, with the knees placed far apart in the stride position; the knees must be sustained by a cushion.

ACTION.—1. The trunk bends slowly backward as far as its flexibility will allow, so as to assume a *reclining* posture, where it remains for a few moments. 2. It then returns slowly to its commencing position; the knees and hips remaining fixed in the mean time. In the cut, the dotted outline indicates the direction and extent of the movement.

EFFECT.—This movement puts the skin and fasciæ and muscles of the anterior portion of the body and legs strongly upon the stretch; it is felt in the groin, the walls of the abdomen, and chest; elevates the ribs, diaphragm, and visceral contents, and expands the chest. The action is chiefly produced by the muscles of the back, which it strengthens.

REMARK.—This and many other back-bending movements frequently occasion keen sensations in the back, especially at the beginning of their employment. This is not because the muscles of that region are strained unduly by the movement; for, the weight of the body assisting the movement from the time it first deviates from the perpendicular, the muscular action is comparatively slight. The sensation is, no doubt, produced by the pinching of the vertebral cartilages caused by the unusual position. The sensation gradually wears away as the cartilages become more elastic, and as the parts adapt themselves to the new requirements imposed upon them. If movements of this class produce an unpleasant tenderness, they must be desisted from for a short time, after which they may be resumed.

VARIATIONS OF NO. 40.—1. The arms may be in *shelter* position instead of *stretch*. In this case the action is not so forcible, and it is, therefore, better adapted to those who are quite feeble.

2. The arms to be extended exactly as in No. 39, but may grasp a couple of weights, as a pair of dumb-bells. The effect in this case becomes much greater, since the added weight acts through the leverage of the arms and body, very much more powerfully upon the whole anterior surface of the body.

3. While the arms are in either of the above positions, the legs may be placed in *walking* position, that is, with one knee presented forward of the body, and the other behind it, and as far apart as convenient. In this case, after the action has been repeated three or four times, the position of the legs may be reversed, by placing forward the leg which was behind, and putting behind that which was forward. The action is now felt much more powerfully in the groin, and the movement is especially useful to strengthen the muscles and fasciæ about the hernial region.

41.—HALF-STRETCH, HALF-WING RECLINED STRIDE KNEELING, TRUNK-TWISTING.

Position.—One arm is extended upward, while the hand of the other is placed upon the hip; the trunk erect, in the kneeling position, with the legs widely apart.

Action.—The side of the extended arm moves forward while the opposite side moves backward, *twisting* the body upon its axis. This action is to be repeated four or five times with each side. The reader is referred to No. 37 for an explanation of this movement; it is to be remembered that in this movement the position is that of kneeling, with the body a little bent backward.

Effect.—This movement is felt at the sides, and in the arm which is in stretch position; also across the abdomen, at its lower portion, pressing somewhat the contents of the abdominal cavity, and strengthening these regions as well as acting derivatively.

42.—HALF-STRETCH, HALF-WING, WALK-KNEELING, TRUNK-TWISTING.

Fig. 43.

Position.—One arm is stretched, the hand of the other being upon the hips; the trunk erect; the knee on the same side with the stretched arm is placed as far back as is possible; the opposite knee placed as far forward.

Action.—The side on which is the stretched arm moves forward, while the opposite side moves backward, twisting the body on its axis, as far as practicable. After this motion has been repeated four or five times, the knees change their respective positions, the back one being placed forward, and the forward one back, and the motion is repeated as before. The cut shows the position *after* the body has twisted.

EFFECT.—This movement acts strongly upon the abdominal muscles and fasciæ, and especially those of the groin, and increases the power and resistance of those parts.

43.—ARMS-ANGLE RECLINED KNEELING, ARMS STRETCHING.

Fig. 44.

POSITION.—The arms are in *angle position*, that is, the elbow is bent while the upper arm is near the side parallel with the body; the trunk kneeling, knees wide apart, but leaning back from the perpendicular.

ACTION.—1. The arms are slowly stretched till they become parallel with each other, and in a line with the body, where they remain for a short time. 2. They are then allowed slowly to return to the commencing position. This may be repeated six or eight times. In the cut, the dotted outline shows the position after the first part of the movement, that is, the extreme position. Care should be taken that the arms be not stretched perpendicularly, but exactly in the line of the reclining trunk.

EFFECT.—The parts affected by this movement are the arms, the tops of the shoulders, the region beneath the shoulder blades, the sides of the chest, the diaphragm, and the abdominal muscles, as well as the visceral organs, which are raised by it and moderately compressed.

VARIATIONS OF No. 43.—1. The hands may grasp some heavy objects, as a pair of dumb-bells, which increases the effect upon all of the parts enumerated.

2. The legs may be in *walking* position. In this case the effect upon the abdomen, especially upon the groin, is materially increased.

44.—RACK-RECLINED STRIDE-KNEELING, ARMS BACKWARD-STRIKING.

Fig. 45.

POSITION.—The arms are in *rack* position, that is, extended horizontally forward; the trunk slightly reclining, and kneeling; knees apart or stride.

ACTION.—The arms are thrown horizontally backward as far as the anatomy of the parts will allow. This action is repeated eight or ten times.

EFFECT.—There are but few muscles brought into active play in this movement, and these are situated back of the shoulder. By this movement the muscles of the breast are acted upon, the ribs elevated, and the blood thrown into the hands, increasing their warmth. This movement may be practiced slowly; if more quickly, an increased effect is produced upon the anterior muscles.

45.—WING STRIDE-KNEELING, RINGING.

POSITION.—The hands are placed upon the hips, the trunk is perpendicular, and kneeling; legs in *stride* position.

ACTION.—1. The trunk bends above the hips to one

side, as far as it can. 2. It then returns and passes beyond the perpendicular for the same distance on the opposite side; the motion being somewhat rapid, so that the momentum acquired will be felt upon the convex side. This action may be repeated ten or twelve times. The cut indicates the position and the direction of the movement, but not its extent, which will vary greatly with the powers of the patient and the amount of practice.

Fig. 46.

EFFECT.—This movement acts upon the muscles of either side, and also upon the liver, spleen, and other organs situated in the region affected by the motion, as the abdominal walls and viscera.

VARIATION.—1. The arms may be in *stretch* position. The motion then is much more slowly performed, and the effect much greater, at the same time more gentle.

2. The arms may be in stretch position, and the hands grasping a pair of weights. This variation adds greatly to the effect, making the movement a gentle and very effective one.

46.—YARD STRIDE-KNEELING, SWAYING.

POSITION.—The arms are extended in a line, palms of the hands downward; the trunk is erect and kneeling; the legs apart, or in *stride* position.

ACTION.—The trunk turns on its axis as far as the muscles will allow, from right to left, and then from left to right, and so continues to repeat the action of twisting, without bending the body, the arms being maintained in the same straight line. This may be repeated eight or ten times. This movement affects the coverings of the abdomen, and the muscles of the back generally. It also warms the hands, and is derivative for the chest.

47.—STRIDE-SITTING, ARMS SIDEWISE-RAISING.

Fig. 47.

POSITION.—The arms hang in their natural position by the side, trunk erect, sitting, legs in stride position.

ACTION.— 1. The arms slowly rise sidewise, in the same perpendicular plane with the trunk, the back of the hands uppermost, carefully avoiding all irregular actions, till the backs of the hands meet perpendicularly above the head, where they remain for a short time. 2. They then return slowly to the first position by the side. This action may be repeated six or eight times. In the cut, the dotted outlines show the commencing position, also the horizontal intermediate position, and the circle described by the points of the fingers in making the movement.

EFFECT.—In this movement the muscles of the top of the shoulder, and all of the muscles of the side of the chest, are brought into action, the former concentrically, the latter eccentrically; the ribs are raised and everted, the diameter of the chest increased; the diaphragm is also affected.

48.—STRETCH HALF-WALK, HALF-KNEELING, TRUNK BACKWARD BENDING.

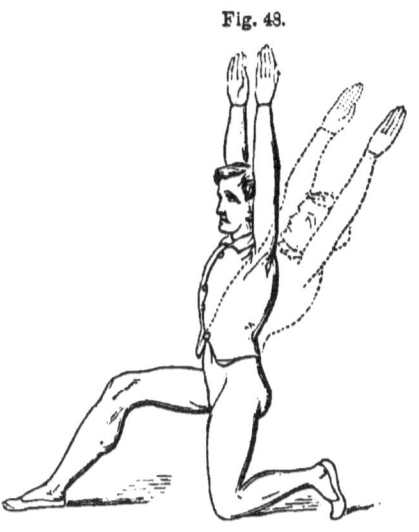

Fig. 48.

POSITION.—The arms are in upward stretch position, the trunk erect; one leg kneeling, while the other is extended forward, with the sole of the foot upon the floor.

ACTION.—1. The trunk bends slowly backward, so as to carry the arms, which must be kept parallel with the head, and in the axis of the trunk, as far backward as possible. 2. It slowly resumes the commencing position. This action may be repeated three or four times, when the position of the legs should be reversed, and the action again repeated. The cut shows the commencing position, and the dotted outline the position at the end of the first part of the movement.

EFFECT.—The lower portion of the abdomen, the groin, and the whole anterior surface of the body are affected by this movement; the parts acted on are strengthened, and those beneath experience a derivative influence in consequence of the action.

49.—HALF-WING HALF-CURVE (WEIGHT HELD) STEP-RECLINED-STANDING, TRUNK SIDEWISE BENDING.

POSITION.—One hand rests upon the hips; the foot of the same side is elevated upon a step or stair; the other hand holds a weight, the forearm resting upon

Fig. 49.

the head; the weight of the body, which is erect, is sustained principally by the leg that stands erect upon the floor.

ACTION.—1. The trunk slowly bends at the waist in the direction of the elevated foot, being assisted by the position of the weight in the hand. 2. It rises slowly to the commencing position. This action may be repeated four or six times, with each side of the body. The dotted outline in the cut shows the direction of the motion.

EFFECT.—This movement allows the muscles of the bent side to remain nearly passive, the bending being mostly produced by the weight; while the muscles of the convex side of the bended body are felt strongly upon the stretch, or in eccentric action. The movement affects the walls of the body upon each side, also the contiguous internal organs.

50.—HALF-WING, HALF-STRETCH, STEP-STANDING, TRUNK SIDE-WISE-BENDING.

POSITION.—In this movement no weight is held, and the arm is in *upward-stretch* position. In all other respects, the position is precisely like that in No. 49.

ACTION.—The trunk bends as in 49, but it is brought into the curve of the terminating position by the action of the muscles of the side. The movement is repeated four or five times upon each side.

EFFECT.—The effects of the movement differ but little from those of 49; the muscles in the present position, however, acting more concentrically.

51.—HALF-STRETCH, HALF-WING, HALF-KICK RECLINED STANDING, TRUNK SIDEWISE BENDING.

POSITION.—One arm in *wing* position; the leg of the same side extended forward in *kick* position, and maintained in place by means of a stool; the arm of the opposite side in stretch position; the trunk reclined, and resting with its weight upon the leg on the side of the stretched arm.

Fig. 50.

ACTION.—1. The trunk slowly bends in the direction opposite the stretched arm. 2. It returns to the first position.

The commencing position is shown in the cut.

EFFECT.—This movement differs from No. 50, in causing much more strain upon the groin and iliac region of the stretched side.

MODIFICATION OF 51.—*Both* arms may be in stretch position, as described in No. 54, instead of only one. The twisting will then be performed in the same direction as before, and the movement in every respect like the one here described. In this case the movement affects the trunk and elevates the ribs more than in the first described.

52.—HALF-STRETCH RECLINED KICK-STANDING, TRUNK TWISTING.

POSITION.—The position is exactly like that in No. 51, and is seen in the cut.

ACTION.—1. The trunk *twists* upon its axis, the

stretched side moving forward, and the opposite side backward. 2. It returns to the commencing position. This action is repeated four or five times with each side.

EFFECT.—This movement affects nearly all the muscles of the trunk.

53.—SHELTER LONG-SITTING, TRUNK FORWARD BENDING.

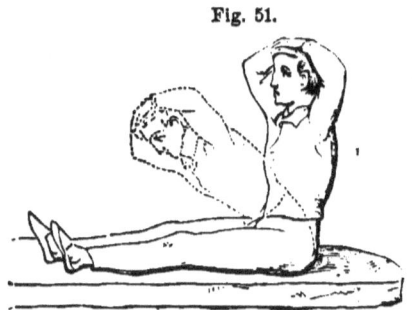

Fig. 51.

POSITION.—The hands are placed upon the head in shelter position; the trunk in sitting posture; the legs extended horizontally, and supported by a cushion.

ACTION.—1. The trunk bends slowly forward as far as possible. 2. It returns slowly to the primary position. This action may be repeated five or six times. The cut shows the first position, and also, by the dotted outline, the direction of the movement.

EFFECT.—This movement elevates the ribs, causes the abdominal muscles powerfully to contract, elevates the abdominal contents, and affects eccentrically the muscles of the back and seat.

54.—ARMS ANGLE, HALF KICK (FOOT SUPPORTED) RECLINED-STANDING, ARMS STRETCHING.

POSITION.—The arms are bent at the elbows, while the upper arm is by the side of the body; the trunk reclines; one leg placed two feet forward, in *kick* position, with the foot supported by a stool; the weight of the body rests mainly upon the other leg.

ACTION.—The arms slowly rise, stretching the elbow, and keeping the extending arms in the direction of the transverse plane of the body till they become straight and parallel with each other, with the head somewhat thrown back; this position is retained for a few moments.

Fig. 52.

2. The arms then *slowly* resume the first position. This action may be repeated three or four times, when the position of the legs should be reversed, and the action again repeated. The dotted outlines of the arms in the cut show their commencing position, and the stretched arms, the limit of the upward motion.

EFFECT.—In this movement the whole of the anterior surface of the body and the tops of the shoulders are strongly acted upon; also the parts beneath the shoulder-blades and the muscles connected with the ribs generally. It develops the muscles of these regions, is derivative for the chest, and is valuable as a means of assisting in its expansion.

VARIETIES.—1. A pair of dumb-bells may be held by the hands, and the movement practiced in all other respects as before. This modification of the movement greatly increases its effect.

2. The movement may commence in the *stretch* position, instead of the *angle*. The effect in this case will be the same in all essential particulars.

55.—YARD RECLINED HALF-KICK STANDING, SWAYING.

POSITION.—The arms are in *yard* position; in every other particular the position is like that of No. 54.

ACTION.—The trunk twists in the lumbar region as far around as it can, while the arms remain in the same relative position, but sway in a circle of which the hands describe the arc, and the plane of which is necessarily inclined to the horizontal in consequence of the reclined position of the trunk. The motion is alternate, and may be repeated fifteen or twenty times, in the mean time changing the position of the legs.

EFFECT.—This movement acts strongly upon the abdominal walls, especially at the sides, and also upon the liver, spleen, and other visceral organs.

56.—HALF-STRETCH, HALF-WING, WALK. TRUNK SIDEWISE BENT, STANDING, TRUNK TWISTING.

Fig. 58.

POSITION.—One arm is in stretch, the other in wing, position; the legs in walk position, with a long distance between the feet; the leg of the wing side being forward, and the trunk bent toward the same side. The commencing position here described is identical with the terminating position of No. 52.

ACTION.—1. The trunk slowly twists upon its axis, the side on which is the stretched arm, as in previous instances, moving forward, and the opposite backward. 2. It returns to the primary position. The cut shows the position after the twisting.

This action may be repeated four or five times with each side.

EFFECT.—This movement puts into powerful eccentric action the muscles of the sides; it is derivative in cases of central congestion, and strengthens the chest and abdomen.

57.—YARD WALK-STANDING, TRUNK BACKWARD BENDING.

Fig. 54.

POSITION.—The arms are extended horizontally on either side, the trunk erect; one foot is placed before, and the other behind, the center of the body, the two being two and a half feet apart.

ACTION.—1. The trunk bends backward as far as it can, where it remains a moment. 2. It then returns to the commencing position. This action may be repeated three or four times, and then the legs should exchange places, and the action be repeated again.

EFFECT.—This movement expands the chest, warms the hands, and strengthens the back.

58.—UPWARD-SIDEWISE STRETCH DOORWAY-STANDING, WALKING.

POSITION.—This is taken in a doorway, the arms being extended upward and outward, and the palms of the hands pressed against the casement; the trunk erect, the feet just behind the middle portion of the threshold.

ACTION.—1. One leg is raised as if to walk, but some-

Fig. 55.

what higher than is common in that action. 2. At the same instant the body is projected forward; but the arms being arrested by the resisting object against which the hands are placed, the center of the trunk is very much curved forward. 3. The raised leg returns to its place beside the other on the floor, and at the same time the trunk straightens, resuming the commencing position. The other leg is next raised and put forward in the attempt to walk, but its progress is arrested, and the trunk bends forward; the whole body afterward returning to the commencing position, as before. This action may be repeated with each leg ten or twelve times. The cut represents the movement at the point when the raised leg and the projecting trunk are falling back into the commencing position.

EFFECT.—This movement acts powerfully in expanding the chest, and tends to develop all the muscles of the front portion of the body. It is easily taken (after being once learned), and requires but little exertion compared with the amount of effect produced. In this respect it very much resembles a true *duplicated movement*.

59.—SHELTER, SIDEWISE-BENT STRIDE-STANDING, TRUNK ROTATION.

POSITION.—The hands are locked upon the top of the head, the trunk is bent far to one side, the legs in stride and the body in standing position.

ACTION.—The trunk is made to rotate, carrying the

REGION OF THE TRUNK.

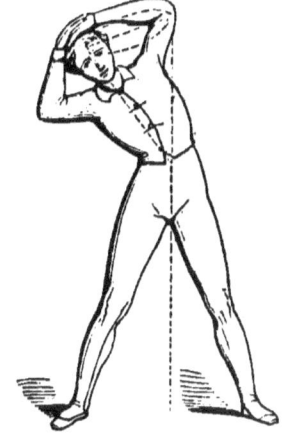

Fig. 56.

head around a circle of considerable extent. The axis of motion is just above the hips. This rotary motion may be performed three or four times each way, when the trunk should bend to the opposite side to the same extent, and repeat the motion as many times more. In the cut, the dotted lines indicate the perpendicular, also the circle in which the head revolves.

EFFECT.—This movement strengthens the parts about the loins, and expands the chest.

MODIFICATION.—This movement may be taken in the *sitting* position. In this case, the body being more firmly supported, the extent of the movement, that is, the diameter of the circle described by the head, may be greater than while standing, and this will, of course, cause greater action of the sides. This movement affects the liver and spleen.

60.—HEAD-AND-HEELS LYING, HOLDING.

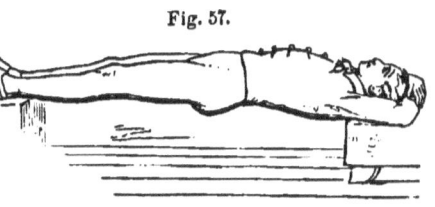

Fig. 57.

POSITION.—The trunk lies in a horizontal position, with the hands clasped upon the head, the legs parallel, the head and the heels only resting on supports, as two chairs, while the remaining portion of the body is quite free.

ACTION.—The body remains in this position for a longer or shorter time, according to the strength.

EFFECT.—The muscles of the back are put into powerful action in this movement. Hence it is derivative in respect to the spinal cord, while it increases the development and power of the muscles of the back.

MODIFICATION.—The supports may be placed nearer each other, as at the shoulders and lower legs. The movement thereby becomes less powerful, and the *holding* may continue longer.

61.—ELBOWS-AND-TOES LYING, HOLDING.

Fig. 53.

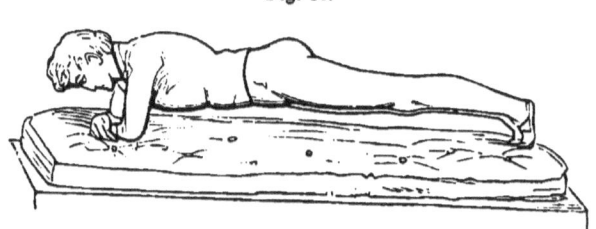

POSITION.—The arms are in *rack elbow-bent* position, the trunk horizontal, face downward; the elbows and toes *only* resting on a mattress.

ACTION.—The trunk is *held* in this position for a few moments, more or less, according to the strength of the experimenter.

EFFECT.—This movement produces a muscular tension and contraction of the whole forward part of the body, the effect of which is especially felt at the lower portion of the abdomen. It presses the abdominal contents toward the diaphragm, and often instantly relieves *prolapsus* of any of the pelvic organs, as that of the womb, vagina, or rectum, restoring the parts to their natural condition and relation. This movement is invaluable in this class of cases. Indeed, all other medical applications designed to meet the ends here indicated, bear no comparison in value with this simple movement. By repetition the weak parts are strengthened, and a radical cure is effected.

MODIFICATION.—While in the position above described, the hips may rise slowly upward, and after a moment, slowly fall to the level of the elbows and toes. This movement may be repeated six or eight times. This mode of taking the movement is often more agreeable, as well as somewhat more positive, and produces similar effects.

62.—ELBOW-AND-LEG SIDEWISE-LYING, HIPS RAISING.

POSITION.— One arm lies upon the trunk, while the elbow of the other rests upon a mattress. The trunk is ex-

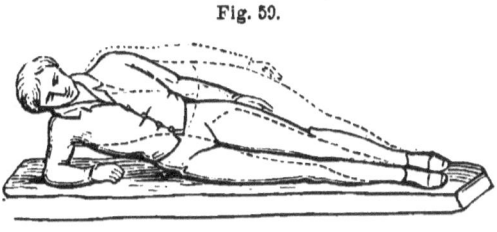

Fig. 59.

tended horizontally, the lower leg lying with its side upon the mattress, the other resting upon it.

ACTION.—1. The hips are raised slowly upward, and remain for a few moments lifted. 2. They return to their first position. This action may be repeated four or five times with each side. The dotted outline in the cut shows the point to which the hips rise.

EFFECT.—This movement is strongly felt at the side of the hip which is under at the time, and acts throughout the whole extent of the side of the body. It also affects the back.

63.—SHELTER BACK-LYING, HEAD AND LEGS RAISING.

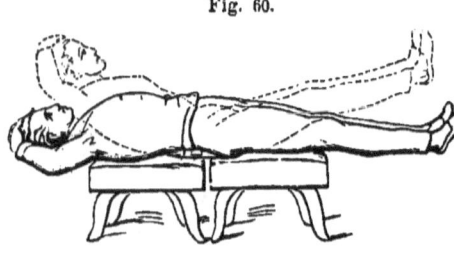

Fig. 60.

POSITION. — The trunk lies horizontally upon the back, supported by a mattress; the hands clasped upon the head; legs parallel.

ACTION.—1. Both the feet and head are raised from the horizontal line at the same time, so as to cause the body to assume a curved shape, and remain for a short period. 2. They return to the commencing position. This action may be repeated five or six times.

EFFECT.—This movement is a very powerful one for the abdominal muscles, affecting the visceral organs derivatively. It also increases the force of the general circulation, and urges the blood into the capillaries of the system at large.

MODIFICATION.—Only the back may be supported, instead of the whole length of the body. The effect is similar. The cut above represents the movement as being taken in this way; the dotted outline indicating the extent of the movement.

64.—BACK LYING, HOLDING.

POSITION.—The arms remain in contact with the body at the sides; the trunk rests with the back supported by a single chair; while both the legs and the head and shoulders are suffered to obey the law of gravitation, and fall below the horizontal position.

ACTION.—The body is allowed to remain for a short period in this position.

EFFECT.—This is chiefly felt in the forward part of

the body, which in this position is *stretched*, or receives eccentric action. The curved position causes considerable pressure upon the abdominal contents.

65.— WING-STRIDE LEG-ANGLE STANDING, TRUNK VIBRATION.

POSITION.—The hands are placed upon the hips; the knees and thighs are bent to the greatest possible extent; the feet rest on the floor about two feet apart; the trunk maintained in a position as nearly erect as the position of the legs will allow.

ACTION.—The body is slightly raised by the exertion of all the muscles of the legs, on which its weight rests, and is directly permitted to return with the force of its weight to the same position. It should rise only a few inches, and repeat the action a dozen times or more as fast as possible.

EFFECT.—This is felt in the perineum, and is propagated to the rectum, exciting its contractility to a noticeable, and sometimes to a remarkable degree. If the posture is maintained with difficulty, the back may be supported by a smooth wall. This movement encourages an evacuation of the bowels in cases of constipation.

66.—OPERATIONS UPON THE DIGESTIVE ORGANS.*

A great variety of motions may be given to one's own digestive organs suited to different constitutions, conditions of disease, development of the region, strength of the person, etc. A few forms are selected for the reader's attention, which, if not entirely appli-

---

* In the inferior animals, the position of whose bodies is such that the trunk is horizontal, the digestive organs are subjected to considerable motion at every step taken; and this motion is greatly augmented with the increase of the pace. The upright posture of man in a degree precludes this motion that is inevitable for the brute. This fact, however, renders it necessary that he should employ his reason and intelligence in order to secure a relief he is so liable to need.

cable for a given case, may at least prove suggestive of some other that may act more to the purpose.

POSITION.—Lying upon a couch, with the shoulders raised and the legs in an easy position.

VARIETIES OF ACTION.—1. *Kneading.*—The two fists, strongly clenched, may be pressed upon the abdomen so firmly as to cause the subjacent parts to yield before the pressure. This action is to be repeated for several minutes over the whole region of the abdomen. The movement excites the muscular contractility of the tube, and promotes fecal discharges.

2. *Shaking.*—The hands are applied to each side of the abdomen, and alternate pressure given to it, producing a somewhat rapid oscillating movement of all the abdominal contents included between the two hands. This movement promotes venous absorption, and removes congestion.

3. *Stroking.*—Each hand is applied to the region of the groin, the tips of the fingers nearly meeting; then each hand is to be drawn slowly, with much pressure, upward and outward. The movement has an effect similar to that of the first.

4. *Circular Stroking.*—The pressure of the hands is made to follow the course of the colon, beginning low upon the right side of the abdomen, passing around beneath the stomach, and terminating on the side opposite. This movement also promotes fecal discharges.

5. *Point Pressure.*—This may be performed under the short ribs; the ends of the fingers are applied from below, and strong pressure made with a tremulous motion. The movement excites muscular and nervous action in the organs reached, and in certain cases relieves pain.

6. *Clapping.*—The extended hands are made to

strike any portion of the frontal region of the body. The blows should be given with each hand alternately, and at such a rate of rapidity and force as to produce no unpleasant sensations. If there be a point where pain is felt, the motion, at each successive application, should for a period be given to surrounding parts, approaching the tender point gradually until the pain disappears.

The doubled fist may be used instead of the flat hand, when it can be borne. This movement promotes absorption, and removes congestion.

VARIETY OF POSITION.—All the above movements may be applied in the standing position, with the trunk a little bent forward, or *stooping*.

EFFECTS.—The above motions are but imperfect imitations of a few of the duplicated movements that may be applied to the part; their effects, however, are often highly salutary.

It is not necessary in practice to procure each of these effects in a distinct form, because in every pathological state there is a general similarity of condition to that of other such states; and it is pathological states, more especially, that these movements meet. Indeed, the effects above described merge into each other as do the applications themselves. With congestion of the mucous membrane, there may be dryness and costiveness; or there may be an attempt at relief by serous effusion or diarrhea; but either of these is relieved by overcoming the primary cause. In either case the surcharged capillaries need to have their contents impelled along their course. In either case, too, the subjacent muscle needs more nutrition and power; in both the circulation needs to be equalized, and nutritive absorption promoted. These results, the motions above described, and others analogous, tend in an eminent degree to secure.

67.—AGITATION OF THE ABDOMEN AND DIAPHRAGM.

POSITION.—Wing stride sitting.

ACTION.—This movement consists in contracting the abdominal coverings and diaphragm by strong efforts exerted in rapid succession, thus producing an oscillatory motion of the entire abdominal contents. This may be continued for several minutes.

EFFECT.—This movement promotes the contractile power of all the muscular tissues participating in it, and the functional action of all the organs affected by it.

Chapter Eleven.

REGION OF THE ARMS.

REMARKS ON THIS REGION.—The region of the arms is intimately connected with that of the chest. This connection is not only suggested by its contiguity to the chest, but indicated by the anatomical conformation and relations of the parts. The arms are connected with the chest by large and strong muscles spreading themselves over a good portion of its surface. The blood-vessels and nerves of the chest also extend along the arms. The gymnast who uses his arms vigorously and habitually, never fails to secure an ample development of the chest. We see this fact further illustrated in the use we make of the arms in certain *duplicated movements* for the purpose of overcoming various deformities and even grave diseases of the thoracic region.

Several movements have already been described in which very potent effects are incidentally experienced in the arms and hands. Indeed, movements of the chest and arms are so connected that no absolute and precise distinction can be drawn between those of the two regions, the one being necessarily affected by the operations designed to influence the other. Power may be exerted by the arms in every direction, in each of which there will result a distinct effect appertaining to both the arms and the chest.

But it is often highly proper to employ such movements as chiefly affect the arms. The cases in which one arm is much stronger than the other are almost universal, indicating how general is the reprehensible habit of making partial use of these important members. So, too, an arm becomes useless from nervous shocks, especially in children, and its growth partly ceases. It then continues powerless, because the parent or physician does not employ the means in his hands to direct the nutritive actions into the channels in which they are now so especially needed. These results are only more conspicuous in the arms, the principle being equally true in its application throughout the body.

In all cases of great feebleness, the treatment must at first be of a kind that husbands the strength, while it is necessary, at the same time, to direct the energies and the nutrition of the system outwardly. The blood of central congestion needs to be removed to external members deficient in it. The use of arm movements, forcible in proportion to the general strength, is the proper mode of commencing the treatment of these cases. By this means the pressure in the large central vessels is relieved, and thereby a most important advantage is gained in the treatment of the disease. The novice will pay a costly forfeit if he neglects this essential portion of the treatment, even in cases proper for its application, especially as diseases situated in the superior cavity of the trunk are the most difficult and dangerous of all under any kind of treatment. By using these precautions, however, the treatment becomes quickly and certainly beneficial.

The reader will notice that in the examples given of movements of the lower extremities, advantage is taken of the *weight* of the body or of some portion of it, which **weight** is made to act upon the regions to which the movement is principally directed. In this way effects are produced that somewhat resemble those of the *duplicated movements*. So, also, as we approach the upper portion of the body, advantage derived from this source may be obtained by taking such positions as throw a portion of the weight of the body upon the arms.

68.—STRETCH BACKWARD-LYING, WEIGHT-HOLDING.

POSITION.—The arms are *stretched*, the trunk extended upon the back, with the crown of the head pro-

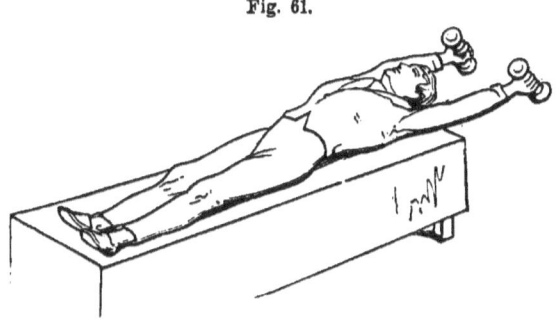

Fig. 61.

jecting a little beyond the edge of the couch; weights are held in the hands.

ACTION.—The weights are held for a length of time proportioned to the strength, the action consisting in a *holding*. The cut shows the position.

EFFECT.—The weights not only task the muscles of the under sides of the arms, but the arms serve as levers, by the action of which the ribs are raised and the chest enlarged. There is little voluntary effort in this movement, but much valuable effect is produced. It is particularly advantageous for strong persons, but useful also for the weak, if not carried too far.

VARIETY I.—1. The arms may be slowly raised, maintaining their parallel relation to each other until they reach the perpendicular, when, 2, they are allowed gradually to fall back again. This may be repeated six or eight times. This mode of performing the movement is somewhat easier than the first, and is attended with similar effects.

II. The arms may describe an arc of a horizontal circle on each side, repeating the motion three or four times. This mode of employing the movement calls other muscles into play, which it is sometimes desirable to develop.

69.—RACK GRASP, FORWARD FALL-STANDING, ARMS ANGLING.

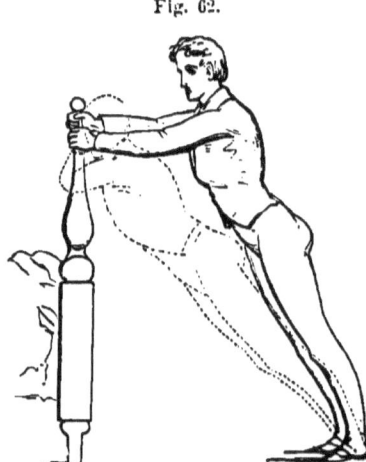

Fig. 62.

POSITION.—The arms are extended forward, grasping with the hands some convenient object, as the edge of a mantel or top of a bedstead; the body is in forward-fall-standing position, forming an angle of about forty-five degrees.

ACTION.—1. The elbows slowly bend outward, while the body falls forward, till the head is brought into the immediate vicinity of the object of support. 2. The elbows now slowly *stretch*, bringing the trunk again into the commencing position. This action may be repeated four or five times. The dotted outline in the cut indicates the extent of the movement.

EFFECT.—In this movement not only the arms are affected, but the chest is expanded, and the anterior muscles of the abdomen are acted upon.

REGION OF THE ARMS. 231

VARIETY.—Some means of support, about half as high as that represented in the above cut, may be employed.

In this case the strain is greater upon the arms and hands, and the influence upon the anterior muscles of the abdomen is increased so as to elevate the ribs and visceral organs.

70.—STRETCH-GRASP STANDING, HIP ROTATION.

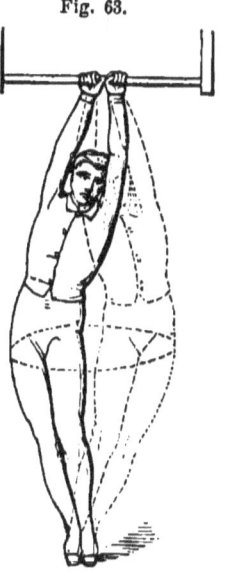

Fig. 63.

POSITION.—The arms are *stretched*, and a transverse pole, eight or ten inches below the point of utmost reach, is grasped by them directly over the feet—these, as well as the hands, being placed close together.

ACTION.—The hips bend to one side, and then revolve in a circle of which the diameter is as extensive as the position of the body will allow. The revolutions are performed eight or ten times in each direction. The cut shows the position, and the dotted outline the circle, in which the hips revolve.

EFFECT.—The hands and arms sustain nearly the whole weight of the body, and the motion affords action alternately to nearly all the muscles of the arms. The same effect is also experienced in nearly equal degree by the shoulders and chest, the ribs being elevated. The size of the chest and the action of the respiratory muscles are increased. The strong tension of the arms also produces a derivative effect upon the chest, and the hands are warmed. There is but little exertion of the will expended in this movement, and consequently there is but little fatigue.

71.—HALF-STRETCH GRASP STANDING, ARM TWISTING.

Fig. 64.

POSITION.—One arm is *stretched* upward, and the hand grasps a transverse pole placed at about the height it can conveniently reach, while the body is standing erect.

ACTION.—1. The trunk turns quite round, without moving from its standing-point, which, as the grasp of the hand is maintained, causes the arm to be *twisted*. 2. It then turns in the opposite direction, not stopping till the arm is *untwisted* and *twisted* again in the opposite direction. This action may be repeated four or five times with each arm.

EFFECT.—This movement causes all the muscles of the arm to act strongly and eccentrically, it affects all the blood-vessels, small and large, is strongly derivative, and warms the hands.

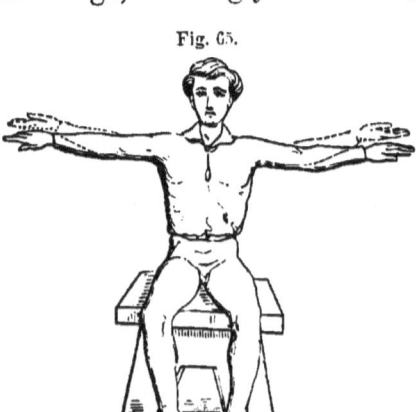

Fig. 65.

72.—YARD STRIDE-SITTING, ARMS TWISTING.

POSITION.—The arms are extended at either side in the same straight line, body in a sitting position.

ACTION.—The arms are *twisted* upon their own longitudinal axis, first forward, then backward, alternately; the same position being maintained. They may be *twisted* eight or ten times each way. The position is shown in the cut.

EFFECT.—This movement engages all the muscles of the arms in both concentric and eccentric action. It is highly stimulant to the circulation, warms the hands, and is derivative for the chest.

73.—STANDING, ARMS ROTATING.

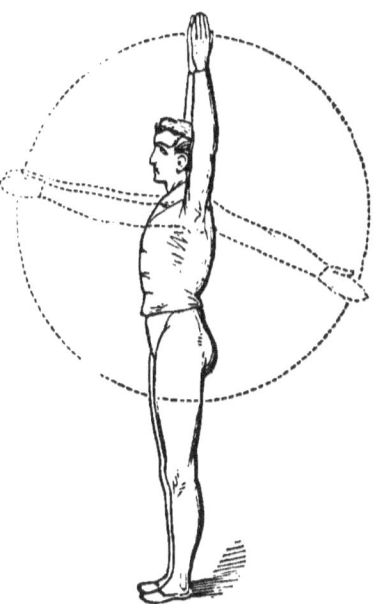

Fig. 66.

POSITION.—The arms are *stretched* in the *upright standing* posture.

ACTION.—The arms are made to describe circles, perpendicular and parallel with the body, the diameters of which are twice the length of the arm. After revolving in one direction ten or a dozen times, the direction of the motion is reversed. The cut shows the position, and the dotted circle the course traveled by the hand.

EFFECT.—This movement causes the blood to be retained in the arms and hands, because the centrifugal force attained by the rotation counteracts the return of venous circulation; while, at the same time, the arterial flow is assisted. The consequence is, that the hands become not only warmed, but absolutely swollen with blood, and the tendency to cold hands is overcome. The movement also relieves congestion of the chest. Besides these effects, all the muscles and ligaments about the shoulder joint, including those that are spread over the chest, are strengthened.

MODIFICATION.—1. One arm may be in wing position, while the movement is performed, as described, by the other arm, but changing after a suitable number of revolutions. The effect of this mode of performing the movement is, perhaps, greater than if both arms revolved at the same time. The body accommodates itself better to the single than to the double movement, and the object is achieved in a shorter time, and with less tendency to fatigue. This last advantage will be especially appreciated by the feeble invalid.

2. Let the commencing be the *rack* position. One arm may be brought backward on a nearly horizontal plane, as far as it can extend, with a swinging motion, and while returning to the commencing position the other arm may be in the act of performing the same motion backward that was before performed by the first. These alternate motions may be kept up till fifteen or twenty are performed. The dotted outlines indicate the positions occupied by the arms anteriorly and posteriorly in this movement. The body is required to be in a more lax state in this than in the principal movement.

74.—HANGING, SWINGING.

POSITION.—For this movement it is necessary to provide a swinging apparatus, to consist of a pole about three feet long, suspended horizontally by ropes attached to it at each end, and so high that it can be just reached by a person standing upon the floor. The higher the ceiling from which the apparatus is suspended, the greater the arc through which the body swings, and the more desirable the arrangement. The two hands are to grasp the pole, as represented in the cut.

Fig. 67.

ACTION.—The person gives a spring with the feet, throwing himself powerfully forward, and hangs by his hands. The momentum thus acquired causes him to swing for a time like a pendulum, the feet describing the arc of a large circle, of which the suspended ropes and body together are the radius. This motion may be continued as long as the body can be sustained by the hands.

EFFECT.—This motion does not occasion fatigue, since the will is but slightly exerted, but the effects are very important. A powerful derivative effect, having reference chiefly to the central portions of the body, is produced, caused, 1. By the strong action of the muscles of the hands, arms, and shoulders, required to sustain the body, the prolonged tension occasioning a subsequent rush of the blood into the arms. 2. The swinging motion produces a very great centrifugal effect, which, acting upon the circulating fluids, causes them to flow into, and be retained in, the lower extremities. In other words, the venous circulation is for the time retarded, while the arterial is accelerated, and the result is an accumulation of blood in the lower extremities, expanding the vessels and increasing the nutrition of that region. While these objects are being attained, the equally important one of diminishing the amount of blood in central portions of the body is also secured, and the circulation is equalized.

Another desirable effect produced by this movement is the elevation of the ribs, with consequent expansion of the chest. It will be seen that the weight of the body is suspended by the arms. But the arms being connected by muscular attachments with the ribs, both before and behind, the body is really suspended at the walls of the chest in such a way as to force them outward, and to allow the inspired air to occupy a larger space.

It is evident that in this movement most of the indications for the treatment of chronic pulmonary affections of the various grades are fulfilled. The same may be said in respect to the treatment of affections of the liver, and the dyspepsia usually connected with it. Hence, for chronic invalids of nearly every class, this is a movement as important as it is grateful and easily performed.

75.—SWING-HANG-STANDING, TRUNK ROTATING.

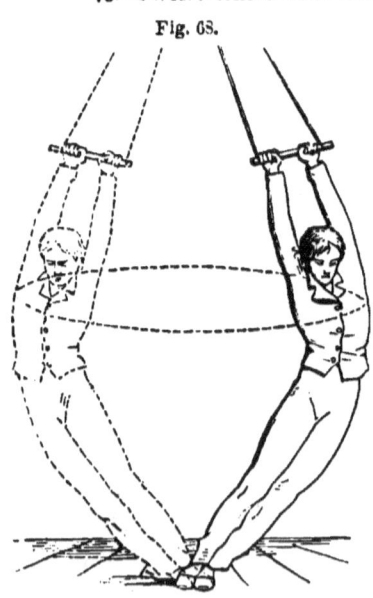

Fig. 68.

POSITION.—The hands grasp the swing, in the same way as in No. 74, *but the feet remain upon the floor.*

ACTION.—The body falls to one side by its weight; but being sustained by the swing, it bends at the side or shoulders, while the feet, or rather the toes, remain on the floor, directly under the point of suspension.

ACTION.—The body now, by a little effort, is

made to revolve in a circle, the longest diameter of which is at the shoulders, care being taken to keep it looking constantly one way. It may revolve several times in each direction.

EFFECT.—In this movement every part of the surface of the body is *stretched*, as the weight is thrown upon it, and *relaxed*, as the revolution throws the weight upon other muscles. The intercostal muscles and those of the arms are particularly subjected to the action, as are also the muscles of the abdomen, back, and legs. As this movement is accomplished with little effort, it is very grateful and refreshing. It also develops the the chest and respiratory apparatus, and is useful in dissipating the unpleasant feeling of fatigue, or any incipient congestion that may have been produced by the expenditure of too much power in the practice of other movements.

MODIFICATION.—Instead of revolving in a circle, the body may remain stationary at any given point in the circle; as, for instance, *looking forward*. In this case the anterior portion of the body is convex, the feet being placed far back, and strong action is produced upon the muscles of the chest and abdomen.

76.—TRUNK FORWARD-FALL HANGING, HOLDING.

POSITION.—The hands grasp firmly some object about as high as the shoulders; the feet and legs are extended backward, the toes resting on the floor; the body takes on a curved shape, the convexity being anterior.

ACTION.—1. The trunk straightens itself, so that it forms a line diagonal to that of the arms. 2. It then falls back into its curved position. This may be repeated two or three times. The dotted outline in the

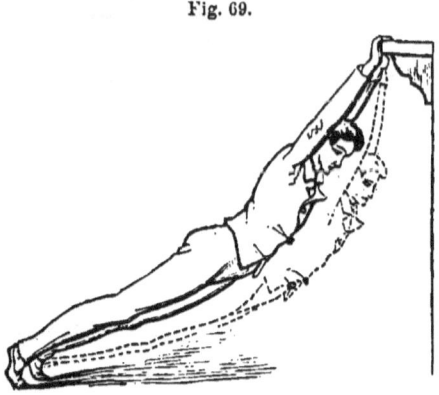

Fig. 69.

cut indicates the *commencing* position, while the figure shows the position attained by *stretching*.

EFFECT.—This movement affects the hands and arms, the chest, the abdomen, and the legs, upon their anterior portion.

MODIFICATION.—The body may take the position shown in the accompanying cut, and *hold* for a few moments. The effects are very similar to those of the above movement, but perhaps a little more marked. The top of a bedstead or a mantel will answer perfectly well as a means for obtaining the position.

77.—BACKWARD-FALL ELBOWS-SUPPORT LYING, HOLDING.

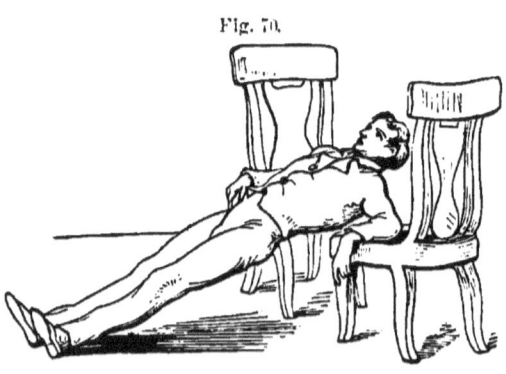

Fig. 70.

POSITION. — The arms extended on either side, in yard position, but the elbows may be bent; the trunk is in backward-fall position, and is supported by a chair or cushioned stool under each elbow, while the back of the heels are supported by the floor, the body being carefully maintained in the straight line.

ACTION.—The position may be continued for about one minute. The cut shows the position and action.

EFFECT.—This movement affects the back of the arms, the muscles between the shoulders and under the shoulder blades, and also those of the back; it strengthens these parts, and is derivative for the spinal cord.

78.—HALF-STRETCH SUPPORT HALF-STANDING, STRETCHING.

POSITION.—One arm is extended horizontally, and being in contact with some object, helps to maintain the upright position of the body; the other arm is stretched; the leg of the same side resting with the foot upon a stool, while the other leg is free; the trunk is erect.

Fig. 71,

ACTION.—The action in this movement does not consist in change of place, nor in *holding*, but in putting *all* the muscles of the standing side of the body into a state of tension; the action of each muscle being exactly balanced by that of its antagonist. In other words, all of the muscles of one side of the body are *stretched* by a strong exertion of the will. After the action has continued for a minute on one side, the other side may undergo the same discipline. The cut indicates the position.

EFFECT.—This movement is quite fatiguing, and is strongly derivative in its effects; it may be used on one side, when that side is much weaker than the opposite, as in partial hemiplegia, curvature of spine, etc.

79.—STRETCH-STRIDE STANDING OR STAR-STANDING, STRETCHING.

Fig. 72.

POSITION.—The arms are *stretched* upward, and a little outward; the legs are in the stride position, trunk erect.

ACTION.—An effort is simultaneously made by nearly all the muscles of the body to *reach higher*, and this action is continued for a minute.

EFFECT.—This is a very fatiguing movement, since it calls for a powerful exertion of the will to maintain the simultaneous action of so many muscles. The effect is derivative, and equalizing to the circulation, and also to the nervous and nutritive forces, for it stimulates at once all these powers to harmonious and vigorous co-operation. It drives the blood toward the skin, and if continued, soon excites perspiration.

Chapter Twelve.

REGION OF THE HEAD AND NECK.

REMARKS ON THE REGION OF THE HEAD.—The motions of the head are due to the action of the muscles of the neck, some of which have their attachments at the base of the skull, and to the framework of the chest. The neck is provided with numerous and powerful muscles, enabling the head to assume an extensive range of positions, and to perform a variety of most important movements. These movements are useful, in a hygienic and medical point of view, chiefly as they affect the circulation of the blood to and from the head, and also as enabling us to modify, to a limited extent, the circulation and nutrition of the throat, and the several organs of sense, as the eyes, ears, nose, etc., all of which are liable to disease or weakness. These muscles of the neck are also called upon to assist in removing certain natural and acquired faults of position, or deformities, not only of the neck, but also of the spine, of which it is a part. In treating of the several movements of this region, it is more convenient to refer them to the head, since it is the change in the position of the latter that constitutes their most conspicuous result, although it is the neck that is the region to which the movement is really applied.

Fig. 73.

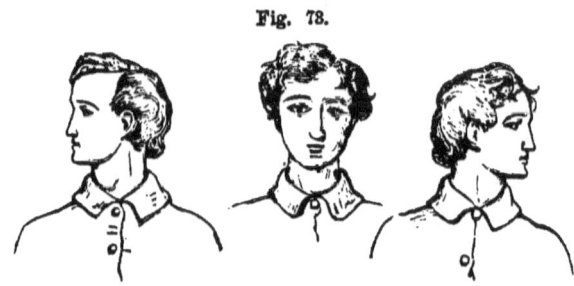

80.—HEAD TURNING.

POSITION.—The body may be in either sitting or standing position, with the head erect, as in the central figure of the cut, which is the commencing position in all head movements.

ACTION.—The head turns upon its axis to the right, so far as it can, and then, in the same manner and to the same extent, to the left, thus twisting the neck. The terminating positions of the movement are shown in the right and left figures of the cut. The action may be repeated six or eight times each day.

EFFECT.—This movement brings all the muscles of the neck into strong action, thus causing them to press upon the vessels, and so aiding the circulation of the blood in this region.

81.—HEAD FORWARD BENDING.

Fig. 74.

POSITION.—This is the same as is represented in No. 80.

ACTION.—The head is bent directly forward, as far as it can go, bringing the chin close to the breast, as in the cut. It is then carried up to the commencing position. This action may be repeated six or eight times.

EFFECT.—This movement is concentric for the front

part of the neck, and eccentric for the back. It is sometimes advantageous on account of its influence on the vertebral vessels, in removing headaches. It is also useful in affections of the throat.

82.—HEAD BACKWARD BENDING.

POSITION.—This is the same as that shown in No. 80.

ACTION.—The head is carried backward as far as possible. It then returns to its first position. This action to be repeated six or eight times.

EFFECT.—This is nearly the same as that in No. 81. The *kind* of action, however, is different; the eccentric action being in this case exercised by the anterior muscles, while the concentric is effected by the muscles at the back of the neck.

83.—HEAD BACKWARD BENDING AND TWISTING.

POSITION.—The same.

ACTION.—1. The head bends backward, and assumes the position represented in fig. 75. 2. It then turns to the right while thus bent, and then to the left, and so on, alternating the motion exactly as in No. 80.

EFFECT.—This movement acts much more powerfully upon the front of the neck than that in No. 80. It is useful for its derivative effect upon the laryngeal mucous membrane in case of congestion of that surface.

84.—HEAD BACKWARD BENDING AND TWISTING (SCREW RAISING).

POSITION.—The head is bent forward and sidewise.

ACTION.—The head slowly bends backward, turning

Fig. 77.

the face upward, while at the same time the head turns upon its axis until it looks toward one shoulder. The motion is like the turning of a screw. The head may return to the primary position, and then rise and turn in the direction opposite to that previously taken. This action may be repeated each way five or six times.

EFFECT.—This movement is useful much in the same way as those previously described. It is also useful in lateral curvature of the spine; but in this case the turning should be of course in only one direction.

PART III.

THE PATHOLOGY OF SEVERAL FORMS OF CHRONIC DISEASE.

Chapter Thirteen.

THE RELATIONS OF MOVEMENTS.

REMARK.—No attempt will be made in the following pages to go into any particular account of the symptoms and progressive stages of the several affections that we have selected as the theme of remark. Such an account would so far swell the size of our volume as to defeat its object. Besides, if such an effort were possible within our present limits, there are many excellent popular treatises, written in the interest of different medical systems, that embrace a similar design, and do such ample justice to the subject as would render any further attempt on our part in the same direction a work of supererogation, to say the least of it.

In the following chapters, therefore, we have thought it best to presume some knowledge on the part of the reader in regard to the nature and symptoms of the diseases noticed—a degree of knowledge sufficient, at any rate, to enable him to refer the particular complaint under discussion to some general class. It should further be understood that the principles of the Movement-Cure, which generally aim at the correction of the primary, radical causes of disease, regard the secondary symptoms as merely *effects,* and consequently as demanding less attention than they do in those plans of remedial treatment in which the suppression of these is regarded as the prime object of the practitioner's solicitude.

The account of himself given by the patient to the physician is really nothing more than a statement crudely rendered of the evidences of the operation of abnormal causes which it is the function of the latter, through this deceptive vail of symptoms, to recognize and remove. To suppress or ameliorate the symptoms while the cause remains, is but to practice a sort of deception at the expense of the patient; to sing the song of *peace! peace!* in the time of trouble; to attempt to purify the stream while the work of corruption is proceeding busily in the secret depths of the fountain.

It will be my chief endeavor, in the following pages, to expose the essential nature of certain maladies in connection with their causes; not in the light of the ordinary, or what would be termed *orthodox therapeutics,* but in that *better, truer* light, as we think, that is shed upon the subject by the Movement-Cure. We shall endeavor to make manifest to the reader's mind, what is clearer than noon-day to the writer's, to wit, the entire therapeutic *appropriateness* (and we use the word in its full, original meaning) of the "*cure*" to the many morbid conditions to which it is now beginning to be applied; and hence the propriety of claiming for it the distinction of being, in the best sense of the term, a philosophical system. It can not be said that the views of pathology herein set forth are in the interests exclusively of either of the two great antagonistic theories of medical science, the *chemical* or *humoral,* or the *vital.* The curative process, properly so called, is regarded as eminently a *physiological* process, in distinction from the *critical* and *artificial,* and *therefore pathological* actions that are the result of the means used by nearly all other schools of medical practice extant. These processes, it has been shown, present both chemical and vital features; and that the *movements* promote these processes, we have made it our business to demonstrate in these pages. It will be seen that the function of any defective locality may be exalted to the healthy state, the circulation be made equable, innervation directed to needy quarters, and so the health be restored, not by excitement and violence (which are ever followed by depression and functional anarchy), but by gentle, gradual, and harmonious tonic impressions.

These results are reached in an eminent degree by the practice of the duplicated movements, the effects of which, I hope to be able to show, may to a considerable degree be realized by the single movements, as explained and represented in this volume.

INDIGESTION—DYSPEPSIA.

Under this general head may be embraced all the common *chronic* disorders of the stomach, with the resulting loss of muscular power and disturbance of the nervous system. The varieties of this disorder so named are many, and the symptoms attending them are legion; but it is unnecessary here to go into a particular enumeration of them, since, being dependent all on essentially the same causes, very little variation in the treatment is demanded for all the countless phases of the complaint.

The digestion of food may be regarded as a central function, upon which the integrity of all the others are, to a great extent, dependent, and all, therefore, are apt to suffer in consequence of disturbance at this point. Indeed, no function of the body can be properly understood when considered apart from its physiological connection; but the control which this exerts over all the others is made painfully evident to the senses in case of any considerable deviation, as many a reader will be quick to acknowledge. Digestion is the first in the order of the changes wrought upon alimentary materials in the system, and when we consider that the supply of this material is under the control of the judgment and will, the responsibility resting upon us for the healthy performance of this act becomes evident.

The term *digestion* simply implies the reduction of alimentary material to a state of fluidity, whereby it is rendered fit to enter the circulation and supply material for the organizing processes of the frame. This act is effected in the *digestive cavity* formed by the alimentary canal, which, with its expansions and convolutions, extends quite through the body, and presents an inner surface of several square feet. Each portion of this canal is adapted to perform some distinct and necessary portion of this act, and the function is incomplete if any portion of the digestive surface is incapable of performing its particular, allotted share of the operation.

This change is effected in food by means of secretions poured into the cavity and mingled with the food derived from all parts of the digestive surface. The extent of this surface is very much augmented by certain appendages to it called glands, whose secretions are conducted into the cavity.

The amount of secretion thus daily poured into this

cavity for this exclusive purpose is very large, and consists in the following substances:

*Saliva	3.30 lbs.	Pancreatic juice	.44 lbs.
Gastric juice	14.08 "	Intestinal juice	.44 "
Bile	3.30 "		

The aggregate of these secretions amounts to more than *twenty-one and a half pounds* of solvent secretions poured into the digestive cavity, whose whole object is the solution of the two or three pounds of food that is daily required to sustain the functions of the body.

These secretions, we all know, are derived from the *blood*, and their quality and adaptation to the purposes for which they are intended, we see at once, must greatly depend on the quality of that fluid.

While we are investigating the causes, and selecting the remedies for *indigestion*, it is necessary to inquire into the separate influence exerted by these several factors that take part in the act—namely, the *food*, the *secretions*, and those accidental or temporary *conditions of the system* that have so much to do in promoting or impairing its health.

1. The *quality* of the food is a matter of much moment, and this is a subject that happens to receive, in our day, much attention from the popular mind; but, unfortunately, this attention proceeds from a most unreliable quarter; for, sad to say, senses perverted by long habits of wrong action are allied to the popular mind, and hence its judgments are generally erroneous. To the healthfully disciplined judgment, enlightened by science and experiment, there is but one test allowed for food—taste, fashion, must be set aside—the only question to be put in regard to any given material is,

---

* Draper's Physiology.

Can it be assimilated? What is its degree of capacity for supporting *all* the functional operations of the system? And here let me say, we must carefully discriminate between *supporting* and *exciting* functional acts, for substances belonging to the class of excitants, though generally mixed with, and often regarded as, food, yet in a true physiological sense do not really bear this relation. Even the mechanical and the imponderable agents may *excite*, but they certainly do not *support*, vital actions. They occasion waste, possibly to a hurtful extent; they never help forward in any direct way the organizing or reproducing processes of the body. The organic actions of the body have two grand objects in view: 1st. The construction of the instruments of vital action. 2d. The maintenance of the vital temperature. To accomplish this there must be a constant supply of materials capable of being *organized* instead of those capable of being *oxydized*. But of all the products of the organic world, whether produced by the plant or derived from the animal, nature restricts food material proper to sustain life to two distinct types. One is the *albuminous*, consisting of vegetable and animal *aliment*, and its derivatives *fibrin*, *gluten*, *casein*, etc., and the saline matters associated with these, all of which contain *nitrogen* in a certain definite proportion. The other class contains no *nitrogen*, and is always of a bland nature, of which starch and oil are examples.

A common cause of imperfect digestion consists in improper food—that is, from a sort of food that does not correspond with this description. Since the system is able to dispose of other matters besides food, one portion by the oxydizing process always going on within it, effecting its destruction, and another portion by its insolubility, the distinctive difference between what *is* and what is *not* food is apt to be lost sight of, and hence the unconscious, but not the less harmful abuse.

Another source of injury to digestion arises from disregarding the proper relative proportion of the correct elements in the use of food. In this case, while there may be an insufficiency of some of the elements, others are in surplus amount, so that while the system is loaded with materials, organization, or rather nutrition, is at a low standard, because the *necessary* elements are not present in sufficient quantity.

Practically, the danger to the health arising under this head comes from two sources: one, the employment of too much soluble—that is, *saccharine* matter; and the other is the rejection of the saline constituents, which are fully as important as the organic. These are apt to be lost by mechanical refining, for the chief portion of the saline elements of the edible grains exists in the outer or coarser portions.

It is also important that the amount of food taken be strictly proportionate to the needs of the system; in other words, proportionate to its power of dissolving in the stomach and intestines, and also of its power of elimination, by means of the oxygen respired. If these bounds be exceeded, the materials thrust into the digestive cavity are no longer *food*, but a harmful foreign mass, perhaps even poisonous matter, affording to the local nerves a cause of irritation that will affect the whole system, and also to the blood a quantity of matter rife with chemical tendencies, over which vitality can exercise but imperfect control.

2. The secretions constitute the next great factor in the digestive process to be considered. It is by these

that the solution of food is effected. If these secretions are *deficient in quantity* or *vitiated in quality* from any cause, an imperfect solution of food must result. A deficiency in quantity can never really exist, because, being furnished by the vital powers of the organism, the quantity must always be graduated to the vital need, so that, practically, the want of a healthy relation, in this respect, resolves itself into an *excess of quantity of food*, the consequence of which was shown when speaking of the relations of the elements of food. There can be no proper digestion unless the peculiar chemical affinities of the true digestive secretions are able to overpower all tendency to other chemical action in the digestive mass.

The cause of a deterioration of the quality of the digestive secretions arises partly from the cause above-mentioned, and partly from a morbid condition of the blood, and of the general nutritive offices of the body connected therewith; in other words, from the general imperfect evolution of vital activity in the system, hereafter to be noticed.

All the causes above enumerated have in themselves an intrinsic and direct injurious tendency, but I am inclined to believe that the train of unpleasant symptoms resulting from indigestion is due, to a large extent, to consequent disturbance *of the nervous system*. The nervous susceptibilities of the digestive organs are aroused by the various causes noticed, and soon become habitually—morbidly active. The perceptions not only become unnaturally acute but erroneous, and the judgment is insensibly led to make false decisions in regard to the conditions of the system. Stomach irritation is reflected through the nervous system to all the bodily organs, and nutritive changes in remote parts of the body are injuriously influenced thereby. But what is of more importance, the *ganglionic centers*, situated near the stomach, and posterior to it, whose function it is to preside over digestion, become inflamed, and rendered incapable of performing their office. There is an *insanity* of digestion, quite as much a disease as that of the brain, and more difficult of cure. The difficulty in either case consists in withdrawing the morbid causes, which are apt to be self-perpetuating in their nature.

The morbid activity of the digestive organs disturbs the digestive process as we have seen by its direct influence, but this is only a portion of the troublesome effects. The attention is concentrated continuously upon the stomach and the digestive process. This is contrary to nature, and is sure to disturb still further the process. No good digestion is possible while sensations in the stomach are habitually aroused by food, improper in kind or amount, by stimulating beverages, or by drugs.

There are two symptoms attending the state of things here described, besides the ordinary ones of loss of power, local or stomach symptoms, pain, acidity, etc., but these appear only in aggravated cases. One is, sensitiveness or soreness at the pit of the stomach upon deep pressure; the other is, a peculiar sensation of buzzing or ringing in the head, generally referred to the region of the ears. There are many evidences that the latter symptom is due to the connection of the nerves of organic life with the cerebrum. The removal of these symptoms is one of the earliest proofs of the restoration of the digestive power.

3. Another, and not the least important cause of indigestion, consists of a defect in the general vital

actions of the system. Viewed with reference to the whole system, digestion may be regarded as being dependent upon the general nutritive actions that are constantly proceeding in every portion of the body. These actions make digestion necessary, and give, at the same time, its peculiar character to the secretion provided for this purpose. The *kind* of digestive action, as well as the *quality of the product*, will therefore depend on the degree of perfection with which all the other processes of the system are performed; for each, as we have seen, contributes to the blood the last result of its action, and it is from blood thus replenished and enforced that the digestive secretions are drawn. Thus it is that an imperfectly elaborated blood, loaded with the results of the imperfect vital action of the tissues, is returned to the stomach and intestines, and is capable of affording only morbid secretions, which must irritate, debilitate, and finally render diseased and sensitive, these important and central organs. It will be recollected that the amount of the digestive secretions that is daily poured into the digestive cavity, nearly equals that of the whole mass of the blood from which they are derived, so that the morbid effects that it is capable of exciting may be concentrated upon these delicate and important parts.

Hence, the cause of indigestion is not confined to improper food, but it is also, in a degree, referable to those voluntary habits which are connected with, and exercise an immense control over, the vital manifestations of the general system. It is to this source that the quality of the digestive fluids is ultimately referable, because they are produced from the blood common to all parts, and by means of the exercise of vital power belonging to the local organs, so that when the vital energy of the general system is low, the digestion is sure to suffer as a direct consequence. It is plain, then, that the digestive process depends no less upon *how we act*, then it does upon *what we eat;* and therefore, that *no amount of dieting, however correct,* per se, *will be capable of doing more than palliate some of the symptoms of indigestion, and can never cure it so long as the movements of the body are insufficient in amount or faulty in kind.*

In cases of indigestion arising from this cause, the amount of pain suffered in the region of the stomach affords no true indication of the severity of the disease. Indeed, there is generally but little, or perhaps no pain referable to that organ, even though the digestive power be very small. The perceptive power of the nerves is deteriorated along with the general power of the system.

The indications of disease afforded through the nerves are very irregular and unreliable, and this fact serves greatly to embarrass the efforts that may be made toward a cure. The dyspeptic patient is generally tantalized, for instance, by a morbid craving for food, and there is little or no sense of satisfaction experienced when food is taken, so that he never knows when to leave off eating, nor when to begin. He also, in this condition of the nerves, craves piquant substances and concentrated food, which is often the worst for him, and shows that the *feelings* of the dyspeptic, especially those accompanying this phase of the disorder, are entirely untrustworthy. Such a patient should first instruct his judgment, and learn to rely upon it, and to *distrust his sensations* scrupulously, and also consider that the physician whose prescriptions are directed to the mere palliation of his present sufferings, is not a safe professional adviser. The dictates of the cultivated judgment must be strictly submitted to, even though opposed to his perverted feelings, if so be he would avoid the abysses of suffering toward which his disease is pressing him, and into which thousands are daily plunging, never to rise till *Death* comes to their relief, or his brother, *Palsy*, quiets the tortured nerves with his benumbing touch.

We are now prepared to understand what are the proper means to be employed for the purpose of overcoming, or, to use the phrase to which the popular mind has been so long accustomed, of *curing* these particular affections. These consist, in the first place, in attention to the quantity and quality of the food. In indigestion, the capacity, not of the *stomach* only, but *of the whole system*, to receive food, is impaired. The quantity of food that may be taken by the system always must depend on the general habits of the individual as well as upon his condition at the particular time; on circumstances exterior to the body, as temperature, as well as those within it, as mental and bodily activity. With the consciousness of a lack of nutrient force pervading the system, it is very difficult to resist the inclination to perform that act which for the time being generally relieves the feeling.

On account of the morbid sensations in the stomach, there is perhaps greater inclination to err in *quality* than in quantity of food taken. As this matter is treated with some elaborateness in another place, it need not be further discussed here. We will now only caution the dyspeptic by suggesting that he can never expect his health and strength to return to him while his system is receiving through the stomach such matters as conflict with the tendency of the acting parts of the body to organize themselves, whether these may be chemical products of morbid action, or food containing noxious elements, as too much alkali, salt, spices, etc., or a larger quantity than can be eliminated by the ordinary physiological processes.

Especially to be deprecated in this disease is the use of drugs, even of the mildest kinds. The temporary relief sometimes gained by this means is quite certain to be followed by a proportionate impairment of power; and the gravest features of the disease are confirmed by an habitual recourse to such palliative expedients, and the unfortunate invalid so treated is apt to lapse into a lamentable and sometimes hopeless hypochondriasis. Even cases which recover *after* (generally, it may be said, in spite of) the use of drugs, serve but as dangerous precedents.

It has been intimated that *voluntary action* is the most important means for maintaining or restoring the integrity of the digestive function. This fact has always been popularly recognized, and in some imperfect manner it has always entered into medical prescriptions of every class.

The general *reasons why* movements should have so important an influence upon the health, have been explained in a former chapter, and are contained in the normal activity which is thereby induced in the *assimilative* and *depurative* functions of the system—the higher vital tone imparted to the essential machinery of life, of which the digestive organs constitute so important a part.

It is particularly to be insisted upon that the digestive power augments with every augmentation of the *respiratory* action, whether induced by exercise or through continued exposure to low temperature, because this act has the direct effect of deterging the blood, and causes the product of vital action to be eliminated through the emunctories, thus relieving the system of those matters that would otherwise contaminate and poison it. The dyspeptic, like the consumptive, is generally a person whose habits of life have been such as injuriously limit the amount of air respired. Persons who confine themselves to the atmosphere of warm rooms, and who seldom expose themselves to currents of cool out-of-door air, find it very difficult to elude the disease in question. Exercise, and especially that afforded by well-directed *movements*, has the effect, we repeat, of urging the blood to the surface. Free contact with the air, aided by baths, tends to the same result. These means greatly stimulate the respiratory process, and scatter, at the same time, those central congestions which, if they give no further trouble, serve at least to cherish the dyspeptic condition of the digestive organs.

While, then, it is a patent and an admitted fact that *exercise* contributes more than all other things, drugs included, to the restoration of the dyspeptic invalid (we have the united testimony of physicians of all schools, as well as of public opinion, to this truth), the admission fails of effecting the good it should effect in consequence of the prevalent crude and unphilosophical notions that obtain generally in regard to the whole subject of exercise as a remedial agent. Every one is conscious that much of the forced exercise he obliges himself to undergo, so far from being beneficial and recuperative, proves decidedly injurious, and so he jumps sagely to the conclusion that *his particular case* is an exception, and that the more quiet he keeps, the better. This difficulty arises from ignorance of the principles we have tried to explain. Nothing is clearer than that when the nutrition is imperfect, the power of exertion must be proportionally limited. In proportion as the muscular power *decreases*, it becomes necessary to *increase* the effort of the will in order to accomplish a given effect. This necessitates an injurious expenditure of nervous power, at the same time causes a preponderance of *nervous* over *muscular* action, which is fatal to the health. No exercise is proper which does not tend directly to augment the capacity for exertion, by increasing muscular nutrition; but this power is not increased, but on the contrary diminished materially if immoderate demand be habitually made upon the nervous system.

Partial exercise, that is, exercise of some one portion of the body exclusively, particularly if it be a central portion, as frequently happens in some of the trades and professions, is also detrimental; for it is apt to excite and maintain congestion in those delicate central organs already affected by disease, or full of the seeds of it, while it withdraws the circulation from the feet and peripheral parts. It is in such cases as these that discouragement is most apt to be experienced in view of the effect of exercise.

When persons are conscious of receiving injury in this way, they should not conclude, as they frequently do, that all exercise must be in the nature of things injurious. Even much stronger exercise, *if of the right kind*, and involving parts remote from the seat of the disease, may be taken, not only with impunity, but with the highest advantage. There is no more important lesson than this for the invalid world to learn.

All passive exercise, such as riding on horseback, or in carriages, or by railroad, and also by sailing, are generally very advantageous in this disease. These passive movements husband the will-power, remove impediments in the capillary circulation, and assist those actions in relation with which all nutrition takes place. The aeration of the blood is also greatly assisted, as well absorption, both from the digestive surface and from the system generally. In this way all the powers of the body are equalized, and the organic or formative processes are promoted.

Special movements are well adapted to fulfill all the indications in this immensely large class of diseases. The prescription should be so made as to affect all parts of the body successively, commencing with the respiratory region, and including at last the feet, legs, abdomen, liver, and the stomach. This latter organ should, at first, be attacked cautiously and tentatively, or be let alone entirely. A difficult case of *indigestion* requires the duplicated movements, both because there is too little strength for the single ones, and because of the amount of control over the circulation which it is necessary to acquire, and to which the *single movements* can not attain. But the *single movements* are eminently useful for a large class of persons that need to guard against the approaches of disease, or to overcome its milder forms; also for the after-treatment of a case cured by duplicated movements. The plan of treatment in this disease does not materially differ in its more important particulars from that which is appropriate in pulmonary affections. The most important indications in both are to expand the chest, stimulate the circulation in the extremities, also in the peripheral portions of the body, and to promote the concoction of well vitalized blood in all the tissues throughout the framework.

EXAMPLES OF PRESCRIPTIONS.*

1. Half-wing, curve (weight held), kick-support half-standing, trunk sidewise bending. Change. No. 48.
2. Forward-fall head-support standing, leg-raising. Change. 25.
3. Wing stride-standing, curtseying. 9.
4. Yard-sitting, arms twisting. 72.
5. Support half-standing, leg-rotation. Change. 23.
6. Yard-kneeling, arms-swaying. 46.
7. Sidewise-lying, hips-raising. Change. 62.
8. Half-wing, half-stretch, short-sitting, trunk-twisting. 37.
9. Half-lying, abdomen-kneading. 66.
10. Hanging, holding.

After a formula like the above has been used for a while, movements that affect the central portions of the body may properly be used.

1. Arms angle reclined kneeling, arms stretching. 44.
2. Shelter, back lying, legs raising. 59.
3. Shelter, sidewise-bent, stride-standing, trunk rotation. 59.
4. Stretch, half-walk, half-kneeling, trunk backward bending. 48.
5. Sidewise-lying, leg-raising. 28.
6. Wing-stride kneeling, ringing. 45.
7. Half-wing, half-stretch, walk-kneeling, trunk-twisting. 42.
8. Half-standing, leg backward raising. 19.
9. Wing-sitting, legs twisting. 24.

---

* The figures at the end of the line describing the movement refer to its *number* as arranged in Part II. of this work.

Chapter Fourteen.

NERVOUSNESS.

The suffering of many chronic invalids, especially those afflicted with disorders of the digestive organs, consists in general not so much in absolute pain as in a peculiar and somewhat indefinite morbid sensation, which, for want of a more significant term, they denominate *nervousness*.

Nervousness is apt to be regarded by people in health as a trivial symptom. This opinion is founded, perhaps, on the peculiar, and often even ludicrous nature of the phenomena, mental, moral, and physical, which accompany it. If, however, it be regarded with reference to the real suffering experienced by the invalid, or to the permanent nature of the malady, it must be admitted to be one of the most serious and important of the diseases which the physician is ever called upon to treat.

In regard to the essential nature of the affection, there would not seem to be room for much difference of opinion. When the result of physiological action is imperfect, we are at liberty to presume that there must be a fault in some one or more, or all of the processes whereby it is produced; and such faults are often called, in a general way, a perversion of the true function which it is the office of the part to perform. Nervous symptoms may be attributable to imperfect nutrition of the nerve-centers in which all nerve-force originates; and this again, as we have seen, is dependent on the other physiological functions whose work it is to maintain the general nutritive processes of the body in harmonious co-operation.

Nervous symptoms exist in many grades of intensity, even in the same person; sometimes they arise through depressed, sometimes through irregular, and sometimes through greatly heightened functional actions of the nerve-centers. The impressions which these centers receive affect the consciousness at times to a degree greatly beyond that to which it is accustomed. This may not, however, be entirely due to the physiological state of the centers themselves; but in many cases probably the intensified consciousness is owing to a general morbid condition of the whole system, of which the nerves of sensation make report, in their own peculiar and unmistakable way.

In nervousness, the judgment itself suffers sadly from the irregular action of the nervous system, for it is obliged to depend, to a great extent, on the evidences which the senses afford. Now, the more the sensations and feelings are excited, the greater becomes their control over the higher powers in council; and their perverted action insures wrong mental decisions. In nervous disease, the sensorial powers immensely preponderate, and the whole man is overwhelmed with influences due to the action of a depraved and rampant nervous system.

It unfortunately happens, that the state of the nerves, and consequently that of the mind, re-acts on the physiological condition in such a way as to perpetuate this condition of things in spite of all that can be done through the most judicious medical treatment. To the mind of the suffering individual, no evidence in regard to his condition and wants equals that of the senses; and these senses being perverted, the subject is constantly inclined to make improper choice of means and materials for the supply of his wants and the rectification of his disorders. He eats improperly, drinks improperly, acts improperly; because the nerves that in health speak truth, now have taken to speaking falsely. Under the guise of friendship they deal treacherously with him, and before he well knows what he is about, he has been led into all sorts of errors and vices of conduct, from the effects of which it may take him a long time to recover.

Imperfection in the various nutritive actions has been mentioned above, as a common cause of nervous disorders; and it was also intimated that such diseases are most liable to occur in persons of intellectual habits, and of delicate and refined tastes and sensibilities. The reasons for this are very obvious. The aspirations for honor or fame, fulfilled or otherwise, and the perplexities and trials consequent thereupon, of which such persons are always the subjects, occasion a great waste of the vital power which should go to the nutrition of the organs. The *intense* ardor, indeed, with which affairs are conducted by the great mass of the people of this country, obliges the nervous systems of men and women to *act*, that is, to suffer waste and repair, to a degree greatly disproportionate to th with which actions proceed in the other vital structures. The consequence of this is, that the organic or vegetative life of all other tissues of the body is depressed. A general depressed tone of vitality accompanies all excessive or inharmonious action; and where the causes continue to act, results must follow, as we see them in the multiform nervous complaints about us. One thing we may set down as certain and incontrovertible: nervous diseases do not occur in the absence of nervous abuse. It matters not how the invalid may protest to the contrary as respects his own particular case, the existence of the symptoms in question is conclusive evidence against him. The ignorance of the sufferer, alas! does not reverse physiological laws. That he has only been led by the *dicta* of a conventional system is not a plea that will serve to bring about a commutation of the sentence already pronounced upon him. He may bring forward the evidence of the senses in favor of his habits, and the approval of the consciousness; but these arguments only prove a perverted state of the senses, which his bad habits have fostered.

The victim of this form of disease is apt to complain that his suffering is greater than that occasioned by other diseases. He should remember that the arrangements of his system which give rise to pain are conceived in the highest wisdom, that the experience of pain is designed in mercy by our Creator, and that the objects of such experience are not fulfilled till he has been stimulated by his sufferings to trace out their sources, and thus enabled to pursue a wiser course in future. In this light, pain is really the invalid's kindest instructor, and as strictly a blessing as enjoyment, though a blessing in disguise. This class of diseases furnishes to the physician a deeper study than he has generally the time or patience to investigate thoroughly, and the sufferer seldom meets, from any quarter, with the amount of intelligent sympathy which his case deserves.

The nervous powers may be abused, and nervous disease induced by causes operating through either the physical or the mental system. The first class of causes affect the sensory nerves, and those of organic life, by direct impressions made by improper substances. The habitual use of fragrant and pungent seasonings and inspiring beverages, which are stimulating and temporarily refreshing but not nutritious, is a most common mode of abusing the nerves. The organic needs of the system demand only materials that are strictly nutritive. Whatever is received into the stomach of a different quality may impress the nerves and rouse their action, and very agreeably, perhaps; but this action is not in the direction of, nor satisfying to, the healthful wants of the system. This is so, because the stimulant substance is not adapted to the purposes of growth and development; thus is established a depraved habit of the central nerves, from which spring, as from a poisoned fountain, those morbid feelings, wrong thoughts, and insane judgments that characterize so many in every community.

Another cause of nervous distemper, and perhaps quite as important as any other, is one perfectly similar in mode of operation to that last mentioned, and this is medication in general. The physician, whether he so intends or not, addresses his remedies mainly to the already too sensitive nerves. For as the perception of suffering is mainly through these, so by addressing this department of the organism is the consciousness of pain frequently most readily overcome. Indeed, the *cause*, in the estimation of both physician and patient, is of secondary importance, but both unite in seeking present freedom from pain, or what in general supplies the place of it, *obliviousness* to the *existence* of the morbid condition. But though quietude, artificially induced, may be grateful for the time, the injury done to the misused nerves is permanent. Though slight and almost inappreciable at first, this injury increases with the repetitions of the cause, and a diseased habit, degrading the whole physiological and moral man, is induced. This remark is directed against no particular method or school of medication, but it is equally applicable to all systems, that of the Water-Cure included, so far as they seek to attain their purposes by making strong impressions upon either the internal or external nerves of sensation, or those of organic life.

The second, not perhaps second in importance, of the two great classes of causes affecting the health of the nervous system, we term the *mental.* If we take delight in those pleasures that are derived through the senses, those that are obtainable by means of the emotional nature exercise an equal, or even greater, fascination. From the sensorial we rise to the region of the feelings, and thence to that of pure intellect, but each of these fountains of enjoyment depends, after all, upon a material and physiological source for supply. The purest, holiest, and most commendable impulses and actions, if cherished or pursued without a wise regard to physiological interests, work mischief, and death at last. This is because all the organic powers run to the support of those actions which do most loudly call for them. Men are too apt to shut themselves up in certain parts of the wondrous tenement of their being. Some domicile themselves in the emotional, some in the intellectual apartments, and never think of occupying, much less of furnishing and keeping in order, the other portions of the building.

In this class may be reckoned the multitude of human desires and ambitions fulfilled and disappointed—

the perplexities, jealousies, and strifes incident to the battle and race of life, as well as the solicitudes, the alternating hopes and fears resulting from the political, moral, and religious movements in the community. In Europe, where these latter questions are questions of the state, in which the mass of the people are not expected or allowed to take any considerable interest, and where, also, the condition of the people, as regards the pursuits of life, is mainly fixed, these diseases are much less prevalent.

The causes above stated are amply sufficient to give a nervous character to the diseases of chronic invalids. Especially must this be true, for reasons named, in our own country. The reader will perceive the want of relevancy of the ordinary medical means to meet the exigencies of such cases. It is a condition which discreet, conscientious physicians declare to be beyond the province of ordinary medical skill, while they still regard it as amenable to the milder, yet more potent influences of hygiene, such as change of climate, scenery, and mode of life. Hence, such are the means principally advised by the more experienced and careful among physicians, and often with great advantage, though it must be confessed, at other times, with wholly unsatisfactory results. It is reasonable to presume that incapacity for restoration in the invalid is *not* the cause of failure in these attempts, but the real cause of the failure lies in the imperfect or improper system, or to that want of system that characterizes the endeavors of many physicians in bringing these important means to bear upon the sufferer.

Those who have conceived a tolerably correct idea of the character and *modus operandi* of *movements* must be convinced that they are eminently adapted to this class of affections. Practically, the treatment by movements operates with all the certainty and directness of effect of a *specific*. The value of the treatment by the Movement-Cure has become apparent to the thoughtful and scientific of many differing schools of pathology.

And why should it not be so? If it be conceived by the practitioner that the indications for treatment in a given case are for *detergents*, most abundantly do the movements supply the means for accomplishing these. If, in another, the general nutrition needs to be stimulative, the movements furnish the means in amplest measure for accomplishing this. If congestion is to be removed, where will you find instrumentalities that will do it more readily and thoroughly than the movements? If the peripheral circulation is to be exalted, here are certain unfailing modes of securing this object.

The principles involved in the Movement-Cure furnish a ready explanation of the power exerted by movements over the many forms of *nervousness*. The doctrine of *balance* or *equipoise*, in the relative activity of functions, will be more fully explained hereafter.

The system of movements has it in its power to *elect* what function or force shall predominate in the man brought under its influence. The several organic actions may be, as those of nutrition, of the circulation, of waste, etc., waked up, so to speak, by movements in any part or parts where they have become languid and insufficient, while at the same time undue action in the nerves is brought under control.

It is important to notice that nervous symptoms, when they come on with acute paroxysms, are most frequently owing to visceral obstructions and derangements, the nature of which, though often apparent, are sometimes obscure. A morbid change suddenly occurring in the contents of the alimentary canal may generate a peculiar product that poisons the blood or irritates the nerve-centers of organic life, producing symptoms sometimes severe and occasionally of a strange and fantastic character. These acute paroxysms generally subside spontaneously in a short time, and medical interference with them is of but little account, though it often gets a great deal of undeserved credit. The treatment by movements should be directed to the perfecting of the digestive powers, to the augmentation of the functional activity of the liver, and to the restoration of the secretions generally. By thus preventing the occurrence of the morbid conditions named, these troublesome attacks may be avoided. And if ever an ounce of prevention is worth a pound of cure, it surely is found to be so in our experience of nervous disorders—to the patient particularly. To the *doctor*, indeed, especially if he happens to be possessed of a homœopathically small practice, and an infinitesimal conscience, it may look differently.

The Movement-Cure supplies the means for arousing directly the action of the nerves, but **this** is not usually called for in these cases. Usually **it is** only necessary to treat the invalid of this class with reference to his general health, to the condition of the stomach, liver, bowels, circulation of the head and feet, etc. The patent disorder is usually a concomitant and symptom of some other—perhaps far graver—affection which the judicious and acute physician will discover, and when this is overcome, the nervousness will surely—gradually, it may be—sometimes very quickly—subside.

If the invalid reader has read carefully the chapters treating of the rules and principles which are laid down as the basis of the movement practice, he will now be able, without much difficulty, to frame a prescription suited to his own particular case. We take it for granted, of course, that he possesses a reasonable degree of intelligence and judgment.

SEMINAL DISEASE.—This peculiar and distressing affection is an indication of a diseased state of the nerves, rather than of the organs to which it is commonly referred. It very frequently accompanies that state of general *nervousness* described above; but sometimes those nerve-centers that are situated in the lower section of the spinal cord, from which these organs draw their power, are the principal seat of the trouble. In either case there is a very great amount of mental depression and lassitude accompanying this disease, the person so afflicted being generally unfitted for business and society, and for any of the enjoyments of life. The abuse of this portion of the nervous system probably brings down upon the sufferer regrets more bitter and a remorse more stinging than that of any other—a fact which indicates the important relations these functions sustain both to the material and the mental system; and we all can understand how it is that intense mental pain should make a part of the penalty attached by nature to such abuses. But, independently of certain special and well-known causes, the affection often appears as one of the results of general nervous debility or irregular distribution of nerve-power; and in all cases its treatment, to be successful, must be general rather than topical. Indeed, topical treatment, in these cases, is often much worse than useless.

Persons afflicted with these symptoms are commonly the easiest dupes in the world of audacious charlatanry.

Their intense desire for restoration disposes them to be credulous, and to grasp at straws, while the necessary weakness of the investigating faculties which accompanies the disease, alike unfits them for the perception of their true condition and for a choice of proper remedial means. Thus, frequently, the victim continues to swallow nostrums which, by increasing the nervous irritability of his system, can only aggravate his disorder, till finally he becomes a confirmed hypochondriac, or some more formidable disease sets in, and death ends his woes.

The prime indication in this affection is to allay nervous excitability. The mode of effecting this has already been pointed out. The treatment required in this class of cases does not differ essentially from that required for general nervousness or for neuralgia. The morbid nutrition of the nerve-centers, upon which this and the other forms of nervous disease depend, can not be perpetuated at the same time with full and complete nutrition of the muscles, and the general satisfactory state of the organic life which attends this condition of the muscles. In persons much emaciated, and especially those who have passed far into the hypochondriacal condition, the general health must be so far restored that these latter symptoms shall disappear before the difficulty in question can be entirely removed. But if the health be not too far wasted, the relief of this difficulty is in general very speedy. In some cases, treated by duplicated movements, the disease has been cured without difficulty.

It can hardly be expected that the single movements will be so efficient in the treatment of this malady as the duplicated, in cases especially where the nerves are greatly disordered. Yet I doubt not their judicious use would prove all-sufficient in a large number of cases, if persons now resorting to other expedients— expedients that can not bear the test of common sense and true science—would but try these simpler and truly rational means.

NEURALGIA.—This is a disease characterized by great suffering; but it is usually unaccompanied with the other ordinary concomitants of inflammation, such as swelling, heat, and redness, and frequently there is an absence even of soreness. Hence it is presumed that the cause of the pain is confined to the nervous structure itself, and is not referable to any morbid condition of the vital structures to which the painful nerve is distributed. Neuralgia may attack any portion of the body, whether internal or external; it may be confined to a particular locality, or it may affect the general nervous system through all its ramifications.

To understand this affection at all, it is necessary to inquire first into the nature and causes of *pain*. As this phenomenon is exhibited by the sensory nerves, it is evident that it bears a relation to their ordinary function. Indeed, pain, as well as sensation in general, has its uses, which consist in informing the mind, not only of the nature of objects in contact with the nerve, but also of the incompatibility of certain of them with the vital purposes.

We know but little of the chemistry of the intercellular fluids. It is not unlikely that the peculiar quality these juices in some depraved states of the system acquire may give rise to the symptom in question, without sensibly affecting vital structures of any other kind. However this may be, the affection seldom yields to ordinary medical influences; but it is generally treated with reference merely to its palliation—by means which obliterate, for the time, the consciousness of pain, rather than remove its cause. This can be done by stupefying drugs; but, alas! the pain returns when the effects of the anodyne pass off.

It is absurd to entertain the expectation that this disease will vanish while the nutritive processes are carried on in an imperfect way. The system must be relieved of its burden of effete matter, and arterial blood, rich in oxygen, must again find its way freely to every structure before any permanent benefit can be experienced.

How it is that movements effect the removal of neuralgic pain, will be obvious upon a little reflection. The analogies afforded by certain physiological phenomena throw light upon this matter. For instance, the amount of force put forth by a muscle corresponds with the amount of change that takes place in that muscle during its action. In like manner we argue from manifestations of nervous power the extent of the changes going on in the substance of the nerves, both centers and conductors. Pain, however severe, is but the result of functional play, and is the representative of nerve-power, and consequently of nutritive change in the inner tissue of the nerve itself. If the nerve be so much diseased, or have undergone such a structural change as not to be able to perform its function, one is no longer conscious of pain in the part. Pain, then, is not simply a result of action, but of excessive action of the nerves in the direction in which they manifest their power, and it consequently implies excessive, though perhaps perverted, nutrition of the nerve-substance.

The therapeutic indications deducible from these

principles are plain. The restoration of nervous action to the healthy standard depends on a depression of the activity of the nerves involved. This effect readily follows the excitement of muscular action. For it is found that in proportion to the increase of the nervous activity, is there an abatement of muscular nutrition. The limb afflicted with sciatica becomes weak, and it is noticeable that the neuralgic subject generally has but little muscular power; the nutritive effort is concentrated upon the excited nerves. That this perverted nutrition of the nerve-substance is an important element in neuralgia is forcibly proved by the immediate subsidence oftentimes of neuralgic pain when the activity of contiguous muscles has become exalted. That this is so is unquestionable, whatever theory may be adopted in regard to the philosophy of the matter. It is a most significant fact that robust people are but little liable to attacks of neuralgia. Those most afflicted with the disease in question, are the weakly; those who have imperfect digestion, sallow complexions, and are poorly nourished. To perfect the nutritive operations, we consider the most important indication in our treatment of these cases. To effect this purpose, the movements are entirely sufficient. By these the functions of the outlets of the body are encouraged, and waste matters are dismissed; so that those matters wanted from the alimentary canal, to subserve nutritive purposes, are selected and conveyed by the blood to their various points of destination. This is especially the case with those saline elements of the blood, without which the organizing processes can not take place.

The most painful cases of neuralgia are those attributable to mineral poisoning, incident to the practice of various trades, such as the working of gold with mercury, or other metals, or their salts. The use of mineral drugs, as a medicine, is also a fruitful source of this affection. Many a person, in consequence of a course of mercury, is ever after subjected to attacks of neuralgia. Even in these obstinate cases, the movements would probably prove useful, since no other means are so effectual as these in dislodging and conveying foreign matters from the system.

The prescription for a case of neuralgia should be so arranged as not only to include every part of the body, affecting all the blood-purifying and blood-making processes, but especially so as to act upon the part subject to pain. With duplicated movements the application can be nicely adjusted to the needs of the local nutrition, and an important part of the prescription will be the *passive* element, consisting of stroking, clapping, punching, etc., as the case may require. The single movements will be the next best substitute, and the passive portion may be applied by one's self to such regions of the body as can thus be reached. It is not necessary to say that when the neuralgic disorder is local, such movements should be chosen as will act on the muscles of the part, especially upon those near to the seat of the pain.

Chapter Fifteen.

SCROFULOUS AFFECTIONS.

The scrofulous diathesis manifests itself in a great variety of symptoms, differing according to constitution and age. In children, it is denoted by a peculiar pallor of countenance, dullness of complexion, hypertrophied or inflamed mesenteric glands, and tumid abdomen, bowels alternately loose and costive, capricious appetite—frequently too urgent—shrunken limbs, fetid breath, indisposition for play. Eruptions of various kinds may occur upon the skin of the face or other parts of the body, and swellings upon or about the neck of an indolent character often appear. The scrofulous child often presents a haggard, almost wild appearance, and its blue veins are painfully prominent. Sometimes the head becomes abnormally developed, accompanied occasionally by a precocity of intellect, which may be accounted for by the larger amount of nutrition diverted to the head, in consequence of impediments in the peripheral circulation, while the extremities are at the same time illy nourished. Not unfrequently serous effusion and death by dropsy are the final results of this unnatural flow of blood and nervous influence to the head.

In youth, the most striking symptoms of the affection are enlarged glands of the neck, fragility of form, narrowness of the chest, and a strong tendency to cough and lung disease, which not unfrequently terminate in pulmonary consumption.

In adults, the morbid action is apt to center in the lungs, in disease which, as commonly treated, is generally incurable.

The intelligent reader hardly needs to be told that in this malady there is a period anterior to that of its outward manifestation, when it exists in an unrecognized and latent form, and is associated immediately with its producing causes, when vicious physiological action is clearly seen to depend upon vicious atomic relations; a period, in short, when sufficient knowledge and a correct practice would furnish an effectual bar to its further progress. But as such knowledge is only acquired under the spur of feelings resulting from the presence of the disease in its developed state, we must be content to bring into requisition as *curative*, means that ought to have proved *preventive*.

It is evident that in this disease the results of the vital processes are incompletely attained. The mesenteric glands and lymphatic vessels become clogged with the materials of an imperfect nutrition, while the skin and lungs execute their functions in an unsatisfactory manner. The result is, either that the nutritive elements become imperfectly vitalized, or else that the matters destined to be cast out as waste from the system, fail to become converted into the usual soluble forms of carbonic acid, water, and urea, the legitimate products of these important processes. Hence occur the excess of albuminous material, and the imperfect and irregular cells that characterize the scrofulous deposits of the lungs, glandular system, etc. Disease being essentially incomplete or ineffectual action (pathology being simply a modified physiology), it can occur only through defect of the conditions essential to the perfect development of the system in all its parts and functions. The *nature* of the mischievous agents that concur in the production of these conditions is learned only by a study of the disease during its development and subsequent progress.

In this way we discover among the prominent causes of this disease, *insufficiency of pure air, light, and exercise, and want of cleanliness.*

We have only to look into the abodes of poverty and squalor for confirmation of this statement. Every city physician has abundant opportunities for studying all forms of this disease in connection with these causes.

But the wealthy, and those who have it in their power to command the conditions of health, are quite as apt to be afflicted with scrofula in one or other of its forms, and in their case it is evidently the result of the same causes that produce it among the poor. For the real hygienic condition of those whose circumstances and social position are so different, are often very much alike. For while the one class is deprived of fresh air and sunlight by being confined in low and crowded localities, the other suffers an equal deprivation through the agency of shutters, heavy window-drapery, and interior rooms, aggravated by the choking dust and corrupt air, which are the inevitable concomitants of fashionable upholstery and carpeting. In both cases, respiration is rendered ineffectual, through lack of healthful motion and purity of the air, and these effects are aggravated by want of exercise and good habits on the part of the persons thus exposed.

We must call the reader's attention to the fact, that it is not the uncleanness which is *external* to the body that exercises the most deleterious influence upon the health. It is not till matters foreign to the purposes of the body become constituents of its substance, that they can interfere to any great extent with the vital operations. The liability of being poisoned through the lungs is evidently immeasurably greater than of being poisoned through the skin, for volatile and soluble poisons are brought in contact with the blood through the one avenue, while through the other there can penetrate only insoluble and solid matters. Indeed, no amount and thoroughness of washing and bathing are effectual if other habits are such as to preclude a free access of air to the skin and lungs. There are no hygienic or medical procedures which can possibly compensate, or begin to compensate, for this want. Thorough cleanliness preserves the blood as well as the external cuticular covering uncontaminated. The illy clad children of the street, though they may suffer untold deprivations, and be subjected to the most unwholesome dietetic regimen, yet for the most part enjoy good health; because, though unwashed, they are essentially purified within through the wholesome effect of the air to which they are through so many hours of the day exposed; while the occupants of the dark and dusty chamber (a luxurious one, it may be) are sickly and scrofulous from the contrary condition of things. Even the dumb animal, caged and treated after a similar cruel fashion, suffers from scrofula and consumption, and manifests symptoms throughout the progress of the disease similar to those under which his fellow human sufferer languishes.

The interesting question in regard to the origin of scrofula is frequently broached. There is no doubt but that hereditary influences may properly be recognized as among the most important conditions determining this form of disease. For the original form of the body is undoubtedly inherited, and the narrow chest of the scrofulous child not less than the color of his eyes or contour of his face. But the practice of the Movement-Cure instructs us that the shape and size of the members and regions of the body may be wonderfully modified by judicious training, as may the slighter temporary or local effects of physiological lapses be counteracted by appropriate medical means. There is, indeed, much reason to believe that if all the conditions of health were supplied to the greatest extent possible, they would quite neutralize the power, immense as it is, of bad hereditary influences, and restore the faulty constitution, after a generation or two, to its pristine vigor. But we all know how fearfully rapid is the decline of persons of originally defective constitution, when subjected to unfavorable influences. The knowledge of such quicksands in the channel of life should be effectual in inciting persons to make that acquaintance with the physiological chart that shall enable them to avoid the dangers that are ever threatening to wreck them or their posterity after them.

With the indications for the treatment of scrofula that are derived from a careful examination of its causes, it is strange that that such palliatives of symptoms as gross animal oils, alcoholic and narcotic stimulants, iodine, etc., should ever have been proposed as *curatives.* How, we ask, can any agent prove curative while the causes above mentioned continue to operate in full force? What is evidently required is, the securing of a greater degree of energy in all the formative or organic actions of the system. Especially must those agencies which favor the oxydizing processes in the blood and solid tissues be brought into active play, such as *light, exercise*, and wholesome and invigorating food. With these indications fulfilled, there are no others left for the drug to accomplish. Through the assimilation of oil or spirits, the disease may be temporarily masked, and iodine, holding much the same chemical relation to the system as oxygen, only less potent, may do some good, but it must needs be temporary and uncertain.

Movements affect the scrofulous subject more like a specific than any other known means. They give direction and energy to the vitalizing processes throughout the body, cause a renewal of the fluids of the clogged glandular system, and so relieve glandular congestion, and are the most direct and powerful means for supplying oxygen to the impoverished blood. In this way the non-vitalized and imperfectly vitalized matters of the blood, and of the body generally, are reduced, and the system relieved from them; the chest is enlarged, and the power of the system to *continue* its multiform operations in a healthful manner, maintained and augmented.

The scrofulous subject needs to press into his service every available hygienic resource. He can not effectually combat the advancing disease simply by attending to one or two particulars of remedial hygiene. By so doing he will be as apt to encourage the approaches of the malady as to oppose them. He should particularly heed such suggestions as we have advanced under the head of Hygiene, regarding abstinence from all drugs, condiments, heating beverages, stimulants, etc., and should adhere to a simple nutritious diet, selecting such food as possesses the particular elements he needs. He must not compel his digestive apparatus to reduce needless matters to the necessary forms in which they may find their exit from the body; for all such matters require the oxygen that might and ought to be employed in eliminating the disease.

The strength, in these cases, is generally already impaired, and the patient, consequently, should avoid such exercises as tend to exhaust the physical powers. *Riding* and *driving* are particularly beneficial to him, because, while so engaged, he is not only in contact with the best air constantly renewed, but the shaking that he thus gets is particularly useful in assisting the clogged and sluggish circulation, both of the glandular system and of the general capillaries. Long journeys, if the circumstances of the patient permit of such indulgence, are highly useful, because thereby the above-mentioned advantages are not only secured, but they are *continued* for a length of time. Besides, the invalid is thus carried beyond the sphere of the particular influences that at first planted and afterward served to foster his disease. We can not be too explicit or emphatic upon this point.

It has been noticed that in this disease, as in consumption, want of compass in the breathing organs is a prominent impediment to recovery, though it is probable that defective action of these organs is the more common one. The deficiency in dimensions may be either congenital or acquired. In either case it is susceptible of remedy, and it should be one of the first objects of our attention in entering upon the treatment of such a case, whether the subject be either child, youth, or adult. The circumference of the chest and waist may be astonishingly increased by proper disciplinary measures, and the several cubic inches of increased capacity that is thus afforded to the lungs of course increases the respiratory ability in a commensurate degree. The change in the health for the better, after entering upon such a course, immediately becomes manifest. The food is thereby not only reduced to fluidity, and enabled to pass the digestive surfaces into the blood, but becomes transformed into the healthy vital element of the body, instead of those low organic forms which afford an obstruction, instead of an assistance to the healthy growth of the system. A higher vital tone and energy is thus secured, and good health is the natural and necessary consequence.

The duplicated movements are demanded if the case be a formidable one, and these should be continued for several weeks, or until evidences of improvement become apparent. At a later day, or even to begin with, if the illness be not severe, the single movements may be employed with profit.

The movements prescribed for a scrofulous patient should be similar to those recommended for pulmonary affections, but they may from the first be used somewhat more energetically. All portions of the body should be included in the movements taken, so that all the organs and functions of the system may share the effect. But the *special* indication, or indications, of the case should not be slighted. If there be a tendency of blood to the head or weakness of eyes, the prescription should begin with movements for the lower extremities, afterward for the arms and chest. If there be constipation, movements adapted to *this* particular complaint should be included. If there be no special indications, it should begin with movements for the chest.

The following formula will serve as an example:
1. Wing sitting, feet rotation. 7.
2. Stride sitting, arms twisting. 65.

3. Swing holding, rotating. 75.
4. Stride-kneeling, swaying. 39.
5. Doorway-stretch, span-standing, walking. 58.
6. Stretch-kneeling, trunk rocking. 45.
7. Heel-support kneeling, trunk forward falling. 12.
8. Support half-standing, leg rotating. 23.
9. Half-stretch, half-wing stride-sitting, trunk-twisting. Change. 37.
10. Backward-stretch lying, weight holding. 68.

Chapter Sixteen.

PULMONARY AFFECTIONS—CONSUMPTION.

The principles of the Movement-Cure cast new and important light upon the nature of most of the grave affections belonging to this class. By simplifying the pathology of these diseases the patient can be brought to understand, as well as the physician, if he will read with care, the suggestions that are made, and the value of the practice here taught will be demonstrated at every step. We give the outlines of a treatment appropriate, direct, and efficacious—a treatment satisfactory to both patient and physician. The practice of movements affords new indications to the practitioner, as well as furnishes new means for fulfilling such as are recognized by the schools.

Viewed in the light (or darkness) afforded by ordinary medical science, the diseases that we are now considering are involved in much mystery. Those thus afflicted, as is well known, almost infallibly continue to decline, in spite of the most vigorous application of all the means known to and recommended by the highest medical authorities of the land. Persons possessed of what is termed the " consumptive habit," are regarded as *fated*, even before the disease makes its appearance in any decided manner. This fact indicates the extent of our knowledge of the pathology of these cases, and it takes no argument to show that the conditions from which originate the disease in question, are miserably misunderstood.

A too common reference of the disease to remote and intangible causes disposes of the case and precludes further investigation. Thus, people are in the habit of saying, and with a learned look sometimes, that such subjects have *originally defective constitutions*, are exposed to a poisoned atmosphere, inhabit unfavorable localities, are unfortunately endowed with too great intellectual activity, etc., without explaining how it is that the constitutions of some persons and not of others are affected by these circumstances. Physicians, taking advantage of popular ignorance and misconceptions, content themselves with pleasing their patients by the exhibition of all sorts of injurious palliatives, and resort to devices that at the best but do the sufferers some temporary good. The short-sighted and hopeful invalid is satisfied to be made to *feel better* for the time, and often mistakes the transient relief for returning health. The plan of treatment commonly pursued is effectual for vailing the real nature and relations of these affections from the minds of both physician and patient. No wonder that such small progress is made in the pathology and treatment of these diseases, or that nostrums and quacks, and their victims, should so abound in the community! The poor invalid, to be sure, is troubled at times with many sad doubts in regard to the efficacy of these *cure-alls*, and he goes, tossed by his doubts, from one nostrum to another, and sometimes will swallow a dozen at once, supposing that in so doing he is increasing the chances of hitting upon the right thing at last. By such wholesale dosing the poor victim is rapidly and surely getting rid of whatever restorative capacity the ravages of disease may have left him. And so it generally happens, that between popular and professional ignorance, and the empiricism that is the result of both, persons threatened with diseases of the lungs seldom escape a fatal termination.

We ought not to expect curative effects which are real and permanent in diseases of this class, unless we direct our treatment point blank at the radical causes. It will avail us little to attend exclusively to the symptoms as they appear, looking for nothing beyond these. We must trace out the circumstances, and physical, mental, and social conditions in which the disease has its origin, and settle ourselves in the conviction, that no medical means whatsoever, that fall short of removing these, can be of any positive and permanent service. Then, and not till then, we shall be prepared to combat with remedies of unquestionable applicability and potency those incipient forms of the disease which, when the subject is only under the influence of palliatives, must inevitably pursue a regular and destructive course of growth.

My observations in pulmonary affections—and they have been extensive—have brought me to the conclusion, that *the tendency to pulmonary affections is always in inverse ratio to the amount of respiratory power*. My belief in this doctrine, which is now daily gaining converts, is amply confirmed by evidence both of a physiological and pathological character. There is no dispute in regard to the nature and relations of the morphological products of the disease, nor as to its general diagnostic features, and what may seem to be exceptions to the above rule, are found upon further investigation rather to confirm it than otherwise.

1. One of the first signs confirmatory of this view

of the disease is the greatly *diminished size of tne chest*, noticeable in those in whom chronic pulmonary disease has resulted fatally. I have been at the pains to make careful examination of the skeletons of a number of persons known to have died of consumption, and found the circumference of the chest to be from three to five inches less than that in persons of the same height, who died of other diseases. In the frequent measurements made by me in the treatment by movements, I have found the same fact to exist invariably; the consumptive is always either narrow-chested or else deformed, one side (that diseased) being shrunken. This condition of things is so patent to all observers, that a resort to measurements to prove it has seemed superfluous.

2. Another invariable condition attendant upon this disease is *diminished mobility of the walls of the chest*. The chest seems, sometimes, to heave with considerable force, but a closer observation shows that the motion is confined to a limited portion of its walls, while the average extent of motion is less, generally very much less, than normal. The change is always apparent in the relative extent of the inspiratory and expiratory movements, but the observer is apt to be deceived in regard to the total amount of mobility of the breathing organs. The efficiency of the respiratory act is far from being in exact proportion to the amount of effort made to effect this act. The necessity for effort proves the presence of an impediment to the performance of the act, as well as the fact that the amount of respiration is less than the system requires.

3. The *increased frequency of the pulse* is an evidence of the diminished efficiency of the respiratory apparatus. The action of the circulatory organ is not under the

direct control of the will, and it is a law of the economy that the circulation, or at least the activity, of the arterial system increases with the increased need of the system for oxygen; as, for instance, in a healthy person during strong exertion either of the muscles or of the brain. The principle holds as well in disease, which in fact is, as we have said, but metamorphosed physiological action. When the respiration has for a time been imperfect, as under the influence of an elevated temperature, or through the ingestion of too great a quantity of food, the pulse of respiration afterward rapidly quickens, so as to bring the blood more speedily and thoroughly in contact with oxygen. This is one of the conditions in *acute disease*. Similar effects are brought about by drugs. So also when, by disease of the lungs, the respiratory capacity is materially diminished, or when, through a want of due development of the muscles engaged in the respiratory act, the amount of air breathed is too small, the pulse necessarily becomes quicker, in order to insure the contact of the blood and air along the diminished respiratory surface.

4. The pulse becomes slower, and a sense of relief and rest is always experienced, by any accident or device that facilitates the aeration of the blood. This object is often secured by a removal of the invalid to a locality where there is exposure of the person to winds, as for instance, to the Western prairies, to southern climes, to islands of the sea. An ocean voyage is often of great benefit. If an invalid suffering from *hectic* rides on a fair day in a carriage, his pulse becomes appreciably slower. If a consumptive be exposed to an increase of atmospheric pressure of six or eight pounds to the square inch, the pulse is also retarded, because this

pressure facilitates the changes effected in respiration. Herein lies the efficacy of what is termed the *compressed air bath*. Thus the most distressing symptoms, in the several forms of pulmonary disease, are shown to arise from insufficient respiration.

5. Another and hardly less conclusive evidence of the truth of the doctrine here laid down is found in the means required to overcome this disease. If movements are made to serve the purpose of increasing the aerating power of the lungs, the pulses are found soon to decrease in frequency, the strength begins to return, and all the more distressing symptoms gradually abate, and in a degree proportionate to the amount of energy imparted to the respiratory efforts. Even during a single trial of a prescription of duplicated movements, the pulse will often fall ten or more beats per minute. If they are followed up, the capacity of the chest soon begins to augment, and along with this increase of breathing power various cheering signs appear.

The amount of air respired in a chest collapsed by disease or disuse, compared with the amount respired after being expanded and strengthened by training it, would be very difficult to compute, even approximately. This increase of efficiency is the effect of two causes acting conjointly; one of these is the increased amount of residual air contained by the lungs; the other, the increased amount of motion secured to the walls of the chest and the diaphragm. If we suppose that by this gain in their mobility the lungs are enabled to admit only a single inch more of air at each respiration, in the course of the day, the increase would amount to fifteen cubic feet! Even this trifling amount of increase in respiratory power, the reader can readily conceive, would be capable of effecting a great change in the quality of the blood and the general nutrition of the system. But when this is multiplied by several cubic inches—a result often attained—the good accomplished is great indeed.*

The habits of life of the consumptive invalid are such as constantly to repress the development of the lungs, or a defect here may be due to original conformation. The diminished capacity of the chest of course implies imperfect respiration. A direct consequence of this insufficient respiration is increase of the frequency of the pulse. The maintenance of this accelerated speed of the pulse occasions a *wear* of and perpetually increasing demand upon the powers of the organism incompatible with that quiet play of the functions, which is health. Had we no facts to prove it,

---

* The following remarks of Lehmann are strongly confirmatory of the view here given:

"While the advances of the science of medicine have taught us that of all the vast accumulation of remedies which in the course of time have been collected together, very few are of any value at the bedside, and while the enlightened practitioner is disposed to attach at least as much importance to a rational dietetic as to a specifically therapeutic mode of treatment, the value of investigations on normal respiration, in reference to the science of medicine, can never be overrated; for when once the fact is universally admitted that the first thing to be considered in many diseases is to furnish a copious supply of oxygen to the blood which has been loaded with imperfectly decomposed substances, and to remove as speedily as possible the carbonic acid which has accumulated in it, these observations will have afforded us the true remedial agents which exceed almost any other in the certainty of their action. We may, perhaps, aid a tuberculous patient quite as much by recommending him to respire a moist warm air, as if we prescribed *Lichen Carragheen*, or *Ol. jecoris Aselli*.

"Instead of tormenting an emphysematous patient, suffering from congestion and hemorrhoidal tendencies, with aperient and saline mineral waters, we might relieve him far more effectually by recommending him to practice artificial augmentation or expansion of the chest in respiration (filling the lungs several times in the course of an hour), *or to take exercise suited to produce this result*, while *we should forbid the use of spirituous drinks*, and *not prescribe tinctures which might hinder the necessary excretion of carbonic acid*. We abstain, however, from offering any further illustrations of these assertions, since the reflecting physician will not blindly follow any guide, while the mere empiricist can never learn thoroughly to heal any disease, whatever his knowledge of physiology and pathological chemistry."—*Physiological Chemistry*, vol. ii., p. 471.

we should suppose from analogy that congestion of the pulmonary tissues would be likely to occur from the excessive labor imposed upon this organ, and a deterioration of the morphological elements of the blood, and a consequent deposition in the form of tubercle need not be an unlooked-for consequence.

When the respiration is below the requirements of the system, either one of two things may occur: either the blood, not being purified, and the secretions becoming clogged and changed in quality, colds, or the more grave and decided forms of fever, follow, with a quickening of the pulse and of the respiratory movements, and failure of the appetite; or the oxydizing action being less energetic, the materials accumulated in the blood may be able to resist it. Tubercle seems to be a degraded form of vitalized matter which continues to resist the oxydizing agencies at work within the blood. The quick pulse and breath are never able to balance each other perfectly. If, now, in this condition of things, an increase of respiration can take place, unaccompanied by the evils resulting from quick breathing and the rapid pulse, the chances of restoration are at once immensely increased.

The *available* power a person enjoys does not equal the absolute product of vital action; it is only that part of the total force of the system which remains after the amount is expended which is needed for organic purposes. It is clear that when the rate of the pulse is one hundred and twenty, and the respirations thirty-two per minute, the expenditure of force is much greater than when the pulse is sixty and the respiration sixteen.

It follows, from this theory of the pathology of pulmonary disease, that the chief remedial indication is, to increase the size of the chest and the mobility of its walls.

The arrangements of nature are designed to secure the perfect performance of the respiratory act, and consist of means which affect the size and mobility of the chest.

1. *Temperature.*—The lower the temperature to which the body is exposed, the greater the impression made by it upon the whole sensory surface. This impression is a direct stimulant to respiration. Whether the impression affects the whole, or only a limited portion of the surface, the result is the same; for a given amount of heat expended, an equivalent amount of air is respired. The average temperature of the atmosphere is forty to fifty degrees below that of the body.

2. *Exercise.*—This, in the plan of nature, is rendered as necessary as temperature. All movements, whether spontaneous and involuntary or voluntary, necessitate the use of oxygen derived from the blood by the acting vital organs. Hence the degree of perfection reached by the respiratory act is strictly proportionate to the vigor of the muscular action; and we find that such action powerfully promotes respiration, and improves the mobility of the walls of the chest.

Properly directed exercise may prove advantageous to the respiration in two ways: 1. By directly increasing this action. 2. Indirectly, by developing and perfecting the mechanism by which this act is performed.

Chronic pulmonary diseases are of two principal forms: congestion and ulceration of the pulmonary nervous surface—the surface in contact with the air; and a deposit of non-vitalized organic matter in the parenchyma of these organs. Both forms are referable to the imperfect aeration of the blood at the point where this fluid accumulates, waiting for its noxious matters to become eliminated by the means above pointed out, and both forms disappear generally upon the restoration of the natural movements of the walls of the chest.

The reader must be warned against rushing upon the inference here, that indiscriminate movements may be employed in this disease. Nothing, in fact, is likely to prove more harmful, in diseases of the lungs, than improper use of exercises, while, if they are practiced in accordance with the principles and under the conditions prescribed by the Movement-Cure, injurious effects are scarcely possible. To enable us to guard against these harmful results, let us analyze the respiratory process.

Respiration is composed of two distinct actions—in the filling of the lungs with air, or *inspiration*, and the exclusion of a portion of the air contained by these organs, or *expiration*.

Inspiration is effected by the contraction and consequent depression of the diaphragm, and the simultaneous contraction of the muscles lying between and covering the ribs, which elevates them and turns them outward. *Expiration* is produced simply by the relaxation of these same muscles, allowing the walls of the chest to return to the position they occupied at the commencement of inspiration, thus narrowing the space included in the chest, and driving out the air.

These actions are properly enough compared to those of a *pump;* but the venous blood is exposed to similar conditions with those securing the rush of air into the lungs, and it of course acquires the same tendency toward the chest, so as to meet the air which it is intended to receive.

It follows that if the respiratory act be forced beyond a certain moderate extent, while other portions of the body are at comparative rest, this tendency of blood to the chest will be beyond the power of the heart to control, and the pulmonary organs become congested. As a consequence, various disagreeable sensations are experienced about the chest, and these may be followed by serious indisposition; inflammation may set in, or rupture of vessels may occur. Especially if the pulmonary organs be weak or previously diseased, the effect of such movements thus taken may be disastrous and irreparable. Such consequences have sometimes followed the use of the inhaling-tube, so often recommended to invalids of this class.

The indications for the treatment of pulmonary affections plainly are, *first*, to remove the congestion that always lingers about the chest in these complaints, and certainly to guard against the possibility of its occurrence. This is easily accomplished by the aid of the duplicated movements, and also, if the patient retain a moderate amount of strength, by the single movements. The prescription, to begin with, must include in its first part such movements as are strongly derivative applied to the extremities, while the central organs should be approached cautiously. Only after a marked effect has been produced upon the extremities should we employ such movements as tend to expand the chest, because these draw the blood from the extremities. A physician of tact will so manage as to combine these effects of derivation and expansion from the first, thus greatly facilitating the progress of the patient. After the derivative prescription has been continued for some time, with an improvement of all the symptoms, those which increase the size of the chest may be applied more boldly, never omitting, however, to alternate them frequently with those of the first-named kind.

It is always best for the patient, if treating himself, to commence proceedings by taking accurate measurement of his chest, both at its upper section and at its lower, or across the short ribs. By repeating the measurement occasionally from time to time, he will be able to judge of the amount of improvement he is making, and thus encourage himself more than he possibly could by merely noticing the improvement in his feelings, because he is impressed with the idea of the permanent character of this result. In using the duplicated movements, some invalids have experienced an increase in the circumference of the chest of an inch or more for each of three or four consecutive weeks. But even when much less than this is gained, nearly all patients will attain results that will be quite satisfactory and cheering, especially if compared with the results effected by other kinds of medical treatment.

The reader must not suppose that all the good accomplished in this way for the lungs is indicated by the dilatation of the chest. The contracted and diseased lungs are incited by the stimulus of the movements to take on a more efficient action; the vitalizing air is made to penetrate and dilate the collapsed air-cells, or to displace the secretions with which they are filled. The improvement from this cause, even before the circumference of the chest has perceptibly increased, is in many cases very decided. Many respectable physicians, who have examined my patients while under treatment, have testified to this fact very emphatically, as this is the improvement that is easily detected by the skillful auscultator.

For the consumptive patient a formula of movements like the following may be employed.

EXAMPLES OF PRESCRIPTIONS.

1. Stretch (weight held), backward lying, holding. 68.
2. Wing-walk standing, forward-knee bending and stretching. Change. 14.
3. Door-way standing, walking. 58.
4. Arms angle (weight held), reclined walk-kneeling, arms stretching. 43.
5. Sitting, arms sidewise raising. 47.
6. Stretch-stride kneeling, trunk transverse swaying. 45.
7. Stretch grasp, forward fall standing, trunk bending and stretching. 76.
8. Half-stretch stride sitting, trunk twisting. Change. 37.
9. Yard-stride sitting, arms twisting. 39.
10. Trunk support half standing, leg twisting. 13.

The movements should be varied to meet the exigencies of each particular case. If there be great feebleness, a formula like the following would be more appropriate to begin with:

1. Wing long sitting, feet rotation. 5.
2. Rack grasp standing, feet stretching. 1.
3. Standing, arm perpendicular, rotating. 73.
4. Yard kneeling, arms horizontal, swaying. 39.
5. Stretch half-walk, half-kneeling, trunk backward bending. 48.
6. Step half-standing, trunk sidewise bending. 49.

7. Support half-standing, curtseying. 10.
8. Elbow-support, backward fall standing, holding. 77.
9. Hanging, swinging. 74.
10. Hang standing, trunk rotating.

It is useful for the invalid thus practicing to apply at the same time rapid and light friction over the whole surface of the body, with free exposure of the naked person to the air, as often as twice every day, and to lave the chest thoroughly with a coarse towel wetted with cold water. He should also bathe the whole person in water as cool as he can well bear, say 80° or 90°, and he may likewise take a hip bath at 75°, for ten minutes, to excite the respiration; both these daily if the strength will allow.

In addition to the above the *swing* may be used for five or ten minutes several times every day.

Chapter Seventeen.

PARALYSIS OF THE NERVES OF MOTION.

The Movement-Cure supplies new hope to the victims of this peculiarly obstinate affection. It does not merely add another to the catalogue of "promising" remedies, but the patient who tries it is often at once convinced of its appropriateness to his condition, he is inspired with a new confidence. Hundreds who had become disheartened by witnessing the futility of ordinary medical treatment have had their courage thus renewed as if by magic. We *reject* such remedies as strychnine, stimulants, galvanism, electricity, for although the application of this class of remedies may afford encouragement by their temporary effects, and may seem occasionally to do a great deal of good, yet experience proves that by such practice the recuperative powers are in the end exhausted, and the case becomes less amenable to treatment than it otherwise would be.

The treatment of paralysis by duplicated movements, by myself and by others under my observation, has resulted favorably in a large majority of instances; many have had members that had become useless and burdensome, partially, some entirely restored to their original integrity and usefulness, while many others have left my hands in the confident hope that their own efforts persistently followed up would finally result in complete restoration. So far as I have learned, these patients have continued to improve to a satisfactory extent. One of the most encouraging cases on my list is that of a gentleman who came to me with complete paraplegia of over two years' standing, who after three weeks' instruction returned home, and applied the knowledge he had acquired to such purpose, that in a short time he was restored to health and the pursuit of his professional avocations. We may understand the peculiar appropriateness and success of the treatment if we will take the pains to examine the pathology of the disease.

Modern physiology explains the *cause* of paralysis to be some defect in the health of *nerve-centers* located in the spinal cord and at the base of the brain, from which the incentive to muscular action proceeds. These centers consist of the gray substance of the cord, and they hold communication by means of countless radiating *nerve fibers* with all the muscular tissue of the body.

The *actual* pathological *state* of these nerve-centers in paralysis is often a matter somewhat obscure. Sometimes it is found upon examination that the walls of the capillary vessels supplying the part with nutrition have been ruptured, and effusion of a clot, pressure, and a sudden shock, depriving the parts or muscles connected therewith by means of the nerve fibers, of power, is the consequence. The extent of the paralysis will in this case depend on the location, as those portions of the body connected with the cord *below* the seat of disease suffer from its effects.

Another cause may be serous effusion into the membrane inclosing the cord, which may by its pressure gradually produce similar symptoms. Sometimes, again, a disease of the substance of the cord occurs called softening, which destroys the function of the cord and of the parts connected with it. The reader will understand from this that the *muscles* are not primarily affected, but their action becoming suspended, they are deprived of nutrition, and consequently become weak and flabby, and are often greatly diminished in bulk. Neither are the nerve filaments which *conduct* the nerve influence from its central seat necessarily implicated. They cease to conduct impressions, simply because they receive none in the disabled state of the central organ.

The reader may now be ready to inquire, with a skeptical smile, "How can exercise of the muscles, which are not the seat of the disease, restore functional power to the disabled nerve?"

The following considerations will serve to throw some light upon what may perhaps appear a rather dark subject.

1. The spinal column is inclosed in the bony case formed by the vertebral column, in which, the more effectually to protect it from injury from external sources, it is suspended, and surrounded through its entire length by fluid. By this arrangement, injury to the cord from any sudden twist or shock is prevented.

But this is not all. Along the exterior surface of the column is situated the largest and strongest muscular mass belonging to the body, which is employed in sustaining and giving flexibility and mobility to the trunk. Every action of these muscles necessarily affects the circulation of the contained and contiguous vessels, and modifies also the condition of the organs contained *within* the vertebral canal. Now the lateral, forward, backward, and diagonal inclinations of the body in the duplicated and the single movements are eminently *derivative* for the cord itself, and serve as a powerful means for relieving congestion of the spinal membranes and nerves, or even for removing serous effusion.

2. But, in perhaps a majority of cases, the spinal lesion has been recovered from spontaneously, as the result of the *patient waiting* which is enforced by the very nature of the affection; still, the power of motion is not as a consequence restored. Whether nature has, after a time, effected so favorable a change in the case, we can have no means of directly knowing; we must be content to wait for the results of treatment to enlighten us on this point. Whether it has or has not, the paralysis generally continues, because the conductor, having once ceased to perform its duty, continues inoperative even after the original source of nerve-power is restored by time. It is evident that the muscles will remain inactive so long as the nerves refuse to convey motive force to them. It is inferred that this state of things may often exist for the simple reason that very frequently paralysis is speedily removed by movements, while this could not possibly happen if the cord itself, the source of all muscular power, remained diseased. The cure does not, in this case, consist so much in the removal of disease as in the restoration of a function. This only is wanted: *the power to move;* the germ of the power still exists; this is to be encouraged and cultivated. The disabled muscles must *be moved,* and *be helped to move themselves,* till they have regained the ability to work unassisted. So are children's muscles trained at the outset of life. What more natural, simple, and philosophic!

Thus, again, the will is enabled to send its mandates like lightning from the brain to every portion of the physical domain, and at once healthful and harmonious action is restored to the whole economy.

The duplicated movements affect the diseased nerves often in a most favorable manner. They may be applied along the course of the conductor or over the spinal centers.

The Movement-Cure overcomes this formidable disease by removing any pressure that may exist at the nerve-centers, by restoring the flow of nervous force to its original channels, while the general expenditure of nerve-power is at the same time carefully husbanded; by tranquilizing the whole system, and especially the diseased organs; and by re-establishing the conditions for healthy nutrition throughout the body. The Movement-Cure deprecates the employment of all means whatsoever designed merely to *stimulate* the nerves to functional activity, whether applied to the general system or to diseased parts. It would evoke no manifestation when there is not behind an abundant capacity to sustain it, supplied through the nutrient energies of the organism, the grand primary source of all functional power. It discards all beverages, excepting simple, unadulterated water; the use of tobacco, which observation proves to be frequently the cause of the disease; the use of condiments of all kinds, which only task, never replenish, the nerve-power. For the same reason, it enjoins abstinence from all exciting business, and everything calculated to arouse the emotions or awake anxious or laborious thought; for these things tend certainly to debilitate the nervous system, and must necessarily aggravate disease where it exists, and counteract, in a greater or less degree, the beneficial effects of the movements.

It is a question that deserves serious consideration, whether the prevalence of this form of disease is not referable, to a much greater extent than the public seem to be aware, to the habits of the individual. *Excessive venery*, every practicing physician knows to be a fruitful source of this disease. The reflecting mind, indeed, may well ponder how it is that so many escape with only milder and comparatively tractable forms of nervous disease, when it considers the self-indulgent habits of so many in the community.

In the treatment of these cases the duplicated movements are nearly indispensable in the beginning. It is absolutely necessary that the patient understand the various principles and methods of the *cure*, in order that as he advances in strength and in self-command he may be able to take the treatment into his own hands and conduct it to the desired consummation.

The prescription must embrace *bendings*, *fallings*, etc., in such positions as call the muscles of the back, and especially of the neck, into active play. It should also include attempts at the restoration of power in the defective members. It is found that the *liver* is nearly always affected in cases of this disease, perhaps often as a consequence of it, induced by mere inaction. It should be roused into activity by regulating and restricting the diet, together with the appropriate movements; many of the duplicated movements of the passive kind are important here, for the toning up not only of defective nerves, but also of those organs whose actions are limited through lack of nervous supply, as well as to sooth and tranquilize the nerves themselves. Such movements are to be applied very cautiously in the vicinity of nerve-centers, more freely along the conductors.

It is important to direct the attention, and with it the nerve-force, into the affected part, by means of attempts to *move* the debilitated or disabled part. These attempts must be *successful* in order to be *beneficial*, and the lacking power must be supplied by an assistant. Unless the patient *sees* a result accomplished by his own endeavors, he will be disheartened and give over his efforts. If a paralytic can not, for instance, raise his hand, he must at least *try*. The effort will of course be fruitless till the power to raise the last ounce of the weight is developed, *and the invalid does not know that he exerts any power until he has exerted enough to accomplish his purpose*. But if *assisted*, he can be made to feel that he overcomes a part of the resistance, and is thence encouraged to continue and multiply his efforts.

The paralytic invalid must be cautioned against making violent efforts, or attempting quick movements; all his motions should be deliberate and gentle. The time of the movement should not only be prolonged, but the part moved should be *sustained* during a period of rest at the terminal position. In this way the object of the movement, which consists in establishing and improving the communication between the nerve-centers and muscles, is secured as far as is possible. It is only further necessary to *repeat* the same movement at the same time, in the same way, daily, and an increased, if not a perfect control of the weakened part is quite certain to result. But if, on the contrary, the movements be taken at irregular times, or practiced rapidly, violently, or carelessly, the fund of power will be exhausted rather than increased, and injury will result rather than benefit to the experimenter.

These remarks apply to duplicate as well as to single movements. It is only necessary to add that the application of single movements is limited, but being employed according to the invalid's ability in the mode and with the cautions above indicated to the afflicted extremity, the result will amply repay in returning health the attention thus devoted.

Chapter Eighteen.

CONSTIPATION, DIARRHEA, AND PILES.

Among business, professional, and studious men, and those engaged in sedentary avocations, no condition is more common than that of constipation of the bowels, and none more disregarded. With these classes of persons constipation is the first notice given of the commencement of a state of chronic ill health that often proves permanent, rendering them miserable perhaps for life. The approach of this affection is insidious, and it may exist even when the subject of it is not aware of the fact, for though his evacuations may be regular, yet the residual matter occupies a much longer time in its passage through the canal than is compatible with health.

This symptom is often accompanied by disorder of the stomach, and it is also frequently connected with nervous irritability, prostration, hypochondria, etc. It is apt to accompany the first stages of pulmonary disease, and indeed nearly all persons afflicted with chronic disorders are troubled with costiveness.

Prominent among the causes of this condition are, *sedentary habits, anxiety of mind and severe thinking, a prolonged use of improper food, and the indulgence in aperients and other drugs.* Constipation may be connected with other symptoms which constitute the main disease, but generally it is the fruit of one, or of a combination of the causes above-mentioned. Persons of active habits who do not unduly burden themselves with the cares and anxieties of this mortal life, are not apt to be afflicted in this manner.

We may easily understand how the above-mentioned causes operate to the production of this distressing result. The organs whose function it is to expel the insoluble matter of the canal, need to be acted upon by the superficial muscles of the abdomen, which are brought into play only in vigorous exercise of the limbs and trunk. Of course these organs in the sedentary are denied this mechanical stimulus. *Mental anxiety* diverts the nutritive material from the digestive organs, and employs it in a remote portion of the body, the brain, and thus robs these organs of the nutrition necessary for a proper performance of their duties. *Improper food* poisons, rather than nourishes the body, induces congestion of the alimentary canal by the irritation it sets up, and the effects upon the system of the products of the chemical changes it undergoes in that canal. *Cathartic drugs* are foreign to the vital purposes, wear down the delicate vital susceptibility, and aggravate the disease for which they are applied. The relief they afford is of the most transitory and deceitful kind; their direct and permanent effects are entirely pathological, and their continued use is well known to be eminently subversive of the vital welfare.

Under the combined influence of improper habits and aperient drugs, the invalid is apt to go on from bad to worse, unless arrested in his career by some accident, till seized by acute, violent, and perhaps fatal disease, or till he lapses into a state of nervous disorder most difficult to overcome. Many persons are constant slaves to the *enema*, the only substitute which they know for the pill or bolus. This is perhaps a more harmless remedy, but it is still but an unsatisfactory palliative at the best. Indeed, we can not well cure the disease which causes the retention of fecal matter, while we confound this symptom with the disease itself.

As might be inferred from what has been said respecting the causes of constipation, it is not usually attributable to a defect of any one part. We must look for these causes at several distinct points, and then we shall be able to remove them by simple means happily at our command. I will enumerate a few of these causes:

1. Weakness of the muscular coat of the alimentary canal exists, in consequence of which its vermicular and expulsive power becomes insufficient.

2. There is generally defective power of the lower section of the spinal cord. The defective power of the expulsive muscles, especially those of the inferior portion of the tube, results partly from want of nervous supply from this source. This is the natural consequence of the nervous fund being too largely drawn upon from other quarters—the brain, the stomach, etc. What is chiefly wanted to overcome this obstacle is, that this draft should cease, and also that appropriate means be used to give employment to the nervous power in the part of the body where it is especially needed. The lower section of the cord should be roused to action chiefly by means of the muscles supplied from this source—sometimes also by more direct operations.

3. There frequently exists congestion of the *mucous membrane* of the alimentary tube, in some portion of its course, which causes a deficiency of the required

secretions. This state of the mucous membranes calls for the exercise and development of the abdominal coverings, for the purpose of drawing off the blood from the congested into the acting parts, and thus relieving that state. Motion applied to the membrane, or, rather, to the organs of which the membrane is a part, is also indicated for the purpose of assisting the capillary action in the membrane.

4. The abdominal muscles, whose function it is to assist the expulsive efforts, are, in constipation, flabby, doughy, and weak. They fail both to maintain the abdominal contents in the proper situation, and to act with sufficient force to aid materially in the contraction of the tube. This state may be readily remedied by such exercises as are adapted to develop these muscles.

5. The liver is generally torpid and congested. Sometimes this state is indicated by tenderness in the region of this organ. This condition manifests imperfect oxydation of the blood, and a consequent retention of matters that ought to have been reduced, through respiration, to a soluble and volatile form, and dismissed from the body. These retained matters are proximate elements of the bile which the liver is incapable of taking up in sufficient quantity. The tissues are wanting in moisture; the refuse materials of the system are not thoroughly reduced, as they should be, to carbonic acid and *water*. To remedy this state, such movements as improve the respiratory action are demanded, together with a curtailment of the amount of food taken. In this way the harmonious co-operation of the digestive and respiratory functions is restored.

6. In this form of disease, coldness of hands and feet also exists. This results from too great a plethora of the

large central blood-vessels. Movements for the extremities to draw the blood toward them, are necessary to effect a wholesome distribution of the circulation.

From this view of the nature of the impediments to be overcome, the reader will see at a glance the entire appropriateness of movements in the treatment of this most common and troublesome affection.

Let us now briefly consider, by way of contrast, the *modus operandi* of an aperient medicine:

1. The drug being mixed with the homogeneous contents of the intestinal tube, and impregnating the whole of the contained mass, unfits it for the purpose for which nutritive matters are designed; the absorbents, therefore, refuse to take up these matters thus contaminated. Hence nutrition is suspended, and there is for the time a general decline of strength.

2. The mass now having become offensive to the organic instinct, is acted upon by the emunctories with great power, which action is the ready and only way of freeing the system from impending harm. By this means the whole intestinal mass, rendered partly fluid by imperfect digestion, is forced rapidly through the entire length of the tube.

3. Some portion of the offensive matter has been already absorbed into the blood, but it is directly returned to the canal as being the appropriate way of egress. This portion is mingled with serum drawn from the blood, so as to dilute the noxious principle, and thus prevent, in a degree, the injury resulting from its immediate contact with vital parts.

4. In the operations just described, but one advantage has been gained, and this is incidental and indirect, and occurs in this way: While the nutrition is

prevented in the manner described from entering the blood, the *respiration continues as usual.* It follows that the effete and noxious matters of the system, which are most prone to become destructive, have been reduced in the ordinary way, that is, in the manner in which these actions happen in health, so that they have rapidly made their exit from the system.

Or, in other words, the effects produced by cathartics are of the same kind, only inferior to those produced by abstinence from food. All the good effects of the process are much more promptly, surely, and easily obtained, without loss of strength, without abuse of the digestive organs, by *abstinence.* In the cathartic process nothing has been accomplished in the way of removing any of the difficulties above-mentioned, and which are *the true cause* of constipation, and by consequence, this difficulty exists in a greater degree *after* the operation of the medicine than before. The prominent system has been relieved, only for the moment, while the disease thus masked has acquired fresh power.

All the indications for the radical cure of constipation are, on the other hand, completely fulfilled by movements. If the case be of great severity, the duplicated movements are called for; but the single movements are competent to subdue the complaint, where there are no perplexing complications, if applied with due accuracy, care, and discretion.

The following formula of movements will be found powerfully remedial in an ordinary case of constipation:

1. Wing-stride back-support standing, curtseying.
2. Wing legs angle standing, trunk vibration.
3. Wing legs angle backward lying, thighs rotation.
4. Wing backward lying, legs rotation.

5. Elbow and foot sidewise lying, hips raising.
6. Stretch kneeling, trunk sidewise swaying.
7. Forward fall, head support standing, leg raising. Change.
8. Backward lying, abdomen deep kneading.
9. Forward bent support standing, chin knocking.
10. Shelter long sitting, trunk forward bending.
11. Wing stride short sitting, leg outward stretching. Change.
12. Shelter backward kick lying, legs separating and closing.

All the above movements affect with more or less directness the abdominal and pelvic contents. There are several others which act more remotely upon the same parts. In making a formula of treatment, some three or four of the above movements may be selected, and these should be connected with such others as are derivative movements for the feet and hands, of a character suited to the strength of the patient.

EXAMPLE 1.

1. Standing, arms swaying.
2. Wing sitting, legs twisting.
3. Half-wing, half-stretch, step standing, trunk twisting. Change.
4. Wing, leg angle, backward lying, thigh rotation.
5. Wing-stride standing, curtseying.
6. Forward bent support standing, chin knocking.

EXAMPLE 2.

1. Arms angle kneeling, arms stretching.
2. Support half standing, leg rotation. Change.
3. Wing kick backward lying, legs separation and closing.

4. Wing backward lying, legs rotation.

5. Leg angle swing standing, trunk perpendicular vibration.

6. Backward lying, abdomen deep kneading.

These movements may be repeated if necessary. As auxiliary to the treatment, the enema of tepid water may be employed from time to time; but its habitual use should be avoided. The tepid hip-bath may also be used occasionally, if found agreeable to the patient. The reader will understand the futility of employing movements to restore the health of the digestive organs, while he is not at the same time careful to control his general habits, so that his general course of living shall contribute to the same end. If he is an habitually careless liver he will scarcely succeed in accomplishing much good for himself, however excellent may be the curative means he may resort to, or however faithfully and judiciously he may apply them, nor ought he to expect it. Nature's laws were never made to be broken. The transgressor need never hope to escape the penalty of his folly. Nature pays no such premium on wrong doing. Every page of the history of every race, community, and individual contains a warning addressed in thunder tones to nature's offending children. "The day thou eatest thereof thou shalt surely die!" It is terrible to think in how many men, this very day, has death begun its retributive work!

DIARRHEA.—Several causes may be concerned in the production of this symptom, and they may act either singly or concurrently. 1. *Debility*—general relaxation of the tissues—is always present, and this condition, as we have seen, is invariably referable to some imperfection of the primary actions that develop vitality. 2. The presence of crude and irritating matters in the alimentary canal, occasioning spasmodic or uncertain action of the muscular coat, while at the same time absorption of the contents is prevented by the morbid state of the membrane, and the alimentary mass is consequently rapidly dismissed. 3. In case of *sudden poisoning of the blood*, either from spontaneous metamorphosis, as in cholera, or the accidental or prescribed use of some injurious drug, the alimentary canal furnishes the most ready outlet whereby such destructive matters may be eliminated. Oftentimes diarrhea is manifestly a curative operation on the part of nature. In these latter cases the symptoms generally amount to something more than is generally understood by the term diarrhea. The flux, in these cases, is generally sufficient to remove the offensive cause, whereupon the health is restored. 4. An ulcerated patch may exist in the canal, and occasion diarrhea. 5. The relaxation of the abdominal parietes and contents, by the consequent pressure upon the perineum and sphincter muscles, may excite action of the lower bowel and occasion urgent desire to go to stool and much straining—a reflex nervous effect of pressure upon the sphincter. In this case there is prolapsus of the bowels, either *concealed* or *apparent*.

In each of the above cases, except where the action is manifestly acute, what is needed is the production of a greater tonicity of the vital structure. The vital organization is depressed and incomplete, and the true remedy must be something that will restore vital power and activity. The fluids of the system must be conveyed from the digestive center outward to the remote parts of the body, and so become applied to normal *use*. The arterial action is low and requires to be energized; there is venous plethora and feeble respiration. The muscular tissue is lax and weak, and all the organizing processes of the body are carried on slowly and unsteadily. All these difficulties are met and overcome by the application of movements.

It is necessary that at first the movements prescribed should be of the passive sort. It is for this reason that those of the duplicated kind are so efficacious. Such exercises as riding, sailing, etc., are eminently serviceable to move the blood in the clogged capillaries, and thus restore their normal power. All vibratory movements applied to the abdomen produce good effects, and the extent of these good effects are found to correspond with the thoroughness and faithfulness with which they are applied. One may vibrate and knead his own abdomen in either or any of the several ways already noticed with much benefit. At the same time, it is very useful to apply movements to the extremities for the purpose of drawing the blood away from the central organs; also to promote the respiratory process in order to restore the purity of this fluid. If the case be one of ulceration of the bowels, long, persistent, and careful constitutional treatment is required. Short, cold sitting-baths ought always to be resorted to frequently to aid the respiration and to encourage the contractile efforts of the bowels.

PILES.—This affection consists often of a distention of the veins at the posterior termination of the mucous lining of the intestine. It is accompanied by a sensitiveness caused by a sluggishness of the abdominal circulation, and generally an engorgement of the liver may be presumed. The condition of the liver is such as to retard the flow of blood in the portal veins, which return the blood to the heart from the digestive tube; hence the lower twigs of the veins that contribute to the portal circulation become distended—an event which is greatly favored by the influence of gravity, which also retards the upward flow of the contents of these vessels. Abdominal plethora is also generally present. Inflammation succeeds distention of the hemorrhoidal veins, and they often become hardened, ulcerated, and disposed to bleed easily. Sometimes a considerable loss of blood occurs from this cause.

Sometimes, also, there is prolapsus of the rectum, which greatly aggravates the disorder on account of the constant straining efforts the patient is impelled to make to evacuate the bowels, which drives the blood down, or, rather, retards its upward flow, and the vessels of the sphincter become strangulated.

The plain indications of treatment are, first, to relieve the liver of congestion, and reduce the abdominal plethora by an abstemious diet. This aids the contraction of the surcharged vessels, and also removes the impediment to the onward flow of the blood. Secondly, to draw the abdominal contents upward to relieve the pressure upon the sphincter. Thirdly, to remove the capillary congestion of the parts.

Surgical aid may sometimes be demanded, undoubtedly, in grave cases of this disease; but after the principles of the Movement-Cure have become well understood, the proper subjects for such treatment will be scarce in the land.

In lieu of the duplicated movement, single movements may be employed for this affection to great advantage. The object sought in their application should be to affect the liver and arouse the abdominal circulation to greater activity. The following movements are recommended for this purpose:

Elbow and toes lying, holding, or hips raising.
The following movement is also useful:
Wing, leg-angle backward lying, hips raising.
Also:
Stretch grasp forward fall-standing, holding.
Stretch (weight held) backward lying, holding.

Chapter Nineteen.

DEFORMITIES OF THE SPINE.

The application of the Movement-Cure to the correction of spinal curvatures is especially successful and satisfactory. Not that the relief obtained in these cases is more certain than in many others, or that the difficulty to be overcome is so much greater, but because we are constantly furnishing to the friends of the patient ocular demonstration of the good effects of the treatment—effects of a kind that admit of no dispute. One clearly marked instance of cure of this kind, in the popular estimation, is more creditable to the skill and resources of the practitioner, and redounds more to his honor, than would any amount of skill and judgment expended upon the more difficult task of preventing the occurrence of these or other maladies, or even in curing many other forms of diseases of less conspicuous character.

In order to arrive at just conclusions regarding the treatment suitable for this class of invalids, it is necessary, first, to inquire into the origin of spinal deformities. This is to be sought in the anatomical character and relations of the column itself and of its supports. The column consists of twenty-four light, spongy bones, resting by their flat surfaces upon each other, with a cushion of elastic cartilage between. This interposition of cartilage is necessary in order to secure the requisite amount of flexibility and elasticity, to enable it to resist the shocks to which it is so often subjected, and to give the trunk that pliability and freedom of motion necessary in assuming the various positions and performing the various actions of man's daily life.

We see at once, from the form and construction of the spinal column, that of itself it could not possibly maintain an erect position, but would, unless supported, be falling into shapes and inclining in directions that might be quite at variance with the will or wishes of the individual. But in the living body this column is entirely under the control of *muscles* which are attached to it at many points, and which give a degree of motion in any direction to every portion of it, and are capable of supporting it in every position. The muscular connections of the spinal column with other parts are extensive and various; the arms and legs are connected with it by muscles, and consequently the character of their motions is related to the positions of the spine, and the movements of these members, as we shall see, are to a considerable extent capable of modifying its form.

The spinal column, in its normal condition, is far from being straight; it has several curves: one, forward at the neck, another at the lumbar region, and one backward, in its dorsal section, and another at the loins. These curves increase the elasticity of the column, and are necessary to the symmetry of the body, and are evidently intended to favor the natural action of the muscles, if they are not produced thereby, as some affirm.

It is manifest from this that a lateral curvature of the spine is not primarily a fault of the column itself, but of certain *muscles* whose function it is to control the movements and general posture of the trunk. If the natural curves of the spine exceed their appointed limit, there will result some deformity of shape; this occurs from weakness of muscles which should maintain the column in a posture more nearly straight. In this case the weight of the body is not well supported, and the supple column yields at the weakest point.

Lateral curvatures are however more positive evidence of muscular weakness, and form a class of cases for which the movements furnish an entirely satisfactory remedy.

Lateral curvatures may be single or double. In the former case the middle portion of the column deviates from the straight line, causing the body to form a more convex line upon one side than upon the other; while in the latter case the shape of the column somewhat resembles the italic *f*, deviating from the straight line one way at the upper portion, and in the opposite direction at its lower portion, the one acting as a sort of counterpart to the other. In far the greater number of cases the superior convexity is to the right, and the inferior, or that of the lumbar region, to the left.

There is also a twisting of the trunk, the side of the projecting shoulder being carried backward so that the transverse plane of the chest and pelvis do not agree. Spinal deformities assume very many different shapes, scarcely two cases being exactly alike; all of these require a competent physician to distinguish and properly prescribe for. The *cause* for the greater frequency of right lateral curvatures is evidently connected with the greater use, and consequently power, of the right arm and the muscles of the right side, which causes the dorsal vertebræ to be drawn with greater frequency and force in that direction.

Another influence, generally unsuspected, is also active in determining curvatures to the right, and this is, the greater habitual use, and consequently greater development, of the *right* than of the *left* leg. There exists in most persons the same disposition to a greater proportional use of the right leg as of the right arm. One puts the right leg forward oftener, and more frequently rests upon it, than the left—a habit that is not a matter of usual observation, but the ill effects of this habit in persons possessing weak muscles, though insidious, are certain. While one is thus resting upon a single leg, the horizontal plane of the pelvis is caused to incline toward the side imperfectly supported; consequently the spinal column, which rises from the plane of the pelvis at right angles, is forced to deviate from the perpendicular and to incline to the same side. But since this direction of the spine would soon carry the center of gravity of the body beyond the base, which would cause it to fall, it necessarily curves in the opposite direction, and goes far enough beyond the perpendicular axis of the body to compensate for the deviation to the left. It will be seen that the effect of this is to increase the amount of the curve in the thoracic region.

The reader will now understand that lateral curvature of the spine is the product of one of two causes. Either the weakness of the muscles is so great as to leave the column unsupported, in which case it yields to the weight of the superior portion of the body, or the greater use and development of one side of the body interferes with the harmonious action of the opposing muscles of the two sides, and the different portions of the column are constantly forced into opposite directions. In either case the change in the shape of the bones must ultimately take place, and the deformity under all ordinary treatment continues, and the executive power of the body is permanently impaired. The character of the deformity, however, is subject to much variation, scarcely any two cases being alike; it may be modified by a variety of circumstances—such, for example, as the natural shape of the body, the influence of particular habits and postures, such as a habit of reclining on one side, studying, writing, or other occupations that employ chiefly one or the other side of the body, whether in the sitting or standing posture; and it may even follow as the effect of diseases of the internal organs.

Curvature of the spine may also result from the scrofulous diathesis. In this case ulcerative absorption of some portion of the vertebral column takes place, most commonly at the front in the dorsal region, where the inner edges of the contiguous vertebræ are subjected to the most pressure. The effect of this is to cause the vertebra in which this process is going on to acquire more of a wedge shape, or, perhaps, the inner edge of the bone is quite worn away, allowing the column to bend at this point and producing an unsightly prominence or angle. In this case the cartilage being removed, the bones become irremediably united, or, technically speaking, *anchylosed*.

In all the above-mentioned cases, while the causes here set forth continue, the deformity has a tendency to increase, which it sometimes does to an extent which becomes extremely prejudicial to the health. The internal organs may, in consequence, become misplaced, so much so as to prevent the performance of their functions, or the spinal cord may become compressed, producing neuralgia or partial paralysis of the lower extremities. No remedies supplied through the stomach are of the least avail here, and generally the only recourse of the physician has been artificial supports and mechanical extension.

The result of the kind of treatment here referred to, usually at first flattering, is afterward anything but satisfactory. The reason is apparent. The mechanical support affords relief to the fatigued parts and removes the undue and painful pressure on one side. But this very recourse is an effectual barrier to the nutrition and development of the natural muscular supports, in consequence of which their condition, instead of improving, is certain to grow worse, and the disease and accompanying deformity, instead of being removed, are perpetuated. The great majority of the spinal supporters in vogue were contrived to take *the place of the muscles* and to do their duty, which is manifestly an impossibility, and their influence is unqualifiedly harmful, if not actually fatal. They subject the tender and sickly child or youth to a torture that is not only unnecessary, but to the last degree injurious to the general health.

Spinal deformities are the fruit of muscular weakness, which the reader knows is the product of imperfect muscular nutrition, often referable to a vicious stomach and defective digestion. The trouble is, no doubt, often aggravated, and indeed, in some cases, induced by irregular innervation, producing spasm, or at least a rigidity and tendency to spasm of certain muscles. But in all ordinary cases the therapeutic indications are simple, plain, and unequivocal, and consist in *developing the power of the digestive, and especially of the muscular system*, thus enabling the latter to do the duties it has hitherto failed to perform. The means for effecting these objects do not consist in any wonderful and nauseating decoctions to be swallowed at certain times of the day and night, nor in mechanical supports and complex modes of extension, but simply in *exercise* under proper regulations and restrictions; in other words, in the practice of *movements*, which are the only proper and efficient means of calling the needed nutrition into the disabled parts, so as to cause their development and reinstate them in health and power.

In directing the treatment of deformities by single movements, it is only necessary to say that the movements should be directed exclusively to the development of the weaker parts. For instance, in right lateral curvature, the movements should be directed to the left side, and in the ordinary exercises of the invalid the *left side* should always have the preference, while much exertion of the muscles of the right should for a while, at least, be *avoided*. If studious attention be paid to this suggestion, the nutrition of the two sides of the body will soon be equalized, and their muscular forces balanced.

It is not difficult by means of duplicated, and even by single, movements to improve the shape of the spinal column to a certain extent in nearly every case that will present itself, and if the vertebræ are in sound condition, the restoration of symmetry to the form will be complete. But if the vertebræ have become considerably diseased and misshapen, the degree of improvement attained will be less. In such case judicious mechanical aid is useful, but this must not be afforded at the expense of the muscles. This assistance should be directed *solely* to the rectification of the shape of vertebral bones, and consists simply in applying pressure to the projecting point, wherever that may be. This is accomplished by means of ingeniously contrived instruments, nicely adapted to the purpose. But these aids are never to be used save in connection with appropriate and vigorously applied movements, for without these the artificial appliances are valueless, if not harmful.

In a case of simple curvature to the right, the invalid may employ such movements as the following with great advantage:

1. Hanging (left arm).
2. Curtseying (left leg).
3. Left curve (weight held) wing, step standing, trunk to the right bending (four times).
4. Left stretch, right wing backward lying, legs to the left guiding.
5. Left stretch, right wing stride short sitting, trunk to the right bending.
6. Left stretch, right wing stride sitting, trunk forward falling.
7. Stretch grasp to the left fall standing, holding.
8. Shelter stride, to the right bent sitting, trunk rotation.
9. Stretch right side balance lying, holding.

Chapter Twenty.

FEMALE DISEASES.

The women of America, probably to a greater extent than those of any other country, suffer from diseases peculiar to the sex. I am convinced from observation as well from the testimony of distinguished medical men and others at home and abroad, that such diseases of this class are far less common in European countries than here. Diseases of this class are likewise scarcely known among the rude, uncultivated people of any part of the world.

There would indeed appear to be something in the habits and customs of our domestic life particularly calculated to engender and foster these distressing and disastrous maladies. We shall hardly succeed in ascertaining the causes of the prevalence of these affections among us by entering upon an analysis of isolated facts or of the habits of the individual or of society. It is probable that these causes are numerous, and of such a nature that, regarded singly, they would seem very unimportant. We are nevertheless justified in making the inference from analogy as well as from facts that the class of diseases under consideration, like so many others, are to be regarded simply as the effect of such causes as tend to restrain or impede the development of the physical system and interfere with its functional actions. We may enumerate as prominent among these causes, *dark rooms, rooms overheat-*

ed, *illy ventilated apartments, luxurious upholstery, foul air*, such labor as necessitates the excessive exercise of single regions of the body, habits of indolence. To these may be added others of another class, but quite as important, that often co-operate with these, although alone sufficient to produce the results. There are causes derived from the *mental* and *nervous system;* of these may be mentioned, *household cares* and *anxieties*, the annoying whims and caprices of unruly servants, the foolish rivalries of fashionable and unfashionable society, the excitements of parties, balls, the theater, sentimental novels, and tragical romances.

A prime cause of the universal deterioration of the organic systems of our women we believe to be ascribable largely to the undue culture and development of the sensibilities resulting from their too great devotion to the light literature of the day. The morbid effect which this style of reading does confessedly exert upon the mind *must* extend to the body, which it controls. The extent and complexity of the sympathetic actions of the female system, under the influence of this lovelorn and trashy sentimentalism, can only be estimated by one who has studied the feminine branch of human nature in its most obscure and embarrassing phenomena. By the means here adverted to, the nerves connected with and controlling the most delicate and sympathetic function of the female, are subjected to a morbid influence, resulting but too often in grave local as well as general disorder.

The symptoms attendant upon the class of diseases under consideration are such as might naturally be expected to result from the causes above mentioned. The laxity of muscular fiber in these cases is a conspicuous feature. This is manifested even in the expression of the countenance and in the style of the carriage. There is always inability to walk any considerable distance without fatigue, which, as a general rule, is felt mostly in the back and loins, and thence down the limbs. Generally the pain in the back is very persistent. The act of ascending stairs is not only laborious and difficult, but is followed by an aggravation of the distressing symptoms peculiar to the complaint. There is also, generally, tenderness of the lower portion of the abdomen, accompanied by a dragging sensation and pain, urinary derangement, sensitiveness of the lower extremity of the spinal column, often by annoying distress in the head, and other symptoms, local and general, of an extent and severity proportionate to the gravity of the case.

The mental phenomena attendant upon this disease are not less conspicuous than those just described. Nervous excitability and irritability of mind, with frequent depression of spirits, are among the commonest symptoms. Hysterical paroxysms frequently occur after unusual fatigue or mental exertion. One great cause of the depression experienced is the conviction the patient usually labors under, that her troubles are incurable. She feels that her disease must progress, and the unsatisfactory effects of the oft-tried pill and powder tend strongly to confirm her in a state of despondency and depressing irresolution.

The ordinary physician, as well as the specialist, for whom the disease in question affords a grand field for experiment, reaps glorious harvests from this class of cases. The ill success of treatment constantly experienced only seems to stimulate to trials of new doctors and new remedies; and so, while the patient grows worse the good doctor grows rich.

In common medical practice, the attempt is often made to sustain the body with mechanical supporters. These are destructive to the health of the muscles, and hence to that of the general system. It employs stimulant and tonic drugs, the temporary effect of which deceives the patient, and the ultimate effect impairs the assimilative and the general vital power. *It prescribes inactivity*, or suspension of the natural functions, as the grand condition for recruiting the strength. It employs local cauterization, which, though it relieves the congested membrane to which it is applied, yet in the end draws the circulation to the part in greater amount, and hence favors the congestion it is employed to relieve. It makes use of internal supports, which distend and irritate the parts, and disturb their natural functions. These means alternately tantalize the sufferer with hopes and depress her with fears, and prevent both herself and her medical adviser from attending to the real fundamental causes of her misery, and from the employment of the appropriate means for its radical relief.

The existence of the symptoms above enumerated do not always indicate the existence of local congestion nor local disease. Even in cases where they are present in a marked degree, I have often been obliged to differ from physicians whose judgment I sincerely desire to respect, in regard to the presence of organic disease. And even when there is ulceration of the neck of the uterus, hypertrophy of that organ, leucorrhea, etc., the gravity of the case does not reside in these symptoms, but in *the lack of vital energy* which permits these symptoms to occur. The common practice demonstrates every day that these *signs* continually return when they have been treated by the above-mentioned methods. No reliable and permanent cure can be effected while the disease is regarded as residing in the symptoms, which should be considered as only proofs of its existence.

A serious objection to the ordinary practice in uterine diseases is the frequently repeated examinations which it necessitates. The refined woman shrinks from these as from martyrdom, and with reason. In the method of cure advocated in this treatise, such examinations are dispensed with, except so far as they may be necessary in forming a diagnosis in a difficult case.

Let us now take another view of this class of diseases.

The real and essential pathology of these cases consists in such conditions as defective muscular nutrition and tone, defective peripheral circulation, central congestion, defective innervation, heightened nervous susceptibility, and bad digestion, the latter three of which conditions are dependent on the first three mentioned.

The condition of the muscles should not be judged of by the amount of force exerted under any strong mental excitement; for, with the impulsive nervous habit, induced by the disease, great efforts of short continuance may be put forth, but the high degree of nervous action necessary to such display, proves the real lack of muscular power. Such exertion is always followed in these cases by exhaustion and permanent debility.

The causes of the above-mentioned states, constituting the disease, have been already alluded to, and consist of defective early culture, uncorrected by subsequent attention to the needs of both the physiological and moral nature. Society consigns the conditions upon which a woman's capacity for usefulness in life mainly depends, to habitual neglect and practical contempt. Do we wonder that women complain of weak abdominal muscles? Why should these muscles be strong when so little used? and how can they be otherwise than weak when they have been subjected to the constant bandaging necessitated by the prevailing mode of dress? Do any wonder that she is pale and is addicted to sighing and tremors, while she sits the whole day, or a great part of it, at her needle-work or book, or languidly reclines upon the lounge? If she takes exercise, she is very careful that the important regions in question shall be disturbed thereby as little as possible. If driven by *ennui*, she *walks;* the pelvis is *carried* as tenderly as if made of glass. We admit there is a great deal to excuse the common aversion which women feel for any description of exercise, when the affection exists in any degree of severity, for the whole contents of the abdominal cavity which the muscles were made to sustain are suffered to obey the law of gravity, owing to the extensive relaxation and weakness of these supports, and the consequences are, as shown to some extent in the external appearance of the abdomen, a depression of the epigastric region, and a proportionate, unnatural fullness of the hypogastric region. The lumbar portion of the spinal column is dragged painfully forward, which displacement is compensated by an ugly rotundity of the shoulders, which gives the head an awkward forward pitch.

The muscles of the abdomen in all these cases are soft and doughy to the touch, thin and inelastic.

The exterior shape, however, conveys but a slight idea of the extent of the muscular weakness of this class of invalids, for there are a number of other muscles quite beyond the reach of direct observation, which are equally important to the health of these parts with those of the abdomen; such as the internal muscles of locomotion, the rotary muscles of the thigh, and especially those of the floor of the pelvis.

The health of the pelvic organs is dependent to the same extent, as are those of the abdominal, upon the oscillatory motion communicated by the diaphragm in respiration. A decrease of this motion favors congestion in the capillary circulation of those organs which have but little motion from causes within themselves, and which, therefore, become dependent on that received from neighboring muscles.

Fig. 78.

OUTLINE OF THE FEMALE FORM, WITH WEAK MUSCLES AND SYMPTOMS OF PELVIC DISEASE.

Fig. 79.

OUTLINE OF A HEALTHFUL FEMALE FORM.

It appears from this statement that the health of the pelvic organs is dependent very much upon the mechanical effects produced upon them by respiration. But the health of the chest and that of the abdomen are associated in another manner. A glance at the outline cuts shows that with the distention of the lower portion of the abdominal walls, and the gravitation of the contents, the diaphragm, which is the superior boundary of the abdominal cavity, must also descend. The ribs necessarily become much depressed, and the cavity of the chest becomes narrowed, and the breathing capacity consequently diminished. Now, if the ribs be elevated, the diaphragm, which is connected with them, will of course be raised, and there will be nothing to force from their place the contents of the abdominal and pelvic cavities.

We need not repeat the statement, that the proper digestion of food and healthful blood are also dependant on vigorous respiration. Now, at the bottom of all this general muscular weakness of the female lies this faulty condition of the blood. But foul blood does a worse thing than produce weakness; it creates congestion, and just where this congestion shall occur is decided by the law of gravity; the most depending organs, especially such as enjoy no voluntary muscular contractility, as the uterus, are most likely to take on this state. The peculiar congestion preceding and accompanying the menstrual flux may become chronic from imperfection of the vital operation, and add to the trouble. When we consider the universality of these causes noticed, we can only wonder that so many of the women of our day and country manage to escape these difficulties.

The remedy suited to this large and distressing class of complaints is suggested by their pathology. Indeed, it is in cases of displacements of various kinds, congestion, ulceration, etc., of the womb, and affections of other organs associated with it, as the bladder and ovaries, that the treatment by movements has been proved efficacious far beyond any other known, whether surgical or medical. By movements, the organs may be raised to their normal position, and their retention in place is not dependent upon any mechanical apparatus, but upon their restored power—this, too, without any of those indelicate manipulations being necessary which are required by the common treatment. By means of the most simple instructions relative to the principles and practice of movements, the condition of the health of the region in question *is placed under the control of the patient herself.* The very amiable reader may doubt the propriety of thus interfering with the doctor's business, but there must be a satisfaction even to the most amiable in doing thoroughly for one's self what the most learned doctor can do for her not one half so well.

The indications of treatment in these cases are generally the following:

1. To elevate the ribs and diaphragm, and increase the space of the superior portion of the abdominal cavity.

2. To contract the space of the inferior portion of the same cavity by causing a permanent contraction of the muscular walls of this region.

3. To develop the small muscles about the thighs and those constituting the floor of the pelvis.

4. To remove the blood from the internal weak and therefore congested parts to peripheral parts, abdominal coverings, and extremities.

5. To restore health to the mental and nervous systems by diminishing nervous irritability.

6. To impart vital energy to the whole system that shall be radical and permanent.

The particular movements required to fulfill these indications depend much upon the temperament as well as the condition of the health of the patient. If there be great feebleness, the duplicated movements are indispensable to the successful treatment. At least, they must be employed in its beginning. If there be much tenderness of the abdomen, as there frequently is, vibratory and other passive movements for the central portions of the body will be interspersed with such as are more active, applied to the extremities. After a few days the extremities will be better supplied with blood, and the visceral congestion will be diminished to a corresponding extent, so that *pressures, bendings*, etc., will not only be easily borne, but be very grateful to the patient. After this is accomplished, the patient may carry on the cure alone if circumstances make it necessary; or she may begin the treatment with the single movements, if the disease be not far advanced, with such as the following, for instance, confident of speedy beneficial effects.

EXAMPLES OF PRESCRIPTION.

1. Stretch (weight held) backward lying, holding. 68.
2. Elbow and toe lying, holding, or hips raising. 58.
3. Wing backward lying, legs raising. 26.
4. Wing legs angle half lying, thighs rotation. 31.
5. Wing legs angle lying, hips raising. 30.

Repeat—

1. Reclined arms angle kneeling, arms up stretching. 43.
2. Stretch long sitting, trunk forward falling. 53.
3. Stretch twist sitting, trunk oblique backward falling. 34.
4. Head rest forward fall standing, leg raising. Change. 22.
5. Forward bent standing, chine knocking. 32.
6. Wing long sitting, legs twisting. 24.
7. Elbow and foot side lying, hips raising. 62.
8. Wing short sitting, leg outward stretching. 16.
9. Shelter backward lying, legs rotation. 29.
10. Wing sitting, feet rotation. 5.

In selecting movements for these affections, the nature of each case must be carefully considered. Generally, appropriate movements should be applied to the extremities at first almost exclusively. The feebler the case, the fewer the movements directly affecting the central organs should be employed. The movement should be taken once a day, and if there be sufficient ability, No. 2 of the first example, or Nos. 1 or 3 of the second, may be repeated, according to the mode already described, several times in the course of the day.

If the patient be afflicted with *amenorrhea*, the following movements are useful:

Wing chine lean stride standing, curtseying. 9.
Support half standing, curtseying. 10.
Forward fall head support standing, leg raising. 22.
Support half standing, leg rotation. Change. 23.
Half wing support standing, leg outward raising. 21.
Shelter backward lying, legs raising. 26.
Shelter trunk backward lying, legs rotation. 29.

Forward bent standing, chine knocking; and the foot and leg movements generally.

The auxiliary means are important here. The patient must observe a proper and healthful diet, abjure all condiments and stimulants; and all indigestible matters and articles, within their chemical and physiological relations, may properly be styled *poor*, however *recherché* and costly. (See article on Diet.) She must also ride and walk in the open air, without regard to the humidity or disagreeable temperature of the atmosphere—should also be rubbed with the wet hand over the whole cutaneous surface, and then, after drying with a towel, with the dry hand, and if convenient, a shower sitting-bath may be used for two minutes, once or twice in the course of the day.

If she has anteversion, or retroversion, or other serious displacements, her movements should be prescribed by a competent physician. Let this be remembered.

By following the above rules and directions, the woman afflicted with the diseases of this class will generally, in a few days or weeks, find her strength to be greatly improving, and she will again be enabled to *mount stairs* without difficulty, a faculty most desirable in this age of tall dwellings. She will feel the blessed influx of health through all the tissues of her frame. She will rejoice and be glad; and, if of a grateful turn, will be very sure to sing the praises of her deliverer, the *Movement-Cure.*

The above formulas are given as examples only, and are not to be regarded as appropriate to every imaginable case.

Chapter Twenty-one.

MISCELLANEOUS APPLICATIONS OF MOVEMENTS.

MOVEMENTS TO REMOVE FATIGUE.—It is not necessary for one to wholly abstain from motion, in order to secure rest from fatigue. On the contrary, the *continuance* of exercise in many cases is more favorable to restoration than a state of total inaction would be, provided always, that other than the fatigued parts be called into action. Hence the advantage of a frequent change of occupation, especially for the weakly. One can accomplish a vast deal more in a given time by varying his work occasionally, than by expending his strength upon any one particular kind. All animals instinctively *stretch* themselves, that is, cause the muscles situated remotely from the central organs to act, in order to get relief from the sense of fatigue. The operators in the foreign Movement-Cure institutions, instead of resting as laborers commonly do, after two or three hours of the severest exercise, *apply movements to each other*, in order to become rested, selecting such portions of the body as were least brought into action by their professional manipulations. A favorite movement with the female assistants, I observed, was that termed *backward and leg lying, holding*. In this movement the legs are fixed, the body in the backward lying position, while the trunk is unsupported, causing powerful action of the muscles of the abdomen, in consequence of which fatigue of the back (from which they most suffer) is removed. All patients, and especially the female portion, testify to the readiness and permanency with which habitual back-ache is thus removed. In explanation of this we need only refer the reader to the principles laid down in the first part of this work. Severe action of any portion of the body is effectual in calling the circulation, and especially the nervous influence, *from* other portions of the body, which in the instance in question are congested by the previous exercise. By causing different portions of the body to act alternately, they are enabled to act equally, their functions are harmonized, and the sense of fatigue is removed.

The system of movements regards the body as a *reservoir of force*, upon which every action makes a a certain demand. If the demands upon the system for expenditure be *moderate*, the supply is readily kept up equal to the demand by means of the unceasing operations of the organizing processes. If the demand caused by the exertion of power be excessive, or if it proceed from several different portions of the system at the same time, then the organizing processes are not equal to it, and *fatigue* is the consequence. Immunity from fatigue is experienced always in proportion to the degree of perfection attained by the nutritive or organizing processes.

It must not be inferred from the above remarks, that movements are *always* the appropriate remedy for fatigue. If the fatigue be general, absolute repose is of course necessary.

To Stop Nose-bleed.—The remedy for this affection is very simple; nothing more is generally necessary than to *raise both arms to upward stretch position*.

The efficacy of this action for the purpose named, admits of easy demonstration, but *why* the effect follows, is not, at first, so apparent. We would explain it in this way. It may be observed, that if the arms be raised to the perpendicular upright position, and then, after remaining uplifted for a short time, be permitted suddenly to *drop*, the hands will be found suffused with blood. Since a much greater impediment than usual is presented to flow of the blood to the uplifted hands, occasioned by the opposition of the force of gravity, the effort of the arterial vessels upon which this increased labor devolves becomes necessarily much greater than before; and since the arterial pressure in direction of the arms is increased, that toward the head is correspondingly lessened. When, now, the impediment (consisting of gravity) is removed, while the arterial impulse is continued, the blood, rushing to the hands, produces a marked derivative effect upon the circulation of the head, and consequently the flow from the ruptured capillaries of the nasal membrane ceases.

Another mode of stopping nose-bleed, presented by Branting, is as follows: The subject takes a *fall stride sitting posture*, the nose is grasped and rapidly vibrated, while at the same instant the trunk rises, and returns to the erect position. This action may be repeated several times.

To Induce Vomiting.—The method of causing the stomach to discharge its contents by means of irritating the fauces was known long before Marshall Hall explained the reflex powers of the nervous system, upon which the action of vomiting depends. This means of dislodging the contents of the stomach is generally adequate for the purpose, *in those cases where this effect is really desirable*, provided it be managed with sufficient tact. It is much better in most cases than to irritate the stomach with powerful drugs, which course is necessarily followed by great debility of the organ, even if lucky enough to escape inflammation, or more serious chronic disease.

The proper method in these cases is to ply the stomach with *lukewarm* water in large doses, and often repeated, no matter how much this may be in opposition to the feelings and in spite of the protestations of the patient. When the feeling of nausea has arisen to a good degree, something (the finger will do) may be applied to the back part of the mouth. This will generally cause the stomach to contract spasmodically, and eject its contents. Should it refuse to do so, the hand of an attendant may be applied to the stomach, just below the pit, and by making a sudden, but not violent kneading motion in an upward direction, a contractile action of the stomach is suddenly induced, and its contents are discharged.

To Remove Chilblains.—This annoying affection, in ordinary cases, may be quickly removed. The *principle* of cure is that concerned in the removal of congestion of internal organs by means of vibratory movements. The mode of operation is pointed out in No. 6, page 164. Or, the leg of the afflicted foot may rest upon the knee of another person, who deals rapid but light blows upon the bottom of the foot, it being protected by a shoe or boot.

The reason why the congestion of the capillaries constituting the disease is dissipated by this treatment, is quite obvious. The actual condition consists not only of a dilatation of the capillaries, but also in a change in the quality of the blood and the occurrence of the *gelatinous corpuscle*, characteristic of inflammation, which, with the normal blood corpuscle, become adherent to the walls of the capillaries, effectually clogging the channel and preventing the onward flow. The motion communicated in the manner described excites the contraction of the distended walls of the vessels, and at the same time detaches adhering corpuscles, which of course are carried through by the current sweeping onward from the heart. The fresh blood entering brings the conditions for restoring the normal state of the parts. The same reasoning probably holds true for the application of passive vibration by the *duplicated movements*, in all cases of congestion, and, if properly managed, of inflammation even, wherever situated.

To Relieve Headache.—1. Energetic friction applied over the longitudinal, lateral, and basilar sinuses will frequently relieve this affection. The reason seems to be, that contraction is thus induced in the venous walls, which consequently urge the blood forward, relieving them of their distention. This may be done by one's self, or by another. The procedure is as follows: partly close the hands, placing the backs of the fingers in contact, raise the hands to the head, placing the tips of all the fingers over the *longitudinal suture*, or middle line of the head. Now carry the fingers, thus placed, backward and forward on the middle line, making considerable friction upon the scalp. The fingers may now divide and pass down the back of the head at each side to the base, and then along the base at the roots of the hair, continuing the same degree of friction through the whole course.

2. If a *band* be very tightly applied about the head, and, after remaining a few minutes, be suddenly removed, a similar effect is experienced. This effect is probably due to the impulse thus afforded to the circulation in the venous sinuses.

3. Movements tending to warm the feet are always useful in headache.

4. Headache is more frequently caused by a fault in the *quality* rather than in the *quantity* of the blood—in which case, all those means whose influence is to purify or deterge the system ought to be used, and to an extent corresponding with the gravity of the case. In moderate cases, a long walk in the open air is sufficient. If this is not enough, *abstinence* must be practiced till the stomach is purified, the liver relieved of the tenderness and congestion that usually in such cases exists, and the secretions set free. To promote vomiting, in the mode above described, is sometimes necessary; but persons liable to periodical attacks of this affection should learn to avoid them by an improved hygiene, rather than to cure them by *any* process. Nervous headache requires rest and sleep, which may be induced by duplicated movements.

WORMS IN CHILDREN.—These parasites feed upon the imperfectly digested residual of the alimentary tube, and they can never occur without the existence of such food for their sustenance. It is the *bad digestion*, giving rise to worms, rather than the worms themselves, that constitute the disease, and it is evident that they can not exist when the *cause* is wanting. The appetite of the child—which in these cases is always voracious—must be restrained, and the action of the digestive organs promoted, in order that *all* the food taken shall be completely disposed of. When this is effected, the parasites will be expelled. The abdomen of the child must be subjected to a thorough *kneading*, as described in a former chapter, three or four times a day, ten or fifteen minutes at each time.

The abdomen, in these cases, is generally tumid, but the kneading increases the natural motion of the muscular walls of the canal, promotes absorption, and restores a healthy tone to all the visceral contents. The child, if possible, should also be made to ride much in a springless vehicle in the open air. Worms are often expelled from the bowels after a few days' practice of the plan here directed, and this result should be regarded as a *consequence*, rather than the *cause*, of the restoration to health.

HERNIA.—This occurs generally in consequence of weakness of the muscle of the lower portion of the abdomen, the hernial region. The fibers of these muscles are liable to separate, upon a sudden muscular effort being made, thus permitting the intestine to protrude. In many cases of this affection the truss has been dispensed with, and the difficulty removed, through the .... of the duplicated movem...

The proper movem............

Half stretch, half wing, half kick .... twisting. This movement is at first to be performed with one side only, the trunk twisting toward the relaxed side, that is, the side of which the foot is raised. After some progress is made, the twisting should be done in the opposite direction. The kneeling twisting, Nos. 42 and 48, also Nos. 56, 26, and 61, might be employed to good advantage.

PROLAPSUS OF THE WOMB AND BOWELS.—In all cases of this kind there is great weakness of the muscles of the *chest, abdomen, perineum,* etc. The affection is immediately relieved by practicing the movement No. 61. To strengthen the parts that are weak, so as to prevent a return, the muscles belonging to all the regions above mentioned require to be developed by judicious practice of the movements affecting the parts. To accomplish this object, such movements as the following are recommended : Nos. 43, 47, 48, 56, 36, 30, and 31.

TO RELIEVE BACK-ACHE.—When caused by fatigue, such movements as cause the abdomen to act are useful. But this symptom is often caused by laxity of muscles, allowing the visceral contents to gravitate. In this case the movements above recommended for prolapsus will be found effectual.

AMENORRHEA.—All processes tending to strengthen the body, tend to overcome menstrual obstruction. The movements particularly to be recommended are, Nos. 14, 18, 27, 29, 30, 31, and 32, and, indeed, such movements are also useful for constipation.

TO EXCITE ACTION OF THE LOWER BOWEL.—A movement highly useful for this purpose is *wide stride leg angle standing, trunk vibration,* No. 65. The *position* for this movement is the same as the terminating position of No. 9. Also the examples Nos. 29, 31, and 32 are very useful, as well as kneading, No. 66.

Chapter Twenty-two.

DIFFERENT EFFECTS OF VARIOUS COMMON EXERCISES UPON PERSONS IN HEALTH.

WALKING.—This is the most agreeable and natural of all exercises. In walking, the body is free and unconstrained, most parts of it are subjected to gentle action with but a slight degree of expenditure of muscular or of nervous force, these powers being economized to the greatest extent, and the action may consequently be continued for a longer period than almost any other that engages the will. Walking causes the blood to circulate freely in the extremities, skin, and lungs, to refresh, nourish, and invigorate these parts, strengthens the spine, and relieves all tendency to congestion of the internal organs and head. It also supplies the most perfect condition for mental action and enjoyment. It is almost the only exercise which invalids of nearly all classes may engage in without a prescription. But it does not supply *all* the system requires of exercise. It fails to call into sufficient action either the abdominal or the breathing organs, and other exercises adapted to these purposes are required by those who have no occasion to engage in work.

RUNNING.—A good *run* of a few moments is very exhilarating to the spirits and stimulating to the frame. It causes a great expansion of the chest, and a powerful pressure of the blood into the capillaries of the general system as well as those of the lungs. It rapidly produces a large amount of animal heat, soon causes the surface to be wet with perspiration, and increases the discharge by the kidneys. Although a good tonic for the well, especially for those who have a capacious chest, it too rapidly exhausts the powers of the feeble, and might produce unpleasant, and perhaps dangerous pulmonary congestion in persons of narrow and feeble breathing organs.

DANCING.—This exercise has been employed by all nations in all ages, to exhilarate the mind, and to give expression to the feeling of abounding good health, which there is no doubt it contributes to maintain. It has the advantage over most other exercise, in being *social*. Being accompanied by music, both the mental and muscular powers of all those engaged are united in executing the same movements, which is consequently effected without much exertion of the will, so that it secures a large amount of exercise with but trifling fatigue. Dancing harmonizes with the general plan of the organic movements of the body, in being also rythmical, so that it is here allied to the *involuntary* movements. Dancing ought to be cultivated in every family, as an antidote to the effects of the wearisome toil and worry of our modern life.

SEWING.—This and many other sitting occupations in which females engage, call chiefly into action the superior portion of the body, while the trunk and lower extremities are left nearly motionless. Those who are thus occupied should therefore counteract the ill effects flowing from a too constant attention to such labors, by much walking in the open air, to equalize the circulation. The health is much endangered in persons of naturally feeble constitutions by the restraint exercised upon the action of the *diaphragm* and *respiratory* and *abdominal muscles* by excessive use of the needle. Those who are compelled to devote themselves to such labors should habitually practice such movements for the lower extremities and trunk as are described in this work.

Sewing with the machine, on the contrary, affects chiefly the lower extremities, and no doubt there are numerous instances in which the life of the feeble sewing-woman has been preserved by this machine, through its tendency to remove that incipient congestion of the chest and lungs, which is the certain prelude to pulmonary disease. It also affords more time to engage in other and more genial occupations. This exercise is, however, insufficient for the purposes of health, since it does not contribute enough to the expansion of the chest of the weakly female.

AGRICULTURAL LABORS.—The healthful tendencies of these employments are proverbial, when engaged in by the well, and even by those slightly ailing. The energetic action of the extremities throws the circulation into these parts, while the amount of force expended necessitates a large supply of air, and consequently a great expansion of the chest. The respiration is generally not materially quickened, but the air entering the lungs is retained and somewhat compressed, in consequence of the great exertion required by such exercises as sawing and chopping wood, mowing, raking, pitching, shoveling, and many other operations required of the farmer. The health of the feeble is, however, endangered by engaging in many of these kinds of exercise, especially if pursued too continuously, for then they would be likely to induce congestion of delicate parts of the body. The weakly must remember that the development of strength depends on a *careful steady process of training*, and it is destructive for them to exert more power than the system is capable of easily supplying. Such persons must therefore undergo the processes whose tendency is *gradually* to fit them for greater exertion.

PAINTING, SCULPTURE, ENGRAVING. — Labor of this kind generally requires the conjoint exercise of the brain and sensorial nerves, as well as that of the arms and chest. When these parts are used to an immoderate degree, to the neglect of exercise of the lower extremities, it becomes harmful. Such occupations ought therefore to be alternated with a great deal of walking, and other such appropriate exercises as are described in their proper place.

STUDY.—The health enjoyed by the studious class is generally conceded to be below that of the laborer. It would be wrong to infer from this that study is in itself unwholesome. On the contrary, the exercise of the intellectual powers is entirely compatible with good health and long life. The cause of ill health in these cases lies in *omitting* to exercise the general muscular system, and permitting the nervous to be almost exclusively worked, for this disturbs the equipoise of the system.

It is not enough in order that the studious may secure the conditions of good health and long life, that he occasionally relieve the fatigued brain and disturbed circulation by a forced walk. He should develop a reserve force to enable him to withstand the accidents that are continually occurring in life, which every one is being forever unexpectedly called upon to encounter. He must resolve on the start, that life shall not be a wretched ineffectual conflict with disease, yielding no satisfactory experience or real profit, but a hopeful, determined, steady, manly march—a stout persistent contest with *foes without*.

Life is a race, a warfare. A man needs all his faculties and gifts, and they can not be too highly trained. His whole intellectual, physical, and moral nature should be disciplined to the highest possible degree. He can not afford to dispense with a single weapon that nature has furnished for his use. A man to do much good in the world must have a good stomach, and a long wind, and a stout grip, as well as staunch principles and a shrewd brain. He must expand and invigorate his narrow and feeble chest; the relaxed diaphragm must be toned up; the weak abdominal muscles energized; the liver, and kidneys, and pores be made to do their duty as well as the thinking organ.

Chapter Twenty-three.

MOVEMENTS ADAPTED TO THE USE OF SCHOOLS.

No argument would seem to be requisite to convince the world of the importance of *physical* culture for children and youth, while that of *mental* culture is so generally acknowledged as the basis of civilization and the condition of progress. Why the former has been so much left to chance, or whim, or to charlatanry, while so much attention is paid to the latter, is quite unaccountable. This inconsistency has been long apparent to the instructors of youth, and various attempts have been made, in modern times, to develop all the powers and faculties of the human system equally and in connection. These endeavors have met with but moderate success—a success probably far inferior to that realized by the ancients.

The prevalence of incorrect ideas on this subject which characterizes the times, makes it necessary that something should be done to attract the attention of the people to those *principles* which have been so long and so studiously ignored.

The difficulties in the way of the successful training of the mind and body together, have been both practical and theoretical. The faults in the ordinary practice of gymnastics have been pointed out (page 124). Besides being heterogeneous, disorderly, liable to abuse, and injurious to weak organs, such exercises require expensive apparatus, much space, and demand more time for their successful practice than can always be conveniently devoted to them.

Well qualified teachers are also necessary. The physical powers of the child can no more properly be directed without care and study than can the mental; and the consequences of misdirection are far more likely to be permanently injurious in the former than in the latter case.

Calisthenics, for the reason that they have not been considered obnoxious to some of the above objections, have occasionally been used in schools; but the class of exercises bearing this name really are scarcely less objectionable, for they, too, require a greater proportional action of the nerves than of the muscles; and hence, though the respiration and circulation may thereby be driven up to a higher degree of activity, yet the nerve-forces, already overtasked by study, are thus too rapidly expended. (See page 112, *et seq.*)

The government of the kingdom of Sweden and Norway, with great wisdom, long ago directed the use of gymnastics in all the common schools throughout the realm. The intention of this decree has never been satisfactorily realized, owing to causes that we have explained. Prof. Branting, Director of the Central Gymnastic Institute, pupil and successor of *Ling*, has attempted to introduce there what he terms the *Sitting Gymnastic Exercises*. To this end, he has published a formula of movements intended to be performed in the intervals of the lessons, without apparatus of any kind, noiselessly, and even sometimes without the pupils leaving their seats. These movements may be resorted to at any time, as, when the school has been long confined, or suffering from too severe and continuous application. These exercises are entirely accordant with the principles advocated in the present work, and consist, in the main, of movements analogous to examples herein given. The Swedish movements are not, however, exactly adapted to our use on account of the difference in the arrangement of seats in the schools of the two countries. I would therefore propose a formula slightly different from the Swedish, but essentially the same, which it is hoped will be found not only practicable, but salutary.

ORDER OF COMMAND FOR THE FREE-SITTING MOVEMENTS.

No.	Name of Movements.	Words of Command.
I.	Primary Sitting Position.	To movements attend.
II.	Half Stretch, Half Wing Sitt'g, Trunk Twisting.	1. Left hip—hold. 2. Right arm—upward stretch. 3. To the right—turn. 4. Forward—turn. 5. Change position of arms. 6. To the left—turn. 7. Forward—turn. 8. Arms downward—stretch.
III.	Heel Rest Sitting, Ankle Stretching and Bending.	1. Hips—hold. 2. Knees—stretch. 3. Ankle stretch—bend, one! two! 4. Rest.
IV.	Stretch Stride Sitting, Head Forward and Backward Bending.	1. Arms upward stretch, one! two! 2. Head backward bend, forward bend, one! two! 3. Head upward stretch. 4. Arms downward stretch, one! two!
V.	Wing Stride Sitting, Knee Stretching.	1. Hips—hold. 2. Left leg—raise. 3. Left knee—stretch. 4. Knee—bend—stretch, one! two! 5. Change position of legs. 6. Right knee—stretch—bend, one! two 7. Rest.
VI.	Stride Sitting, Arms Upward and Backw'd Raising.	1. Arms forward—stretch. 2. Arms upward—raise, one! two! 3. Arms downward—stretch.
VII.	Stretch Stride Sitting, Head Rotation.	1. Arms upward stretch. 2. Head turn to right, to left, one! two!

ORDER OF COMMAND—*Continued:*

No.	Name of Movements.	Words of Command.
VIII.	STRETCH STRIDE SITT'G, TRUNK SIDEWISE BENDING.	1. Arms upward stretch. 2. Trunk to left—bend. 3. To the right bent, one! two! 4. Rest.
IX.	SHELTER STRIDE SITT'G, TRUNK TWISTING.	1. Hands to the head—grasp. 2. Trunk to left—turn. 3. To right—turn, one! two! 4. Rest.
X.	WING STRIDE SITTING, LEGS TWISTING.	1. Hips—hold. 2. Knees—stretch. 3. Legs inward—turn. 4. Outward—turn, one! two! 5. Rest.

In executing the above movements, the scholars remain in their seats. At the first word of command they drop their books, and proceed to imitate the slow movements of the teacher, who stands in front, in full view of all the pupils. At the signal, *one! two!* a vocal exercise commences. At the word *rest*, the hands of each pupil fall to his sides, and the body returns to its natural sitting posture.

The intelligent teacher will be able to change the formula from time to time as occasion may seem to require, or form entirely new ones, by selecting appropriate examples from Part II. of this book. In this way he may be always supplied with a variety, and avoid wearying his pupils with a monotonous routine.

PART IV.

HYGIENE.

Chapter Twenty-four.

THE PHILOSOPHY OF HYGIENE.

By the term Hygiene we mean, simply, that assemblage of rules and regulations applied to our conduct and mode of living which teaches us what in our modes and practices is right and what wrong—what *is* and what is *not* conformable to physiological law. Of the importance of knowing something about this matter, we do not feel called upon to give any formal demonstration.

The absurdity of employing medical treatment for the cure of disease, while at the same moment a dozen disease-producing causes are in active operation, needs no proof. The inconsistency of such procedure seems still greater when the remedial treatment consists in a *special application of Hygiene*, such as the Movement-Cure has been explained to be. Hence a work like the present, designed for popular instruction on a particular branch of Hygiene, would be incomplete and almost useless if the importance of attending to the subject in all its particulars and relations, both as a *preventive* of disease and as a *remedy*, were not pointed out and enforced.

We take it for granted that a compliance with the

conditions of health is within the ability of every individual; and further, that such compliance is spontaneous and intuitive in a natural and unperverted condition of the system. For it would be monstrous to suppose that God, who is the great and all-wise Friend of his creatures, should so impress his original constitution as to bias him at the outset in the direction of error and misery. Such a supposition would be compounded of absurdity and blasphemy in about equal parts.

Food, drink, air, temperature, light, exercise, and *mental pursuits* are subjects that have entered more or less into previous discussions, but it is due to their importance that a portion of them, at least, should receive some more especial attention in this place.

Food.—That is food, which, being introduced into the stomach, is capable of sustaining the vital actions of the system. We may consider food in relation to *quantity, quality, modes of preparation, times of eating,* etc. It fails to serve its purposes in proportion as it deviates in the above particulars from a correct standard.

Quantity.—The matters which serve nutritive purposes are removed from the system through the instrumentality of oxygen; consequently, the *quantity* proper to be used is limited by respiration and those causes which influence this act. We are wholly unconscious of the rate, and even of the existence, of the oxydizing processes going on within the body by which its constituents are removed, and so are guided, in our use of food, almost entirely by our sensations. The necessities of the system, indeed, are absolute, but the sensations are subject to variation and modification from many, and different, and ever-varying causes; so that to decide as to the proper quantity of food to be eaten at a given time may be a matter of much difficulty, especially in those persons whose gastric nervous systems have become deranged.

Errors in quantity are liable to occur from the following causes:

1. In disease, whether acute or chronic, the amount of oxydized products eliminated from the system is much reduced, and the amount of food taken should be correspondingly diminished. In acute disease, the results of lessened affinity of the blood for oxygen are rendered conspicuous in the character of the urine, the fur of the tongue, and the quickened pulse and respiration—which latter is an attempt to compensate for this lessened affinity. In either case no restoration is possible while there continues an *excess* of food over respiration.

2. Bodily inactivity reduces the need of the system for food, and the ill effect of partaking of the same amount as when actively employed, soon becomes apparent in lessened vigor of health.

3. Elevated temperature necessarily diminishes the amount of carbonic acid and water produced in the system, and consequently the amount of food required is less than is demanded at low temperatures.

4. Confinement in close rooms, out of the reach of currents of air, diminishes the amount of air taken into the system both by skin and lungs, and consequently less food is needed.

5. Anything taken into the stomach that unduly stimulates it, such as spices, sweets, and the various condiments, as well as drugs prescribed for the pur-

pose, perverts and blunts the sensibility of the organ, and inclines it to solicit an undue quantity of food.

All that portion of alimentary material taken into the system over and above its wants, must be regarded as so much foreign matter over which the organism can at best exercise an imperfect control.

No absolute rule can be given in regard to the amount of food which the system requires. To attempt to give any such rule would not only require a superhuman acquaintance with all the internal and invisible present actions and relations of the system, but also the ability to *anticipate* those changes in its condition that, under the influence of accidental circumstances, may within a brief period occur to it. But while the digestive powers are unperverted by bad habits or by disease, there is little occasion for concern in regard to this matter, since the sensations intended to control the alimentary process afford a reliable indication of what the needs of the system are. When, however, the sensations and instincts are blunted or perverted by the above-mentioned causes, there is always great liability to err in this matter.

QUALITY.—Food consists in part of material capable of being *organized* or transformed into the vital structure—in part of matters which are not imbued with this vital quality, but are only oxydized in the body, and thereby reduced to a form easy of elimination. The former class contains *nitrogen*—the latter does not. The nitrogenized class is of uniform composition, represented by *albumen*, and by its modifications, *fibrin*, *gluten*, *casein*, etc. No other substances containing nitrogen are capable of being transformed by vital operations into the instruments of life. The non-nitrogenized class is represented by *starch*, *sugar*, *vegetable acids*, etc.

Certain saline matters, forming the ash of food, are equally indispensable in the organizing processes of the body as the others named.

The errors common in the quality of food are chiefly the following:

1. The distinction between food proper and other matters destined to oxydation in the system, is frequently lost sight of. In this way such substances as alcohol, and its various mixtures, have come to be considered as food.

2. A good proportion of the *saline* constituents of food is generally lost in the mechanical separation effected by the miller. This is a great error, for which the system must suffer. As well might an abundant harvest be expected to spring up from a worn-out soil as that the organizing processes of the system shall be perfectly conducted while a portion of the elements essential to the process is deficient.

3. The habitual use, especially by the sedentary, of much *soluble* food—of food soluble *in water*—is a fruitful source of evil. The system provides secretions *in proportion to its need for nourishment*. Now if food be taken already dissolved, or soluble in water, it *must* pass into the circulation, though it may prove exceedingly injurious, and the system has no means of protecting itself against it.

Ordinary food is not soluble except by these secretions, and therefore, if eaten in proportion beyond the need of the system, is cast off in a disguised form, and is not liable to produce injury, even though in excess as to some of its elements.

4. Very common is the erroneous supposition that the spices, etc., that are added to food are essential or useful parts of it. Such matters only detract from the nutritive value of food, and do harm by forcing the system to labor in their elimination.

5. A disproportion in the nutritive elements received into it to the needs of the system, is a common error. Indulgence in *sweets*, while it loads the blood with hydro-carbons, diminishes the relative proportion of the nitrogenized and organizable constituents of food—therefore renders it *poorer* in quality.

SALT.— Physiologists agree that the salt of the animal fluids does not require constant replenishing, but is retained by the blood to serve its purpose in the economy over and over again. Accordingly, the lower animals require salt only occasionally. That which appears in the excretions is therefore mainly but the *excess* of the needs of the system, and, if given in large quantity, it can not but overtask and diminish the vital power. Christison regards salt as poison, and gives several cases of poisoning by it.

The common practice of employing preparations of the alkalies, *soda*, *potash*, etc., to a large extent in food, is extremely prejudicial to health. These are potent chemicals, and can not act otherwise, when in excess, than to deteriorate the quality of the blood. Alkalies have an affinity for fibrin, and destroy its coagulating property, and by their strong affinities they oppose the vital force and detract from its influence, and hence supply an important condition of disease. The excessive use of saline substances, wholesome enough in the natural and proper quantity, is the gravest error in modern dietetics.

The various causes above enumerated tend powerfully to modify the regular vito-chemical actions of the system, frequently arresting the oxydizing process at some point short of the final, in which the materials which have served the vital chemistry are prepared for dismission from the system. These modifications and this retention are the origin of morbid matter, and are the causes of disease.

What the system needs is such a *mixture** of the different elementary ingredients of food as shall correspond with that characterizing those edible plants upon which all herbivorous animals depend for their sustenance.

PREPARATION OF FOOD—COOKING.—Man has been called the *cooking animal*. This does not indicate that his nutritive wants, considered in a physiological light, differ from those common to all animals, but that, by the use of his reason, he may husband his expenditures for the purely animal wants, and so gain time and opportunities for the cultivation of his intellectual and moral capacities. The object of cooking, then, is *not* to change the intrinsic chemical qualities of edible substances. So far as such changes are produced in the processes of cooking, the nutritive qualities of the food are not benefited, but rather injured. A few instances may be excepted, where noxious qualities belonging to plants are destroyed by the elevated temperature required for cooking. The legitimate province

---

* "It seems placed beyond a doubt by these experiments, that the proportions in which these factors of nutrition are mixed in the food, exert the most decided influence on the welfare of the organism, and that the intermixture of the different factors of nutrition is essential for the metamorphosis of matters. Great as are the fluctuations which nature allows in these proportions, an *undue preponderance of one or other of the factors always* acts injuriously upon the due course of the processes of nutrition. No single part of this process can go on without the concurrence of all these factors."—*Lehmann.*

of cooking may, in general, be regarded as confined to overcoming the mechanical impediments to digestion, so as to render the nutritive properties of the substance promptly available to the digestive organs. This is effected by the aid of *heat and moisture*. By this means the areolar structure of meats (composed of gelatin) is softened or dissolved, starch granules are opened, woody fiber divided and rendered soft, gluten swollen and rendered porous and pervious to the digestive fluids, and the mechanical labor of the digestive organs reduced to the lowest practicable point. In this way the nutritive elements existing in food are all turned to an immediate account, and the powers of the stomach are not exhausted by mechanical efforts, or its nerves irritated by the same cause.

The errors of cooking are chiefly the following:

1. By long custom we come to prefer food which has been subjected to *too high a degree of heat*, which, by decomposing it, injures its nutritive properties, and it is thus made to perform the part of a *spice*. *Bread*, for instance, is toasted, and the juices of meats burned, to gratify an acquired taste, greatly to the detriment of their quality.

2. Injurious additions are made to food in cooking, the effects of which have been previously described. Sugar, oily matters, alkalies, etc., are commonly added to edible preparations, in utter disregard of the proportions of these elements really demanded by the system.

3. Food is also injured by rendering it so porous and soft, that it is swallowed without due mastication, which deprives it of a portion of the saliva so necessary to its proper digestion.

PROPER TIMES FOR EATING.—It is difficult to lay down

rules upon this subject. People engaged in business are generally compelled to take their food after long intervals, and if these intervals are not so lengthy as to transgress natural law, thus inducing alternate exhaustion and repletion, the health is apt to be favored thereby rather than otherwise.

In sedentary life, especially with invalids, whose thoughts are too much occupied with the questions, what they shall eat and what they shall drink, the temptations to take nourishment are more frequent and urgent because not tempered by wholesome occupations. To guard the reader against errors that are often very damaging, it may be remarked:

1. That in a diseased state of the stomach or system in which physiological actions are either perverted or retarded, generally both, the demand upon the digestive organs for a supply of nutritive material thereby lessens, and the digestive process itself is conducted with less energy, and so the need for food is experienced less frequently. In such condition for one to take food as often as in health, must necessarily operate disadvantageously. A good rule to observe in these cases is, to *take no food into the stomach while a residual of the preceding meal remains*. The presence of the residual, acting as a ferment, hinders the succeeding digestive effort. It is even necessary, in many cases, that the distance between meals for a time be greatly extended, in order to effect a wholesome purification of the solvent fluids.

2. In a state of health the digestive process requires *time* for its thorough accomplishment. It proceeds by *stages*, and an introduction of food at the wrong time tends to arrest the process and render it abortive.

DRINKS.—There is in nature but *one* substance which performs in the system the purpose of a wholesome beverage, and this is *water*. All artificial drinks consist of various mixtures, infusions, or solutions of other matters, either solid or liquid, with water, which has become simply the medium of conveying these to the system. Thus, tea, coffee, vinous and spirituous liquors are beverages only on account of the water they contain. To consider the physiological relations of these drinks is to investigate the effect of the potential chemicals in question upon the vital structures. These effects have been shown, in another place, to consist, *not* of nutrition, but of irritation, stimulation, and destruction of organized substance, in various modes and degrees. Their use, in any form, then, is reasonably inferred to be incompatible with any remedial treatment, although it may be consistent with the *palliation* of certain distressing symptoms, generally first sought by the drug method of medical treatment. All drinks save water are therefore proscribed in a strict and consistent hygienic practice.

MILK.—This fluid is frequently drunk by *adults* as well as by children, for whom alone it is intended by nature. It consists of about 80 per cent. of water, holding about twenty per cent. of solid matter in solution, the largest portion of which becomes immediately precipitated upon reaching the stomach. This proportion of dry solid to the watery portion is scarcely less than is found in potatoes, and is much greater than exists in edible fruits and roots. It is hence seen, that though milk may be drank when fresh, it is *not* properly a beverage, in the strict sense of this term, and the inference is legitimate, that to use it as such, is at best but to clog the system, by loading it with nutritive matter, under the pretense of quenching thirst. This, to be sure, may be of little consequence to the growing or laboring person, but will become a source of ill health to the sedentary, and is quite incompatible with a systematic employment of Remedial Hygiene.

Chapter Twenty-five.

TEMPERATURE.

PHYSIOLOGICAL EFFECT OF COLD AND HEAT.—To understand the real relations that the thermometric and barometric changes of the atmosphere bear to the system, would relieve men of much of the anxiety they habitually experience in regard to their effects upon the health. Invalids, especially, are fond of ascribing their depressed spirits to the state of the weather, and often attempt to get rid of a disagreeable sense of personal responsibility by persuading themselves that their symptoms are attributable to some uncontrollable atmospheric cause. This is convenient; but I am persuaded that a correct understanding of the intentions of nature toward us in these changes would lead us to regard them, severe and untoward as they seem to us, when we sedulously unfit ourselves for their effects, as really most friendly to us, and wisely and mercifully adapted to maintain, and even to restore the health.

The average temperature of the air in this climate is not far from 55° Fahr.—the temperature of our bodies 98°; hence the average difference between the heat of the body and that of surrounding things is not far from 43°; but the thermometer sometimes falls considerably below zero, effecting a great increase of this difference, from which it is apparent that it is the intention of nature that the animal body should be subjected not only to a high or a low, but to a *variable* temperature. It is the nature of heat to be forever seeking an equilibrium. Hence all bodies, whether animate or inanimate, having a temperature *above* that of the atmosphere, soon lose their excess, unless constantly replenished. The rapidity with which an object loses heat depends on the amount of *difference* between its temperature and that of contiguous objects. But the living animal body loses more heat in a given time than an inanimate body of the same size, weight, and temperature, because it not only, like the stone, parts with its heat by *radiation* to surrounding things, and by contact with them, but in other ways peculiar to itself. The surface of the animal body is always moist, and *evaporation* from it is a most potent cooling agent. The body also parts with its heat through the action of several excretory organs, and a great deal is carried off by the large body of air which is constantly being warmed in the lungs.

The loss of heat which the body is thus compelled to sustain is perpetual, but is exceedingly variable in degree. The temperature of the atmosphere not only has its yearly and daily, its regular and therefore its expected vicissitudes, but it is also subject to hourly and *unexpected* ones. We never know that the temperature will not rise or fall in a few hours a number of degrees above or below the average point for the season. This uncertainty and variableness of temperature obtains to a greater or less degree in all climates, and may be considered as ordained by the Creator for the benefit of his creatures; and we may suppose that a uniformity of temperature would, contrary to the usual opinions of the invalid, be prejudicial to the health.

Let us look now to the arrangements of the human system with reference to temperature, that we may the more easily understand those hygienic principles that relate thereto.

All atmospheric changes so impress the system as to modify its vital and its vito-chemical actions. All parts of the body are pervaded by sensory nerves, which receive such impressions and convey them in every direction. When the surface of the body, or any portion of it, receives an impression of external temperature, every part of the organism related to it in any way is immediately affected thereby.

That function of the body which is directly related to external impressions of temperature, is the *heat-making process*. The point of temperature at which vital actions take place being fixed, and the bodily heat being dependent upon its own resources, it follows that the production of heat is accelerated or retarded to an extent exactly proportionate to the loss experienced—the process undergoing an amount of variation just about equal to that to which the sensory system is subjected.

This regulation of the bodily temperature is connected with the employment of the materials which are necessary to the production of vital phenomena. The system is thus relieved of any surplus of heat which it may have acquired by means of an increased *evaporation from the surface*, while the want of heat that is felt stimulates the *respiratory organs* to greater activity. Thus it appears that impressions from without are as sure to affect the production of heat, either to lessen or to augment it, as pressure upon the key of the piano to elicit a musical sound. The slightest observation verifies these statements. To place the hand, or foot, or any portion of the warm surface of the person, in contact with a very cold substance, as a piece of ice, instantaneously causes an expansion of the ribs and a depression of the diaphragm, and consequently an *unusually profound inspiration, which is involuntarily continued till the heat that is thus lost be fully restored.* The heat of the body, or of any part, may for a short period be depressed without injury, because it requires *time* for the physiological changes now described to complete their effects upon the economy. No artificial supply of heat is required in order healthfully to maintain the bodily temperature; and when, by our fine civilized modes of life we depress the heat-producing operations of the body, we must remember that at the same time we are impairing the respiratory acts, and are doing ourselves more or less harm in proportion to the extent of our misbehavior in this respect.

We may now understand some of the consequences of inattention to the relations borne by the system to temperature. In hot weather, and in hot climates, the respiratory stimulus being less, respiration is consequently diminished, and then results a retention of the materials that should be excluded from the system through this agency. Such materials are not completely reduced to carbonic acid water and urea, but the process is arrested at an intermediate point, and the state popularly termed *biliousness*, which implies the presence in the blood of the proximate elements of bile, inevitably succeeds, unless the person so exposed becomes very cautious as to his diet.

ORIGIN OF COLDS.—The symptom or the form of disease styled "a cold" can never occur except in the condition of the system above described. But it further requires that the body part with its heat under conditions which do not produce a corresponding increase of respiration. In this case, the blood, loaded with the materials to be discharged from the system, fills the capillaries of the respiratory membranes, and not meeting with the requisite oxygen is necessarily retained, causing congestion of the membranes in question, and those other very unpleasant and annoying consequences familiar to every one. A prolonged exposure to a cold atmosphere would, in all of these cases, render the respiratory effect more profound and efficient, complete the physico-chemical change designed and commenced, but now incomplete, and would effectually prevent the occurrence of the symptom in question. The disease is called *a cold*, from the popular fancy that low temperature is the occasion of it, while the truth is, no means are so effectual as this for its cure; for by cold, just those physiological effects are secured which are required to relieve the system of the injurious cause.

The conditions essential to the production of the disorder in question may now be stated:

1. There must be a surplus of materials in the system requiring a certain quantity of oxygen for their elimination.

2. These are moved forward to the respiratory passages by the normal stimulus, which, however, is insufficient to effect its purpose.

This view of the *cause* readily suggests the *remedy*. A more free and abundant exposure to low atmospheric temperature, aided by abundant exercise, is the best protection against colds, and the best remedy when the disorder is once contracted.

When we say that *cool air* is the most natural and important condition of health, it is not implied that those arts of civilization which protect us against its impressions are utterly useless or mischievous. It is only the *abuse* or the *excess* of these appliances that we need to fear. The objects of life, in the physiological point of view, are attained in the development of the greatest possible amount of the available force. The arts of civilization can serve us only as they *economize* our powers, not as they impair or prodigally waste them.

It is, then, *vicissitude* of temperature, and not that avoiding of it that is attempted by means of our heated dwellings and our thick and impenetrable clothing, which the human constitution requires to preserve its integrity and force; and we shall see that, to *restore the health*, alternations of heat and cold, *artificially* brought about, are among the most potent instrumentalities at our command.

EFFECT OF CONTINUED AND GREAT EXTREMES.—In both very high and very low latitudes the physiological necessities imposed on man by climate are not favorable to the development of his nobler powers, but he becomes the slave of his climatic condition, as he often does, in temperate latitudes, to his sensorial faculties. In *cold* climates, because the system loses much heat, it must produce much, and man becomes an apparatus for the combustion of carbon; while in *hot* climates the system is compelled to supply much water to the surface for evaporation, and becomes accordingly an hydraulic machine. In both cases the due physiological balance essential for the development of the highest powers is wanting. But, on the other hand, the frequent changes of temperature which our systems experience in temperate climates, is most compatible with health and the highest development of the bodily powers.

IMPORTANCE OF COLD.—Chronic invalids are generally the victims of the falsest notions respecting temperature. They have become, by long habits of effeminacy, incapable of bearing the amount of cold fitted to the respiratory needs of the body. They exhibit the greatest suspicion and fear of the most beneficent designs of nature. They shrink from the very influence which elicits and vivifies their powers, and so they continue to repress and cramp their already weakened faculties. The importance of developing to a suitable and healthy extent the *heat-making* faculty is quite equal to that of exercise, and is among the first things to which the attention of the chronic invalid should be directed.

The propriety of subjecting the system to the influence of cold is not always to be decided by the sensations, for these, except in perfect health, are not to be trusted unless corroborated by the other faculties. The effect of cold is to infuse into the system an agreeable vigor and elasticity; but in a weakened state of the system and perverted condition of the nerves, the sensations, being abnormally acute, will often rebel. This indicates the need of discipline, the very process required to reinstate the health. It is *only* under circumstances when the withdrawal of heat from the system is not attended with a corresponding increase of respiration, that exposure to cold can be in any degree hurtful; for it is only then that the refuse matter of the system is retained to be subjected to that spontaneous chemical action which will of course conflict with the vital processes.

THE WATER-CURE.—A medical practice, of extensive reputation for its empirical success, has been founded upon the use of temperature as a remedial means. The *Water-Cure*, though a special, is a legitimate practice, because based on important, though perhaps as practiced, insufficient number, of the plain principles of physiology. The practice consists in causing an artificial demand to be laid upon the system, or some limited portions of it, to *produce heat*, and also in repressing the natural production of heat in various parts by withdrawing the incentive thereto. In this way the most important changes may be induced in the circulation, innervation, and nutrition of various portions of the body, often sufficient, when skillfully managed, to restore the harmony and health of the organism.

In this practice, *water*, instead of air, is employed, because it furnishes the means of applying temperature quickly, vigorously, and extensively, and is thus eminently adapted to meet the emergencies of sickness, especially of acute disease. In bathing, it is the *temperature* of the water, rather than the water itself, which is to be regarded as the source of the effects which we often realize by the operation.

THE COLD BATH.—This may be either *general*, applied to the whole surface, or *local*, applied to some portion of the body, as the hands, feet, seat, etc.; in either case the general effect is similar, though the particular effects may be widely different. The first impression of the cold, to whatever part the water may be applied, acting through the sensory nerves, causes the ribs to become everted, and a profound inspiratory effort to be made. The respiration continues thus exalted so long as the body, or any portion of it, is parting with an unusual amount of heat. Nor does even this cease immediately, for if heat be not produced as rapidly as it is being abstracted by the artificial method in question, it continues to be produced through the influence of greater respiration till the equilibrium is restored.

The practical effect of such a process is very apparent, and is susceptible of demonstration. The water coming in contact with the warm body has acquired heat, all of which is compensated by increased respiration and increased respiratory effect upon the blood. A sitting bath, the temperature of which is elevated two degrees, will have caused the absorption by the blood of the oxygen from four or five cubic feet of air, enough to raise a half-pint of water from the freezing to the boiling point, and will have eliminated from the system more than a half ounce of its solid material.

THE WARM BATH.—When the temperature of the air is considerably below that of the body, we know that it receives heat from it at only a very moderate rate; but water does not feel warm to us till its temperature approximates very nearly our own. At 98° it ceases to receive heat from us, and therefore, when the body is submerged in a bath of that temperature, the ordinary incentive to the production of heat ceasing to act, all the physiological processes are retarded, respiration becomes slow and difficult, and the system soon suffers from retained matters. If there has been pain, the bath affords oftentimes a delightful sense of relief, and frequently checks morbid action. These effects become less apparent at slightly lower temperatures; and when still further reduced, the effects experienced are those of the cold bath to a moderate degree.

THE HOT BATH.—In a bath of this sort, heat is imparted to the body, the effect of which is to compel it to take on a reciprocal action and return what it has received, by producing moisture at the surface, to be evaporated. The skin, under the influence of the hot bath, breaks out in a copious perspiration, this effect following with a rapidity proportioned to the temperature. When this effect is produced, the superficial capillaries are filled with blood, and central portions of the body consequently relieved from their engorgement, often, especially in severe internal congestion, to the temporary relief of the complaint. The effect here described can not long be continued, for obvious reasons, without serious detriment to the organism.

The reader will note an important and radical difference between the effects of cold and those of warm bathing. Cold baths, on account of their effects on respiration, are an agency for the removal from the body of its *solid materials;* while warm and hot baths, by the effort they assist the system in making to relieve itself of heat, remove *fluid and saline matters* therefrom. In many cases of disease both of these agents are required.

LOCAL BATHS.—The application of the bath to a limited portion of the body is governed by the same general principles as govern its application to the whole surface. But the response made by the system to the impression of the local bath is peculiar. If the bath be cold, the process causes the heat of the body to depart from it through a circumscribed surface. Now, since the heat is supplied to the cold part through the blood which flows thitherward, the process of local bathing becomes one of calling, or deriving the circulation from the general system in the direction of the cold part. This effect is eminently useful in aiding similar effects produced by movements for the removal of visceral congestions.

Effect on the Nerves.—It will be noticed that temperature, especially a low degree of it, acts primarily upon the nerves, and it is through the intervention of these that its effects upon the circulation, respiration, nutrition, etc., are chiefly wrought. The great majority of people, whose sensory surface is too little exposed, are greatly benefited by the stimulation and vigorous tone that is afforded by the daily morning bath. It counteracts in the sedentary the ill effects of warm air confined next to the person by clothing, and for all who are not constantly out of doors, is an important means for maintaining the health. But serious ill effects may, and *very frequently do*, arise from too much, and injudicious bathing. The abuse here alluded to arises from an ignoring of the principles relating to the harmony of function, insisted on in this volume. It will be understood that all impressions made upon external sensory nerves are accompanied by corresponding action of the nerve-centers situated in the brain, spinal cord, and especially those of the trunk, at the seat of the nerves of organic life. Stimulant impressions, if habitually resorted to, induce hypernutrition, and consequent excited and unbalanced action of the nervous system, which is utterly incompatible with health. Persons who, for a length of time, subject themselves frequently to repeated and intense impressions of heat or cold, by means of water bathing, abuse themselves in a way that will certainly be followed by irregular nervous action, and the various grades of nervous disease—excitability, depression of spirits, neuralgia, hypochondria, etc. Great caution should be used that this mode of stimulation be not made a substitute for the more common nerve stimulants which Hygiene condemns. The *Water-Cure*, so called, is sometimes practiced in the reprehensible manner here pointed out, considerably more to the detriment than to the benefit of many patients.

COMPRESSES.—These consist of linen or cotton cloth, several times folded, thoroughly wetted, and applied to some part of the body. If wrung out from hot water, the application is termed a *fomentation*. This is a very grateful application to painful parts, and affords relief on the principle before mentioned. If cold, it soon acquires the temperature of the body, and produces an effect upon the parts analogous to that of the warm bath.

Wet compresses also supply the conditions for *osmosis*, or interchange of fluids between the different structures of the body. They hence become exceedingly useful in *congestions*, because the absorption of fluid through the capillary walls into the vessels detaches the corpuscles which in this case are apt to adhere to the walls, and aids the escape of the clogged blood from the point of congestion. Compresses also remove the surplus heat of the part, and thus supply an important condition for the normal vital activities. The compress should be continued upon any one part only a portion of the time, otherwise its good effects will be counteracted.

PARTICULAR DIRECTIONS FOR BATHING.

THE AIR BATH.—This consists simply in a full exposure of the whole body, divested of clothing, to the air at the ordinary temperature, after the manner recommended by Dr. Franklin. This may be continued a moderate length of time, and should be accompanied by light, rapid friction over the whole surface of the body with bare hands, or with a few of the examples of movements contained in Part II. The rubbing necessitates much useful bending and stretching of the body in all directions. The skin is greatly refreshed by this process. A good time for it is on going to bed, or on rising.

THE COLD GENERAL BATH.—This should never be employed while the stomach has food in it, nor when the system is fatigued by exercise; neither should it be taken while the body is cold from previous exposure. If cold from internal causes, exercise to increase the respiration should precede it, and it should be, moreover, of very short continuance.

A serious mistake prevails in regard to the proper manner of taking a bath. The directions usually are, to begin by wetting the head and face. This direction arises from ignorance in regard to the true physiological effect of bathing, and of the conditions of the system, for the regulation of which it is useful.

A valuable lesson on this subject may be learned by observation of nature. The dog, cow, and ox, etc., whom instinct (a better reason than belongs to some conceited bipeds) teaches to bathe, *stand* first in the water for a while, to cool off the *feet*, before making a general plunge. Our feet, even, in spite of effeminate precautions, are much exposed to the damp, cold earth. The effect of this is, to counteract the tendency of afflux of the circulation to the head, which is that portion of the body which employs the most blood, and most continuously. To obviate this tendency, the feet and lower extremities should be bathed first, longest, and most. Baths of all temperatures below that of the body should be taken by commencing at the feet.

It is sometimes said that bathing or showering the head affords relief, implying an effect in opposition to the principle above stated. In this case the temporary stimulus is evidently mistaken for a permanent effect, and if the observation be extended, the result will be found to be opposite that supposed.

REACTION.—After a time, greater or less according to the vigor of the system, the heat abstracted from the body by the bath is fully restored to it. This is popularly termed reaction. The real beginning of this process is at the first moment, when the nerves are impressed with the sensation of cold. Reaction is often carried to a point beyond the limits of a healthful activity, producing irritability and tendencies to disease, if not positive inflammation.

The term, *want of reaction*, simply implies that the complete restoration of heat is slowly accomplished. In such cases, the effect desired is more promptly and thoroughly secured by the employment of movements.

Baths should always be taken deliberately, and not with nervous haste, as this occasions fatigue, and tends to defeat the end desired.

SHOWER AND DOUCHE BATHS.—These are highly useful as local applications, readily inducing derivative effects in visceral organs, and at the same time exerting the same general influence as has been previously described. The shower is unfit for the delicate, because it operates too severely upon the nerves. A *small* douche is more manageable and milder. In these baths, the mechanical impression made upon the surface by the running water adds to the stimulating effect. In every case, anything like *shock* should be sedulously avoided as harmful for the ordinary chronic invalid.

Chapter Twenty-six.

LIGHT.

The fact that *light* has powerful hygienic, and even remedial properties, is one too much overlooked. Light is well known to be a most potent chemical agent, both in nature and in the arts. It arouses the vegetable world into life and perfects its products, and without it all animate nature would soon perish for lack of sustenance. In the arts, modern science has wonderfully economized its powers, and makes it serve the most important uses. It is a most potent agent for determining the chemical state of bodies, readily decomposing numerous chemical compounds, and re-combining their elements in new forms.

That peculiar property of light whereby it is rendered a most important hygienic agent, is manifested in its power to destroy noxious vaporous bodies existing in the atmosphere. The surface of the earth, covered with vegetable and animal matter in a state of decay, sends forth under the influence of heat and moisture an abundance of gaseous matter, which, mingling with the air, enters the lungs to poison the blood, and produces various forms of disease. Though existing in quantities too minute to affect the senses, or any known chemical test, yet, through the lungs, these particles are constantly being conveyed into the system, where they accumulate and exert their chemical power in full force, in opposition to the conditions of health.

It is well known that in those localities characterized by a degree of heat and moisture favorable to the most rapid vegetable decomposition, fevers of various kinds abound. These effects can occur only when the noxious products in question are produced more rapidly than they can be destroyed by the agency of sunlight.

We receive the most injury from insidious and disregarded causes. We seldom give a thought what may be the consequences of denying to the rooms in which we dwell, the wholesome and vivifying influence of sunlight, but on the contrary take the most unwearied pains to exclude it. In the absence of light, the invisible causes of disease, entering by the windows and doors, or generated from the gaseous matters eliminated from our bodies, operate with all their force. It is useless to try to counteract the effects flowing from these causes with drugs, or to combat them in any other way, while the causes themselves are operating in full force. Commonly the air and light are shut out together, which is much worse than if the air, newly acted on by the strong light, were freely admitted.

The influence on the constitution of this custom of living in darkness is most favorable to the production of that condition of the blood and of the vital habit from which springs *scrofula*. The pale and dusky complexions, eruptive skins, flabby and weak muscles, and general sickly aspect, which are so frequently witnessed in young children, are, in many instances, mostly attributable to this cause. Of course, *light* is a most important agent to be employed in the cure of affections of this class. It is wonderful and delightful to see how soon a pale, attenuated, miserable child, after being freely exposed to the sunlight for several hours every day, will begin to improve, and the symptoms here described to disappear. Even scrofulous swelling of the glands of the neck, or other parts of the body, will quickly succumb under the magical influence of sunlight and pure air.

Nursing mothers, especially, ︱ ' these hygienic influences to maintain the purity and vigor of their system, that they may not lay the foundation for lasting disease in their offspring, for the child is sure to suffer, even sooner than the mother, the grievous consequences of her physiological errors.

Is it necessary that the parlors and sitting-rooms of our dwellings should be kept so dark and unwholesome? The first reason always assigned by the housekeeper is, that only in this way can she preserve the colors of her carpeting and upholstery, as if the color of a carpet or a curtain was more precious than that of the cheek and lip. In a hygienic point of view, one is led to feel that these household comforts and elegancies do more harm than good, that their advantages are rather more than balanced by their ill effects. However beautiful and costly, *they are necessarily uncleanly.* However well kept, they are the inevitable receptacles of impalpable dust, which yield invisible clouds at every touch, besides, being the reservoirs of air contaminated in the way we have noticed. Carpets, so common a luxury here, are but little used in Europe, except in England, and it would undoubtedly greatly promote the health of our own people were they to be abolished by statute from every habitation in the land.

17

Chapter Twenty-seven.

MENTAL HYGIENE.

The different states of the mind, whether in its departments of thought or feeling, are well known to exert a powerful influence upon the physiological manifestations; but unfortunately the consideration of these relations has been too generally left to a class of writers whose aim is to astonish and amuse rather than to effect any practical good by their disquisitions.

We hear it constantly asserted by invalids, that some peculiar mental trouble, disappointment, or excitement of feeling was the original *cause* of their ill health; but how very few think of looking for relief, or are led to look for it, in a restoration of order and harmony to the disturbed mind. How few seem to know that the forces that exercise such potent control over the organism for the production of disease, may be made equally available for the restoration of health! The ordinary practice of medicine inculcates the notion that the business of the physician is simply to endeavor to supply and regulate certain material conditions, by means of pill and powder, and that when that is accomplished, all has been done that lies within the limits of human ability.

The truth is, the influence of the mind over the body is equally great in health and in disease. No thoughtful observer can doubt this. We have seen that voluntary muscular action gives language to our *ideas*, and that no part of the frame-work of the body is exempt from the duties of aiding in the performance of this interesting and wonderful function. The passions, especially, put into requisition the action of almost every muscle of the body for their expression. Says a German writer,* "Who is unacquainted with the sparkling eye, the free respiration, the glowing color, and the serene brow of the joyous? Who is not familiar with the trembling aspect, the hesitating utterance, the cold ruffled skin, the bristling hair, the palpitating heart, the impeded respiration, the paleness, the low pulse, and the thousand other signs of fear? The slow, oppressed breathing, interrupted by sobs, the cold, pallid, wrinkled skin, the slow tottering gait, and the weak pulse of the despairing? The deep broad blush of shame, or the pallor of miserable envy? The beaming countenance of requited love, or the anguished expression of disappointed affection? The spasmodic constriction of throat and chest which accompanies jealousy? The gnawing pain which torments the heart of devilish hate? The storm in the veins of the angry man, his inflamed countenance, his gasping breath, his bounding pulse, and wild swollen countenance?" All these *external* manifestations depend upon certain changes effected among the invisible elements of matter.

Now the extraordinary states into which the system may be thrown soon subside, and are directly succeeded by the ordinary states, and whether the impressions thus made be wholesome or unwholesome, the effects are not necessarily permanent. But if these conditions be *continued* for any considerable length of time, the consequences must be serious, and may be

---

* Dr. Feuchtersleben.

even fatal. The continued indulgence of malicious feelings by a person, for example, will surely so modify all the internal invisible functional acts of his system as to check and overcome finally its vital power; and thus any latent tendencies to chronic disease that may belong to him will pretty certainly be quickened into active life.

A grave difficulty to be encountered in overcoming states of chronic disease by ordinary medical means is now seen. Diseases are perpetuated, if not produced, by causes over which mere chemical influences can not be presumed to exercise any positive control. This fact may be, often is, tacitly acknowledged by the physician, but he declines to investigate its relations so as to be able to turn them to useful account. He is unwilling to acknowledge in practice, although he may admit confidentially, that the headache, the nervousness, the heart disease, or the dyspeptic qualms which he is called upon to remedy, are only indications of some *peculiar morbid state of the mind or of the emotional nature of the sufferer*, which it becomes him to meet directly, rather than to torment his patient with an eternal round of palliatives. In these cases, every medical prescription must be totally irrelevant (though written in the best Latin) unless it recognizes the operation of causes existing in a sphere quite beyond the reach of the most potent drug. What fatal mistakes may not result when *stimuli* are substituted for *encouragement*, and *physic* for rational *ideas;* when the invalid is advised to try the resources of an inexhaustible pharmacy, instead of bringing common sense to a controlling sway in the organism! Neither physician nor patient can afford any longer to devote his attention exclusively to the superficial and deceptive signs of disease, nor to ignore the fact, that the body is but the incarnate expression of the interior, invisible, imperishable spirit, which is the man.

We can not get rid of the sequences of the important fact, that in the human organism spirit governs matter, by brutishly ignoring it; nor can we innocently treat it as an unimportant matter. Science, like true religion, is learning every day to live more by faith and less by sight.

The jests that used to be hurled at the defenseless head of the practitioner who dared to suggest that the thoughts, and feelings and mental habits of the invalid might need rectifying as well as his bile and blood, are fast losing their point. We are all beginning to suspect that perhaps, after all, a disease may not be the less a disease because its source happens to lie in an unruly imagination, or in excessive activity, or wrong modes of thought. And gradually—very slowly, to be sure—yet really, we think people are waking up to the conviction that these intangible causes are not irremediable. They are beginning to see and understand that by this close union and co-operation of the material and immaterial natures, remedial agents may possibly find access to either or both through avenues that otherwise could have no existence. We have faith to believe that the time is near at hand when the mental aspects and relations of disease will receive an amount of attention equal to that which has always been given to the pulse and tongue, the temperature of the skin, and color and consistence of the excretions.

Blessed will be the day when science shall purge her soul of the dishonor of leaving this interesting and vital subject to ignorance and charlatanry. But even the devil should have his due. As much as we detest quackery, it can not be denied that many quacks meet with a success in the treatment of some diseases that would be very puzzling if we could not refer it in great measure to the mental control they contrive to exert over their patients. In this respect, in practice, the pretender has a positive and oftentimes an immense advantage over the real man of science. He stimulates his patient's imagination, awakens his hope, gains his confidence, whereby the perturbed mind is restored to a condition of tranquillity, and thus a state of the system is induced most conducive to that spontaneous restoration of its harmony and power which is often mistaken for the effect of medicine.

A wholesome co-operation of the mental, emotional, and material forces of the invalid is, indeed, the grand desideratum, and if the charlatan can secure it, he is certainly entitled to the credit of doing what his betters so often and so lamentably fail in their efforts to accomplish.

Every one knows what benefit is frequently derived from a simple *change* of doctors; this benefit is generally much greater than the difference in the courses of treatment will account for. We all know how salutary are the influences of cheerful society, change of scene, and exciting incidents, in some conditions of the system. It is very strange that the abundant experiences of men in this direction should not long ago have convinced them of the existence of a principle so important and fundamental.

We shall make no attempt here at giving specific directions in regard to the best manner of bringing the principles of mental hygiene to bear upon particular cases. We can only direct *en passant* the attention of invalids and physicians to this important subject.

We believe that while some benefit may be derived from discussion of this great question, in the enlightenment of the public mind, no extensive practical advantage will be reaped until these principles are taught in our schools and incorporated into our medical science. The mind itself must be regarded as an available force capable of being aroused and managed in such a manner as effectually to oppose the tendencies of the body toward disease.

It should be understood that the efforts of the physician must be seconded by the patient; and that this concurrence must not be faint and faltering, but determined and earnest. If his energies, or what remains of them, can be thus enlisted in his own behalf, the victory is already half gained. The only hopeless invalid is he who has no resolution—in whose soul faith and courage have utterly died out.

A man may bestow the greatest care upon what he eats and drinks; may regulate ever so nicely his periods of exercise and of repose; learn by heart whole treatises on the art of living long; reflect profoundly on the relation of his feelings, his will, and his thoughts to his general well-being. But more than this is demanded of him. He must learn to *govern*, as well as to *know*, himself. Does the reader say, "Oh, I am incapable of such efforts as are necessary for this." I answer: Your duty in the premises is demonstrable. God, who succors the raven so tenderly, is not a hard master. "You *can* do what you *should* do."

APPENDIX.

BIBLIOGRAPHY.

LAURENT JOUBERT... Treatise on Laughter, containing its Essence,
Paris, 1550.   Causes, and Marvelous Effects—being Curious
                    Researches, Reasonings, and Observations.
J. F. SCALIGER..... The Art of Gymnastics.
Lyons, 1561.
LEONARD FUCHS..... Movements and Repose.
Tubingen, 1565.
AMBROSE RARE ..... On Movements and Repose.
Paris, 1575.
JULES ALESSANDRINI. The Art of Preserving Health; in twenty-three
Cologne, 1575.   Books.
JEAN A. BORELLI.... Animal Mechanics.
Rome, 1680.
PIERRE BRISSEAU..., Treatise on Sympathetic Movements, with an Ex-
Valenciennes,   planation of such as take place in various Ner-
1682.   vous Diseases.
S. F. PAULLINE..... Curious Account of how Blows will often Cure,
Frankfort, 1698.   promptly and well, all kinds of Chronic Diseases,
                    nearly incurable: the whole Proved and Illus-
                    trated by Agreeable and Pleasant Anecdotes, and
                    by Particular Remarks and Interesting Notes by
                    the Author.
GEO. E. STAHL...... Active and Passive Commotions of the Blood—Of
Halle, 1698 to   Horseback Riding, a new Method of Curing
1736.   Lung Diseases—Of the Medical Use of Volun-
                    tary Movements—Of Movements, Diet, and Cold
                    Water, the simplest Remedies—Several other
                    Works on the same subjects.
DE SAUVAGES....... Rational Mechanics in Medicine.
Leyden, 1703.

FREDERICK HOFFMAN. Dissertations on Medical Physics, relating to
La Hague, 1708. Health.
PAUL-JEAN BURETTE. .The Gymnastics of the Ancients, and several other
Paris, 1717. Works.
NICHOLAS ANDRY.... Orthopœdy ; the Art of Preventing and Correcting
Paris, 1741. Deformities of the Body in Children by means at
the command of Parents, and those having Children in charge.
FUCHNER .... On several kinds of Passive Movements, appro-
Halle, 1746 to 1748. priate to certain Diseases—On the Danger of Corporeal Movements, when inappropriately Applied
—Basis of Physiology, deduced from Physical and
Mechanical Principles—Basis of General Pathology, deduced from the Principles of Anatomy,
Physics, and Mechanics.
C. J. TISSOT .... Surgical and Medical Gymnastics.
Paris, 1780.
GUTS MUTHS........ Exercises for Youth.
Paris, 1793.
CHARLES LONDE..... Medical Gymnastics ; or Exercise Applied to the
Paris, 1821. Organs of the Body according to the Laws of
Physiology, Hygiene, and Therapeutics.
ED. WEBER .... Mechanism of the Organs of Locomotion : Re-
Leipsic, 1836. searches Anatomical and Physiological.
J. A. L. WERNER... Medical Gymnastics ; or, the Art of Correcting
Vices of the Bodily Formation, and of Re-establishing the Form and Proportions of the Human
Body according to the Principles of Anatomy
and Physiology.
PETER HENRY LING.. Treatise on Gymnastics, without Apparatus.
1836.
1838 .... Treatise on Sword and Bayonet Exercise.
1840 .... Treatise on the General Principles of Gymnastics.
J. F. LOESCHKE .... Gymnastics in Lunacy.
Leipsic, 1840.
G. INDEBETOE... ... Therapeutic Manipulation.
London, 1842.
H. ROTHSTEIN....... Gymnastics in Sweden, and the Gymnastic System
1841. of Ling.
G. RESMER .... Regular Exercises in Relation to the Physical De-
Leipsic, 1843. velopment of the Young.
WALKER.......... Manly Exercises.
London, 1845.

APPENDIX.

HARTWIG ....The Therapatetic Curative Method; or, the Treat-
Dusseldorf, 1847.   ment of Diseases by Movements.
ADOLF SPIERS.......Manual of Gymnastics for Schools.
Basle, 1847.
G. M. SCHREBER....Medical Gymnastics—Directions for a Healthy and
           Long Life.
GEORGII ....Kinesitherapie, or Treatment of Diseases by Move-
Paris, 1847.   ments, according to Ling's Method.
G. FRIEDRICH ......Gymnastics, as a means of Preserving the Health
Rentley, 1847.   and Curing the Diseases of both Sexes.
ROTHSTEIN..........Gymnastics of the System of the great Northern
Berlin, 1850.   Gymnasiarch, P. H. Ling.
M. ROTH ....Prevention and Cure of Many Chronic Diseases.
London, 1851.
E. A. RICHTER......Organon of Physiological Therapeutics.
Leipsic, 1850.
J. C. WERNER ......Basis of Scientific Orthopœdie.
Berlin, 1851.
ROTHSTEIN ....Journal of the Gymnastic World.
1852.
VON MEDICIN.......The Medical Power of Certain Movements in Ad-
Leipsic, 1852.   vanced Age, as a Means of Radically Curing
           Obstinate Hypochondria, Gout, Rheumatism,
           Oppression of the Chest, Stomach Affections,
           Hemorrhoids, and several other Diseases.
SCHREBER..........Method of Medical Gymnastics, for the Use of
Leipsic, 1852.   Physicians and Others, deduced from Experience.
EULENBURG ....The Swedish Curative Gymnastics.
Berlin, 1853.
A. C. NEUMANN.....Curative Gymnastics.
Berlin, 1853.
C. J. HEIDLER......Vibrations Considered as a Means of Diagnosis and
Braunschwig, 1853.   Cure.
ROTHSTEIN..........Free Gymnastic Exercises.
Berlin, 1855.
RICHTER ··.........Organon of Physiological Therapeutics.
R. W. IDLER.......Manual of Hygiene for the Friends of Long Life.
Berlin, 1855.
SCHREBER..........Medical Gymnastics for the Chamber; being Rep-
   1855.   resentations and Descriptions of Movements,
           without Apparatus or Assistance, and Suitable
           to Perform at all Times, and in all Places, and
           for all Ages—applied to various Affections.

KLOSS..............Movements for Females; an Educational Means
Leipsic, 1855.   of Developing Health and Beauty; with Advice
                         to Parents and Teachers.
WALKER............Manly Exercises.
London, 1855.
M. ROTH............The Prevention and Cure of Chronic Diseases by
London, 1851.   Movements.
1856 ....Hand-Book of the Movement-Cure.
M. DALLY..........Cinesié, or Science of Movements.
Paris, 1857.
C. F. TAYLOR.......Theory and Practice of the Movement-Cure.
   1860.

"Books sent, Prepaid, by Mail, to any Post-Office in the United States."

A LIST OF WORKS

BY

FOWLER AND WELLS, 308 BROADWAY, NEW YORK.

In order to accommodate "the people" residing in all parts of the United States, the Publishers will forward, by return of the first mail, any book named in the following list. The postage will be pre-paid at the New York office. The price of each work, including postage, is given, so that the exact amount may be remitted. Letters containing orders should be post-paid, and directed as follows: FOWLER AND WELLS,
308 BROADWAY, NEW YORK.

WORKS ON PHRENOLOGY.

COMBE'S LECTURES ON PHRENOLOGY. A complete course. Bound in muslin, $1 25.

CHART for Recording various Developments. Designed for Phrenologists. 6 cents.

CONSTITUTION OF MAN. By Geo. Combe. Authorized edition, with Illustrations, embracing his Portrait. 62 cents; muslin, 87 cents.

DEFENCE OF PHRENOLOGY, Arguments and Testimony. By Dr. Boardman. A work for Doubters. 62 cents; muslin, 87 cents.

DOMESTIC LIFE, THOUGHTS ON; its Concord and Discord. By N. Sizer. 15 cents.

EDUCATION COMPLETE. Embracing Physiology, Animal and Mental, Self-Culture, and Memory. One vol. By O. S. Fowler. $2 50.

EDUCATION, founded on the Nature of Man. By Dr. Spurzheim. Muslin, 87 cents.

FAMILIAR LESSONS ON PHRENOLOGY and PHYSIOLOGY. An excellent work for Children. Beautifully Illustrated. $1 25.

LOVE AND PARENTAGE AND AMATIVENESS; applied to the Improvement of Offspring. By O. S. Fowler. 75 cents.

MARRIAGE; its History and Philosophy, with directions for Happy Marriages. Bound in paper, 50 cents; muslin, 75 cents.

MATRIMONY; or, Phrenology and Physiology applied to the Selection of Congenial Companions for Life. By O. S. Fowler. 30 cents.

MEMORY AND INTELLECTUAL IMPROVEMENT; applied to Self-Education. By O. S. Fowler. Paper, 62 cents; muslin, 87 cents.

MORAL AND INTELLECTUAL SCIENCE. By Combe, Gregory, and others. Muslin, $2 30.

MENTAL SCIENCE, Lectures on, according to the Philosophy of Phrenology. By Rev. G. S. Weaver. Paper, 62 cents; muslin, 87 cents.

PHRENOLOGY PROVED, Illustrated, and Applied. Thirty-seventh edition. A standard work on the science. Muslin, $1 25.

PHRENOLOGICAL JOURNAL, American, Monthly. Quarto, Illustrated. A year, $1.

PHRENOLOGY AND THE SCRIPTURES. By Rev. John Pierpont. 15 cents.

PHRENOLOGICAL GUIDE. Designed for the Use of Students. 15 cents.

PHRENOLOGICAL ALMANAC. Illustrated with numerous engravings. 6 cents.

PHRENOLOGICAL BUST: designed especially for Learners, showing the exact location of all the Organs of the Brain fully developed. Price, including box for packing, $1 25. [Not mailable.]

PHRENOLOGICAL SPECIMENS for Societies and Private Cabinets. 40 casts; nett, $25.

SELF-CULTURE AND PERFECTION OF CHARACTER. Paper, 62 cents; muslin, 87 cents.

SELF-INSTRUCTOR in Phrenology and Physiology. Illustrated with one hundred engravings. Paper, 30 cents; muslin, 50 cents.

SYMBOLICAL HEAD and Phrenological Chart, in map form, showing the Natural Language of the Phrenological Organs. 30 cents.

WORKS OF GALL ON PHRENOLOGY. 5 vols., $7.

The PUBLISHERS would respectfully refer Strangers, Agents, and Country Dealers to the principal Publishers in New York, Philadelphia, Boston, or other cities, for evidence of their ability to fulfill all contracts. They have been many years before the public, engaged in the publishing business in the city of New York.

FOWLER AND WELLS' PUBLICATIONS.

HYDROPATHY; OR, WATER-CURE.

IF THE PEOPLE can be thoroughly indoctrinated in the general principles of HYDROPATHY, and make themselves acquainted with the LAWS OF LIFE AND HEALTH, they will well-nigh emancipate themselves from all need of doctors of any sort.—DR. TRALL.

By no other way can men approach nearer to the gods than by conferring health on men.—CICERO.

ACCIDENTS AND EMERGENCIES. By Alfred Smee. Notes by Trall. Illustrated. 15 cents.

CHILDREN; their Hydropathic Management in Health and Disease. Dr. Shew. $1 25.

CHOLERA; its Causes, Prevention, and Cure, and all other Bowel Complaints. 30 c.

CONSUMPTION; its Causes, Prevention and Cure. Paper, 62 cents; muslin, 87 cents.

COOK BOOK, HYDROPATHIC. With New Recipes. Illustrated. By R. T. Trall, M.D. Paper, 62 cents; muslin, 87 cents.

DOMESTIC PRACTICE OF HYDROPATHY, with 15 engraved illustrations of important subjects from drawings. By E Johnson, M.D. $1 50.

EXPERIENCE IN WATER-CURE in Acute and other Diseases. By Mrs. Nichols. 30 cts.

FAMILY PHYSICIAN, Hydropathic. By Dr. Shew. A new and invaluable work for home practice. Profusely Illustrated. $2 50.

HYDROPATHIC ENCYCLOPEDIA. A Complete System of Hydropathy and Hygiene. Illustrated. By R. T. Trall, M.D. In one large volume, with nearly a thousand pages. Price, $3.

HYDROPATHY; or, Water-Cure. Principles and Modes of Treatment. Dr. Shew. $1 25.

HOME TREATMENT FOR SEXUAL Abuses, with Hydropathic Management. A practical treatise for both sexes. By Dr. Trall. 30 cents.

INTRODUCTION TO THE WATER-CURE. With First Principles. 15 cents.

MIDWIFERY AND THE DISEASES OF WOMEN. A practical work. By Dr. Shew. $1 25.

PARENTS' GUIDE AND CHILDBIRTH MADE EASY. By Mrs. H. Pendleton. 60 cts.

PHILOSOPHY OF WATER-CURE. By J. Balbirnie, M.D. A work for beginners. 30 c.

PRACTICE OF WATER-CURE. By Drs. Wilson and Gully. A handy, popular work. 30 c.

PREGNANCY AND CHILDBIRTH; Water-Cure for Women, with cases. 30 cents.

RESULTS OF HYDROPATHY; treating of Constipation and Indigestion. By Edward Johnson, M D. 87 cents.

WATER-CURE IN CHRONIC DISEASES; an exposition of the Causes, Progress, and Terminations of Various Chronic Diseases. By Dr. J. M. Gully. An important work. $1 50.

WATER AND VEGETABLE DIET in Scrofula, Cancer, Asthma, etc. By Dr. Lamb. Notes by Dr. Shew. 62 cents; muslin, 87 cents.

WATER-CURE IN EVERY KNOWN Disease. By J. H. Rausse. 62 cents; muslin, 87 cts.

WATER-CURE MANUAL. A popular work on Hydropathy. 62 cts.; muslin, 87 cts.

WATER-CURE ALMANAC. Containing much important matter for all classes. 6 cts.

WATER-CURE JOURNAL AND HERALD OF REFORMS. Devoted to Hydropathy and Medical Reform. Published Monthly, at $1 a year.

FOWLER AND WELLS have all works on HYDROPATHY, PHYSIOLOGY, and the Natural Sciences generally. Booksellers supplied on the most liberal terms. Agents wanted in every State, County, and Town. These works are universally popular, and thousands might be sold where they have never yet been introduced. Letters and Orders should be post-paid, and directed to the Publishers, as follows:

FOWLER AND WELLS,
208 BROADWAY, NEW YORK.

[Name the Post Office, County, and State.]

FOWLER AND WELLS' PUBLICATIONS.

PHYSIOLOGY, MESMERISM, AND PSYCHOLOGY.

ON PHYSIOLOGY.

ALCOHOL AND THE CONSTITUTION OF MAN. Illustrated by a Diagram. By Prof. Youmans. 30 cents.

ALCOHOLIC CONTROVERSY. A Review of the *Westminster Review* on the Physiological Errors of Teetotalism. By Dr. Trall. 30 cents.

AMATIVENESS; or, Evils and Remedies of Excessive and Perverted Sexuality, with Advice to the Married and Single. 15 cents.

CHASTITY, in a Course of Lectures to Young Men. By Dr. Graham. 30 cents.

CHRONIC DISEASES, especially Nervous Diseases of Women. Important work. 30 cts.

COMBE'S PHYSIOLOGY, applied to the Improvement of Mental and Physical Education. Notes by Fowler. 62 cents; muslin, 87 cents.

DIGESTIVE, PHYSIOLOGY OF. The Principles of Dietetics. By Andrew Combe. 30 cts.

FAMILY GYMNASIUM. With numerous Illustrations; Containing the most improved methods of applying Gymnastic, Calisthenic, Kinesipathic, and vocal exercises to the development of the bodily organs, the invigoration of their functions, the preservation of health, and cure of diseases and deformities. By R. T. Trall, M.D. $1 25.

FAMILY DENTIST; a Popular Treatise on the Teeth. By D. C. Warner, M.D. 87 cts.

FOOD AND DIET; containing an Analysis of every kind of Food and Drink. By Dr. J. Pereira. Muslin, $1 25.

FRUITS AND FARINACEA the Proper Food of Man. With Notes and engraved Illustrations. By R. T. Trall, M.D. Muslin, $1 25.

GENERATION, Philosophy of; its Abuses, Causes, Prevention, and Cure. 30 cents.

HEREDITARY DESCENT: its Laws and Facts applied to Human Improvement. O. S. F. New Edition. Paper, 62 cents; muslin, 87 cents.

INFANCY; or, the Physiological and Moral Management of Children. Illustrated. By Dr. Combe. Paper, 62 cents; muslin, 87 cents.

LOVE AND PARENTAGE; applied to the Improvement of Offspring. 30 cents.

MATERNITY; or, the Bearing and Nursing of Children, including Female Education. O. S. Fowler. 62 cents; muslin, 87 cents.

NATURAL LAWS OF MAN. By Dr. Spurzheim. A good work. 30 cents.

PHILOSOPHY OF SACRED HISTORY, considered in Relation to Human Aliment and the Wines of Scripture. By Sylvester Graham. $2.

PHYSIOLOGY, Animal and Mental, applied to Health of Body and Power of Mind. By O. S. Fowler. Paper, 62 cents; muslin, 87 cents.

SEXUAL DISEASES; their Causes, Prevention, and Cure on Physiological Principles. Including practical directions for home treatment. $1 25.

SOBER AND TEMPERATE LIFE; with Notes and Illustrations by Louis Cornaro. 30 cts.

SYRINGES, Patent Injecting Instruments, best in market. $3.

THE SCIENCE OF HUMAN LIFE. By Sylvester Graham, M.D. With a Portrait and Biographical Sketch of the Author. $2 50.

TEA AND COFFEE; their Physical, Intellectual, and Moral Effects. By Alcott. 15 cts.

TEETH; their Structure, Disease, and Management, with Engravings. 15 cents.

TOBACCO, Works on: comprising Essays by Trall, Shew, Alcott, Baldwin, Burdell, Fowler, Greeley, and others. Complete in 1 vol. 62 c.

UTERINE DISEASES AND DISPLACEMENTS. A Practical Treatise on the various Diseases, Malpositions, and Structural Derangements of the Uterus and its Appendages. By Dr. Trall. Illustrated with colored engravings, $5; not colored, $2.

VEGETABLE DIET, as sanctioned by Medical Men and Experience in all Ages. By Dr. Alcott. Paper, 62 cents; muslin, 87 cents.

MESMERISM—PSYCHOLOGY.

ELECTRICAL PSYCHOLOGY, Philosophy of, in Twelve Lectures. By Dr. J. B. Dods. Paper, 62 cents; muslin, 87 cents.

FASCINATION; or, the Philosophy of Charming (Magnetism). Illustrating the Principles of Life. Paper, 50 cents; muslin, 87 cents.

LIBRARY OF MESMERISM AND PSYCHOLOGY. With suitable Illustrations. In two large volumes of about 900 pages. Price, $3.

MACROCOSM AND MICROCOSM; or, the Universe Without and the Universe Within. By Fishbough. Scientific Work. 62 cts.; muslin, 87 cts.

PHILOSOPHY OF MESMERISM AND CLAIRVOYANCE. Six Lectures. With Instruction. 30 c.

PSYCHOLOGY; or, the Science of the Soul. By Haddock. Illustrated. 30 cents.

EITHER of these works may be ordered and received by return of the FIRST MAIL, postage prepaid by the Publishers Please address all letters, post-paid, to **FOWLER AND WELLS,**
N. B.—Name your Post Office, County, and State. 308 BROADWAY, NEW YORK.

FOWLER AND WELLS' PUBLICATIONS.

PHONOGRAPHIC AND MISCELLANEOUS.

When single copies of these works are wanted, the amount, in postage stamps, small change, or bank-notes, may be inclosed in a letter and sent to the Publishers, who will forward the books by return of the FIRST MAIL.

MISCELLANEOUS.

AIMS AND AIDS FOR GIRLS AND YOUNG WOMEN. By Rev. G. S. Weaver. Price, 87 c.

CHEMISTRY, applied to Physiology, Agriculture, and Commerce. By Liebig. 25 cts.

DEMANDS OF THE AGE ON COLLEGES. An Oration. By Horace Mann. 25 cents.

DELIA'S DOCTORS; or, a Glance Behind the Scenes. By Miss Hannah Gardner Creamer. For the Family. Paper, 62 cents; muslin, 87 cents.

DOMESTIC ANIMALS: A Manual of Cattle, Sheep, and Horse Husbandry; or, How to Breed, Rear, and Manage the Tenants of the Barnyard. Paper, 30 cents; muslin 50 cents.

FRUIT CULTURE FOR THE MILLION; or, Hand-Book for the Cultivation and Management of Fruit Trees. Illustrated with Ninety Engravings by Thomas Gregg. Paper, 30 cents; muslin, 50 cents.

HINTS TOWARD REFORMS, in Lectures, Addresses, and other Writings. By H. Greeley. Second edition, with Crystal Palace. $1 25.

HOME FOR ALL; the Gravel Wall, a New, Cheap, and Superior Mode of Building, with Engravings, Plans, Views, etc. 87 cents.

HOPES AND HELPS FOR THE YOUNG OF BOTH SEXES. By Rev. G. S. Weaver. An excellent work. Paper, 62 cents; muslin, 87 cents.

HOW TO WRITE; A Pocket Manual of Composition and Letter-Writing. Invaluable to the young. Paper, 30 cents; muslin, 50 cents.

HOW TO TALK; A Pocket Manual of Conversation and Debate, with more than Five Hundred Common Mistakes in Speaking, Corrected. Paper, 30 cents; muslin, 50 cents.

HOW TO BEHAVE; A Pocket Manual of Republican Etiquette, and Guide to Correct Personal Habits, with Rules for Debating Societies and Deliberative Assemblies. 30 cts.; muslin, 50 cts.

HOW TO DO BUSINESS; A Pocket Manual of Practical Affairs, and a Guide to Success in Life, with a Collection of Legal and Commercial Forms. Suitable for all. 30 cents; muslin, 50 cents.

HAND-BOOKS FOR HOME IMPROVEMENT (Educational); comprising "How to Write," "How to Talk," "How to Behave," and "How to Do Business," in one large volume. $1 50.

IMMORTALITY TRIUMPHANT.—The Existence of a God, with the Evidence. By Rev. J. B. Dods. Paper, 62 cents; muslin, 87 cents.

KANZAS REGION; Embracing Descriptions of Scenery, Climate, Productions, Soil, and Resources of the Territory. Interspersed with Incidents of Travel. By Max Greene. 30 cents.

LIFE ILLUSTRATED. A New First-Class Pictorial Weekly Family Newspaper, devoted to News, Literature, Science, the Arts, etc. Per year, in advance, $2; half a year, $1.

LECTURES ON THE SCIENCE OF HUMAN LIFE. By Sylvester Graham, M.D. $2 00.

POPULATION, THEORY OF. The Law of Animal Fertility. Introduction by Trall. 15 cts.

THE FARM: A Manual of Practical Agriculture; or, How to Cultivate all the Field Crops, with a most valuable Essay on Farm Management. Paper, 30 cents; muslin, 50 cents.

THE GARDEN: A Manual of Horticulture; or, How to Cultivate Vegetables, Fruits, and Flowers. Paper, 30 cents; muslin, 50 cents.

THE HOUSE: A Manual of Rural Architecture; or, How to Build Dwellings, Barns, and Out-Houses generally. Paper, 30 cents; muslin, 50 cents.

RURAL MANUALS; comprising "The House," "The Farm," "The Garden," and "Domestic Animals," in one large volume. $1 50.

WAYS OF LIFE; the Right Way and the Wrong Way. By Rev. G. S. Weaver. A capital work. Paper, 50 cents; muslin, 60 cents.

ON PHONOGRAPHY.

HAND-BOOK OF STANDARD OR AMERICAN PHONOGRAPHY. By Andrew J. Graham. Muslin, $1 50.

THE MANUAL OF PHONOGRAPHY. By Pitman. A new and comprehensive exposition of Phonography, with copious illustrations and exercises. 60 cents.

AMERICAN MANUAL OF PHONOGRAPHY; being a complete guide to the acquisition of Short-Hand. By Elias Longley. 50 cents.

PHONOGRAPHIC TEACHER; being an Inductive Exposition of Phonography, with Instructions to those who have not the assistance of an Oral Teacher. By E. Webster. In boards. 40 cts.

PHONOGRAPHIC COPY-BOOK, of Ruled Paper, for the use of Phonographic students. 12 cents.

All works on Phonography will be furnished to order.

THESE works may be ordered in large or small quantities. A liberal discount will be made to AGENTS, and others, who buy to sell again. They may be sent by Express or as Freight, by Railroad, or otherwise, to any place in the United States, the Canadas, Europe, or elsewhere. Checks or drafts, for large amounts, on New York, Philadelphia, or Boston, always preferred. We pay cost of exchange. All letters should be post-paid, and addressed as follows:

FOWLER AND WELLS,
803 BROADWAY, NEW YORK.

[Name the Post Office, County, and State.]

www.ingramcontent.com/pod-product-compliance
Lightning Source LLC
Chambersburg PA
CBHW030423300426
44112CB00009B/829